PS M05
National, State and Local Politics

Lee Ballestero
Moorpark College

SAN DIEGO

Thank you for purchasing this book! Cognella Custom is an imprint of Cognella, Inc., a student-founded company with a mission to support instructors in creating engaging learning materials at the lowest possible cost to students. While many textbooks include chapters you'll never read, every piece of content in this book has been hand-picked by your instructor to help you get the most out of their course.

The cost of this book includes the copyright fees required by the original rightsholders. By purchasing this text, you are protecting yourself and your school from copyright infringement, as well as supporting the scholars and authors who spent time developing this content.

If you have any questions regarding this text, please don't hesitate to contact us at orders@cognella.com.

Best wishes for a successful academic term,

The Cognella Custom Team

3970 Sorrento Valley Blvd., Ste. 500, San Diego, CA 92121

Contents

1. *The Constitution of the United States* — 1

2. *Amendments to the Constitution of the United States of America* — 11

3. *Articles of Confederation* — 33

4. *No. 39*
    James Madison — 43

5. *No. 10*
    James Madison — 47

6. *Puppy Federalism and the Blessings of America*
    Edward L. Rubin — 53

7. *The Katrina Breakdown*
    Jonathan Walters and Donald F. Kettl — 61

8. *The Six Suburban Eras of the United States*
    Robert Lang, Jennifer LeFurgy and Arthur C. Nelson — 65

9. *Return to Center*
    Christopher D. Ringwald — 69

10. *The Sprawl Debate: Let Markets Plan*
    Peter Gordon and Harry W. Richardson — 73

11. *The Charter of the New Urbanism*
    Peter Calthorpe and William Fulton — 93

12. *Vote Choice in Suburban Elections*
    J. Eric Oliver and Shang E. Ha — 101

13. *Comparing Absentee and Precinct Voters: Voting on Direct Legislation*
    Jeffrey A. Dublin and Gretchen A. Kalsow — 115

14. *Twentieth-Century Voter Turnout in the United States*
    Melanie Jean Springer — 135

15. *Getting Out the Vote in Local Elections: Results from Six Door-to-Door Canvassing Experiments*
    Donald P. Green, Alan S. Gerber and David W. Nickerson — 161

Bibliography — 175

The Constitution of the United States: A Transcription

Note: *The following text is a transcription of the Constitution in its **original** form.*
Items that are hyperlinked have since been amended or superseded.

We the People of the United States, in Order to form a more perfect Union, establish Justice, insure domestic Tranquility, provide for the common defence, promote the general Welfare, and secure the Blessings of Liberty to ourselves and our Posterity, do ordain and establish this Constitution for the United States of America.

Article. I.

Section. 1.

All legislative Powers herein granted shall be vested in a Congress of the United States, which shall consist of a Senate and House of Representatives.

Section. 2.

The House of Representatives shall be composed of Members chosen every second Year by the People of the several States, and the Electors in each State shall have the Qualifications requisite for Electors of the most numerous Branch of the State Legislature.

No Person shall be a Representative who shall not have attained to the Age of twenty five Years, and been seven Years a Citizen of the United States, and who shall not, when elected, be an Inhabitant of that State in which he shall be chosen.

Representatives and direct Taxes shall be apportioned among the several States which may be included within this Union, according to their respective Numbers, which shall be determined by adding to the whole Number of free Persons, including those bound to Service for a Term of Years, and excluding Indians not taxed, three fifths of all other Persons. The actual Enumeration shall be made within three Years after the first Meeting of the Congress of the United States, and within every subsequent Term of ten Years, in such Manner as they shall by Law direct. The Number of Representatives shall not exceed one for every thirty Thousand, but each State shall have at Least one Representative; and until such enumeration shall be made, the State of New Hampshire shall be entitled to chuse three, Massachusetts eight, Rhode-Island and Providence Plantations one, Connecticut five, New-York six, New Jersey four, Pennsylvania eight, Delaware one, Maryland six, Virginia ten, North Carolina five, South Carolina five, and Georgia three.

When vacancies happen in the Representation from any State, the Executive Authority thereof shall issue Writs of Election to fill such Vacancies.

The House of Representatives shall chuse their Speaker and other Officers; and shall have the sole Power of Impeachment.

Section. 3.

The Senate of the United States shall be composed of two Senators from each State, chosen by the Legislature thereof for six Years; and each Senator shall have one Vote.

Immediately after they shall be assembled in Consequence of the first Election, they shall be divided as equally as may be into three Classes. The Seats of the Senators of the first Class shall be vacated at the Expiration of the second Year, of the second Class at the Expiration of the fourth Year, and of the third Class at the Expiration of the sixth Year, so that one third may be chosen every second Year; and if Vacancies happen by Resignation, or otherwise, during the Recess of the Legislature of any State, the Executive thereof may make temporary

Appointments until the next Meeting of the Legislature, which shall then fill such Vacancies.

No Person shall be a Senator who shall not have attained to the Age of thirty Years, and been nine Years a Citizen of the United States, and who shall not, when elected, be an Inhabitant of that State for which he shall be chosen.

The Vice President of the United States shall be President of the Senate, but shall have no Vote, unless they be equally divided.

The Senate shall chuse their other Officers, and also a President pro tempore, in the Absence of the Vice President, or when he shall exercise the Office of President of the United States.

The Senate shall have the sole Power to try all Impeachments. When sitting for that Purpose, they shall be on Oath or Affirmation. When the President of the United States is tried, the Chief Justice shall preside: And no Person shall be convicted without the Concurrence of two thirds of the Members present.

Judgment in Cases of Impeachment shall not extend further than to removal from Office, and disqualification to hold and enjoy any Office of honor, Trust or Profit under the United States: but the Party convicted shall nevertheless be liable and subject to Indictment, Trial, Judgment and Punishment, according to Law.

Section. 4.

The Times, Places and Manner of holding Elections for Senators and Representatives, shall be prescribed in each State by the Legislature thereof; but the Congress may at any time by Law make or alter such Regulations, except as to the Places of chusing Senators.

The Congress shall assemble at least once in every Year, and such Meeting shall be on the first Monday in December, unless they shall by Law appoint a different Day.

Section. 5.

Each House shall be the Judge of the Elections, Returns and Qualifications of its own Members, and a Majority of each shall constitute a Quorum to do Business; but a smaller Number may adjourn from day to day, and may be authorized to compel the Attendance of absent Members, in such Manner, and under such Penalties as each House may provide.

Each House may determine the Rules of its Proceedings, punish its Members for disorderly Behaviour, and, with the Concurrence of two thirds, expel a Member.

Each House shall keep a Journal of its Proceedings, and from time to time publish the same, excepting such Parts as may in their Judgment require Secrecy; and the Yeas and Nays of the Members of either House on any question shall, at the Desire of one fifth of those Present, be entered on the Journal.

Neither House, during the Session of Congress, shall, without the Consent of the other, adjourn for more than three days, nor to any other Place than that in which the two Houses shall be sitting.

Section. 6.

The Senators and Representatives shall receive a Compensation for their Services, to be ascertained by Law, and paid out of the Treasury of the United States. They shall in all Cases, except Treason, Felony and Breach of the Peace, be privileged from Arrest during their Attendance at the Session of their respective Houses, and in going to and returning from the same; and for any Speech or Debate in either House, they shall not be questioned in any other Place.

No Senator or Representative shall, during the Time for which he was elected, be appointed to any civil Office under the Authority of the United States, which shall have been created, or the Emoluments whereof shall have been increased during such time; and no Person holding any Office under the United States, shall be a Member of either House during his Continuance in Office.

Section. 7.

All Bills for raising Revenue shall originate in the House of Representatives; but the Senate may propose or concur with Amendments as on other Bills.

Every Bill which shall have passed the House of Representatives and the Senate, shall, before it become a Law, be presented to the President of the United States: If he approve he shall sign it, but if not he shall return it, with his Objections to that House in which it shall have originated, who shall enter the Objections at large on their Journal, and proceed to reconsider it. If after such Reconsideration two thirds of that House shall agree to pass the Bill, it shall be sent, together with the Objections, to the other House, by which it shall likewise be reconsidered, and if approved by two thirds of that House, it shall become a Law. But in all such Cases the Votes of both Houses shall be determined by yeas and Nays, and the Names of the Persons voting for and against the Bill shall be entered on the Journal of each House respectively. If any Bill shall not be returned by the President within ten Days (Sundays excepted) after it shall have been presented to him, the Same shall be a Law, in like Manner as if he had signed it, unless the Congress by their Adjournment prevent its Return, in which Case it shall not be a Law.

Every Order, Resolution, or Vote to which the Concurrence of the Senate and House of Representatives may be necessary (except on a question of Adjournment) shall be presented to the President of the United States; and before the Same shall take Effect, shall be approved by him, or being disapproved by him, shall be repassed by two thirds of the Senate and House of Representatives, according to the Rules and Limitations prescribed in the Case of a Bill.

Section. 8.

The Congress shall have Power To lay and collect Taxes, Duties, Imposts and Excises, to pay the Debts and provide for the common Defence and general Welfare of the United States; but all Duties, Imposts and Excises shall be uniform throughout the United States;

To borrow Money on the credit of the United States;

To regulate Commerce with foreign Nations, and among the several States, and with the Indian Tribes;

To establish an uniform Rule of Naturalization, and uniform Laws on the subject of Bankruptcies throughout the United States;

To coin Money, regulate the Value thereof, and of foreign Coin, and fix the Standard of Weights and Measures;

To provide for the Punishment of counterfeiting the Securities and current Coin of the United States;

To establish Post Offices and post Roads;

To promote the Progress of Science and useful Arts, by securing for limited Times to Authors and Inventors the exclusive Right to their respective Writings and Discoveries;

To constitute Tribunals inferior to the supreme Court;

To define and punish Piracies and Felonies committed on the high Seas, and Offences against the Law of Nations;

To declare War, grant Letters of Marque and Reprisal, and make Rules concerning Captures on Land and Water;

To raise and support Armies, but no Appropriation of Money to that Use shall be for a longer Term than two Years;

To provide and maintain a Navy;

To make Rules for the Government and Regulation of the land and naval Forces;

To provide for calling forth the Militia to execute the Laws of the Union, suppress Insurrections and repel Invasions;

To provide for organizing, arming, and disciplining, the Militia, and for governing such Part of them as may be employed in the Service of the United States, reserving to the States respectively, the Appointment of the Officers, and the Authority of training the Militia according to the discipline prescribed by Congress;

To exercise exclusive Legislation in all Cases whatsoever, over such District (not exceeding ten Miles square) as may, by Cession of particular States, and the Acceptance of Congress, become the Seat of the Government of the United States, and to exercise like Authority over all Places purchased by the Consent of the Legislature of the State in which the Same shall be, for the Erection of Forts, Magazines, Arsenals, dock-Yards, and other needful Buildings;--And

To make all Laws which shall be necessary and proper for carrying into Execution the foregoing Powers, and all other Powers vested by this Constitution in the Government of the United States, or in any Department or Officer thereof.

Section. 9.

The Migration or Importation of such Persons as any of the States now existing shall think proper to admit, shall not be prohibited by the Congress prior to the Year one thousand eight hundred and eight, but a Tax or duty may be imposed on such Importation, not exceeding ten dollars for each Person.

The Privilege of the Writ of Habeas Corpus shall not be suspended, unless when in Cases of Rebellion or Invasion the public Safety may require it.

No Bill of Attainder or ex post facto Law shall be passed.

No Capitation, or other direct, Tax shall be laid, <u>unless in Proportion to the Census or enumeration herein before directed to be taken</u>.

No Tax or Duty shall be laid on Articles exported from any State.

No Preference shall be given by any Regulation of Commerce or Revenue to the Ports of one State over those of another; nor shall Vessels bound to, or from, one State, be obliged to enter, clear, or pay Duties in another.

No Money shall be drawn from the Treasury, but in Consequence of Appropriations made by Law; and a regular Statement and Account of the Receipts and Expenditures of all public Money shall be published from time to time.

No Title of Nobility shall be granted by the United States: And no Person holding any Office of Profit or Trust under them, shall, without the Consent of the Congress, accept of any present, Emolument, Office, or Title, of any kind whatever, from any King, Prince, or foreign State.

Section. 10.

No State shall enter into any Treaty, Alliance, or Confederation; grant Letters of Marque and Reprisal; coin Money; emit Bills of Credit; make any Thing but gold and silver Coin a Tender in Payment of Debts; pass any Bill of Attainder, ex post facto Law, or Law impairing the Obligation of Contracts, or grant any Title of Nobility.

No State shall, without the Consent of the Congress, lay any Imposts or Duties on Imports or Exports, except what may be absolutely necessary for executing it's inspection Laws: and the net Produce of all Duties and Imposts, laid by any State on Imports or Exports, shall be for the Use of the Treasury of the United States; and all such Laws shall be subject to the Revision and Controul of the Congress.

No State shall, without the Consent of Congress, lay any Duty of Tonnage, keep Troops, or Ships of War in time of Peace, enter into any Agreement or Compact with another State, or with a foreign Power, or engage in War, unless actually invaded, or in such imminent Danger as will not admit of delay.

Article. II.

Section. 1.

The executive Power shall be vested in a President of the United States of America. He shall hold his Office during the Term of four Years, and, together with the Vice President, chosen for the same Term, be elected, as follows:

Each State shall appoint, in such Manner as the Legislature thereof may direct, a Number of Electors, equal to the whole Number of Senators and Representatives to which the State may be entitled in the Congress: but no Senator or Representative, or Person holding an Office of Trust or Profit under the United States, shall be appointed an Elector.

The Electors shall meet in their respective States, and vote by Ballot for two Persons, of whom one at least shall not be an Inhabitant of the same State with themselves. And they shall make a List of all the Persons voted for, and of the Number of Votes for each; which List they shall sign and certify, and transmit sealed to the Seat of the Government of the United States, directed to the President of the Senate. The President of the Senate shall, in the Presence of the Senate and House of Representatives, open all the Certificates, and the Votes shall then be counted. The Person having the greatest Number of Votes shall be the President, if such Number be a Majority of the whole Number of Electors appointed; and if there be more than one who have such Majority, and have an equal Number of Votes, then the House of Representatives shall immediately chuse by Ballot one of them for President; and if no Person have a Majority, then from the five highest on the List the said House shall in like Manner chuse the President. But in chusing the President, the Votes shall be taken by States, the Representation from each State having one Vote; A quorum for this purpose shall consist of a Member or Members from two thirds of the States, and a Majority of all the States shall be necessary to a Choice. In every Case, after the Choice of the President, the Person having the greatest Number of Votes of the Electors shall be the Vice President. But if there should remain two or more who have equal Votes, the Senate shall chuse from them by Ballot the Vice President.

The Congress may determine the Time of chusing the Electors, and the Day on which they shall give their Votes; which Day shall be the same throughout the United States.

No Person except a natural born Citizen, or a Citizen of the United States, at the time of the Adoption of this Constitution, shall be eligible to the Office of President; neither shall any Person be eligible to that Office who shall not have attained to the Age of thirty five Years, and been fourteen Years a Resident within the United States.

In Case of the Removal of the President from Office, or of his Death, Resignation, or Inability to discharge the Powers and Duties of the said Office, the Same shall devolve on the Vice President, and the Congress may by Law provide for the Case of Removal, Death, Resignation or Inability, both of the President and Vice President, declaring what Officer shall then act as President, and such Officer shall act accordingly, until the Disability be removed, or a President shall be elected.

The President shall, at stated Times, receive for his Services, a Compensation, which shall neither be increased nor diminished during the Period for which he shall have been elected, and he shall not receive within that Period any other Emolument from the United States, or any of them.

Before he enter on the Execution of his Office, he shall take the following Oath or Affirmation:--"I do solemnly swear (or affirm) that I will faithfully execute the Office of President of the United States, and will to the best of my Ability, preserve, protect and defend the Constitution of the United States."

Section. 2.

The President shall be Commander in Chief of the Army and Navy of the United States, and of the Militia of the several States, when called into the actual Service of the United States; he may require the Opinion, in writing, of the principal Officer in each of the executive Departments, upon any Subject relating to the Duties of their respective Offices, and he shall have Power to grant Reprieves and Pardons for Offences against the United States, except in Cases of Impeachment.

He shall have Power, by and with the Advice and Consent of the Senate, to make Treaties, provided two thirds of the Senators present concur; and he shall nominate, and by and with the Advice and Consent of the Senate, shall appoint Ambassadors, other public Ministers and Consuls, Judges of the supreme Court, and all other Officers of the United States, whose Appointments are not herein otherwise provided for, and which shall be established by Law: but the Congress may by Law vest the Appointment of such inferior Officers, as they think proper, in the President alone. in the Courts of Law, or in the Heads of Departments.

The President shall have Power to fill up all Vacancies that may happen during the Recess of the Senate, by granting Commissions which shall expire at the End of their next Session.

Section. 3.

He shall from time to time give to the Congress Information of the State of the Union, and recommend to their Consideration such Measures as he shall judge necessary and expedient; he may, on extraordinary Occasions, convene both Houses, or either of them, and in Case of Disagreement between them, with Respect to the Time of Adjournment, he may adjourn them to such Time as he shall think proper; he shall receive Ambassadors and other public Ministers; he shall take Care that the Laws be faithfully executed, and shall Commission all the Officers of the United States.

Section. 4.

The President, Vice President and all civil Officers of the United States, shall be removed from Office on Impeachment for, and Conviction of, Treason, Bribery, or other high Crimes and Misdemeanors.

Article III.

Section. 1.

The judicial Power of the United States shall be vested in one supreme Court, and in such inferior Courts as the Congress may from time to time ordain and establish. The Judges, both of the supreme and inferior Courts, shall hold their Offices during good Behaviour, and shall, at stated Times, receive for their Services a Compensation, which shall not be diminished during their Continuance in Office.

Section. 2.

The judicial Power shall extend to all Cases, in Law and Equity, arising under this Constitution, the Laws of the United States, and Treaties made, or which shall be made, under their Authority;--to all Cases affecting Ambassadors, other public Ministers and Consuls;--to all Cases of admiralty and maritime Jurisdiction;--to Controversies to which the United States shall be a Party;--to Controversies between two or more States;--between a State and Citizens of another State;--between Citizens of different States;--between Citizens of the same State claiming Lands under Grants of different States, and between a State, or the Citizens thereof, and foreign States, Citizens or Subjects.

In all Cases affecting Ambassadors, other public Ministers and Consuls, and those in which a State shall be Party, the supreme Court shall have original Jurisdiction. In all the other Cases before mentioned, the supreme Court shall have appellate Jurisdiction, both as to Law and Fact, with such Exceptions, and under such Regulations as the Congress shall make.

The Trial of all Crimes, except in Cases of Impeachment, shall be by Jury; and such Trial shall be held in the State where the said Crimes shall have been committed; but when not committed within any State, the Trial shall be at such Place or Places as the Congress may by Law have directed.

Section. 3.

Treason against the United States, shall consist only in levying War against them, or in adhering to their Enemies, giving them Aid and Comfort. No Person shall be convicted of Treason unless on the Testimony of two Witnesses to the same overt Act, or on Confession in open Court.

The Congress shall have Power to declare the Punishment of Treason, but no Attainder of Treason shall work Corruption of Blood, or Forfeiture except during the Life of the Person attainted.

Article. IV.

Section. 1.

Full Faith and Credit shall be given in each State to the public Acts, Records, and judicial Proceedings of every other State. And the Congress may by general Laws prescribe the Manner in which such Acts, Records and Proceedings shall be proved, and the Effect thereof.

Section. 2.

The Citizens of each State shall be entitled to all Privileges and Immunities of Citizens in the several States.

A Person charged in any State with Treason, Felony, or other Crime, who shall flee from Justice, and be found in another State, shall on Demand of the executive Authority of the State from which he fled, be delivered up, to be removed to the State having Jurisdiction of the Crime.

No Person held to Service or Labour in one State, under the Laws thereof, escaping into another, shall, in Consequence of any Law or Regulation therein, be discharged from such Service or Labour, but shall be delivered up on Claim of the Party to whom such Service or Labour may be due.

Section. 3.

New States may be admitted by the Congress into this Union; but no new State shall be formed or erected within the Jurisdiction of any other State; nor any State be formed by the Junction of two or more States, or Parts of States, without the Consent of the Legislatures of the States concerned as well as of the Congress.

The Congress shall have Power to dispose of and make all needful Rules and Regulations respecting the Territory or other Property belonging to the United States; and nothing in this Constitution shall be so construed as to Prejudice any Claims of the United States, or of any particular State.

Section. 4.

The United States shall guarantee to every State in this Union a Republican Form of Government, and shall protect each of them against Invasion; and on Application of the Legislature, or of the Executive (when the Legislature cannot be convened), against domestic Violence.

Article. V.

The Congress, whenever two thirds of both Houses shall deem it necessary, shall propose Amendments to this Constitution, or, on the Application of the Legislatures of two thirds of the several States, shall call a Convention for proposing Amendments, which, in either Case, shall be valid to all Intents and Purposes, as Part of this Constitution, when ratified by the Legislatures of three fourths of the several States, or by Conventions in three fourths thereof, as the one or the other Mode of Ratification may be proposed by the Congress; Provided that no Amendment which may be made prior to the Year One thousand eight hundred and eight shall in any Manner affect the first and fourth Clauses in the Ninth Section of the first Article; and that no State, without its Consent, shall be deprived of its equal Suffrage in the Senate.

Article. VI.

All Debts contracted and Engagements entered into, before the Adoption of this Constitution, shall be as valid against the United States under this Constitution, as under the Confederation.

This Constitution, and the Laws of the United States which shall be made in Pursuance thereof; and all Treaties made, or which shall be made, under the Authority of the United States, shall be the supreme Law of the Land; and the Judges in every State shall be bound thereby, any Thing in the Constitution or Laws of any State to the Contrary notwithstanding.

The Senators and Representatives before mentioned, and the Members of the several State Legislatures, and all executive and judicial Officers, both of the United States and of the several States, shall be bound by Oath or Affirmation, to support this Constitution; but no religious Test shall ever be required as a Qualification to any Office or public Trust under the United States.

Article. VII.

The Ratification of the Conventions of nine States, shall be sufficient for the Establishment of this Constitution between the States so ratifying the Same.

The Word, "the," being interlined between the seventh and eighth Lines of the first Page, the Word "Thirty" being partly written on an Erazure in the fifteenth Line of the first Page, The Words "is tried" being interlined between the thirty second and thirty third Lines of the first Page and the Word "the" being interlined between the forty third and forty fourth Lines of the second Page.

Attest William Jackson Secretary

Done in Convention by the Unanimous Consent of the States present the Seventeenth Day of September in the Year of our Lord one thousand seven hundred and Eighty seven and of the Independence of the United States of America the Twelfth In witness whereof We have hereunto subscribed our Names,

G°. Washington
Presidt and deputy from Virginia

Delaware
Geo: Read
Gunning Bedford jun
John Dickinson
Richard Bassett
Jaco: Broom

Maryland
James McHenry
Dan of St Thos. Jenifer
Danl. Carroll

Virginia
John Blair
James Madison Jr.

North Carolina
Wm. Blount
Richd. Dobbs Spaight
Hu Williamson

South Carolina
J. Rutledge
Charles Cotesworth Pinckney
Charles Pinckney
Pierce Butler

Georgia
William Few
Abr Baldwin

New Hampshire
John Langdon
Nicholas Gilman

Massachusetts

Nathaniel Gorham
Rufus King

Connecticut
Wm. Saml. Johnson
Roger Sherman

New York
Alexander Hamilton

New Jersey
Wil: Livingston
David Brearley
Wm. Paterson
Jona: Dayton

Pennsylvania
B Franklin
Thomas Mifflin
Robt. Morris
Geo. Clymer
Thos. FitzSimons
Jared Ingersoll
James Wilson
Gouv Morris

Amendments to the Constitution of the United States of America

---

Articles in addition to, and amendment of, the Constitution of the United States of America, proposed by Congress, and ratified by the several states, pursuant to the Fifth Article of the original Constitution fn1

Amendment I fn2 [Annotations]

Congress shall make no law respecting an establishment of religion, or prohibiting the free exercise thereof; or abridging the freedom of speech, or of the press; or the right of the people peaceably to assemble, and to petition the Government for a redress of grievances.

Amendment II [Annotations]

A well regulated Militia, being necessary to the security of a free State, the right of the people to keep and bear Arms, shall not be infringed.

Amendment III [Annotations]

No Soldier shall, in time of peace be quartered in any house, without the consent of the Owner, nor in time of war, but in a manner to be prescribed by law.

Amendment IV [Annotations]

The right of the people to be secure in their persons, houses, papers, and effects, against unreasonable searches and seizures, shall not be violated, and no Warrants shall issue, but upon probable cause, supported by Oath or affirmation, and particularly describing the place to be searched, and the persons or things to be seized.

Amendment V [Annotations]

No person shall be held to answer for a capital, or otherwise infamous crime, unless on a presentment or indictment of a Grand Jury, except in cases arising in the land or naval forces, or in the Militia, when in actual service in time of War or public danger; nor shall any person be subject for the same offence to be twice put in jeopardy of life or limb; nor shall be compelled in any criminal case to be a witness against himself, nor be deprived of life, liberty, or property, without due process of law; nor shall private property be taken for public use, without just compensation.

Amendment VI [Annotations]

In all criminal prosecutions, the accused shall enjoy the right to a speedy and public trial, by an impartial jury of the State and district wherein the crime shall have been committed, which district shall have been previously ascertained by law, and to be informed of the nature and cause of the accusation; to be confronted with the witnesses against him; to have compulsory process for obtaining witnesses in his favor, and to have the Assistance of Counsel for his defence.

Amendment VII [Annotations]

In Suits at common law, where the value in controversy shall exceed twenty dollars, the right of trial by jury shall be preserved, and no fact tried by a jury, shall be otherwise re-examined in any Court of the United States, than according to the rules of the common law.

Amendment VIII [Annotations]

Excessive bail shall not be required, nor excessive fines imposed, nor cruel and unusual punishments inflicted.

Amendment IX [Annotations]

The enumeration in the Constitution, of certain rights, shall not be construed to deny or disparage others retained by the people.

Amendment X [Annotations]

The powers not delegated to the United States by the Constitution, nor prohibited by it to the States, are reserved to the States respectively, or to the people.

Amendment XI fn3 [Annotations]

The Judicial power of the United States shall not be construed to extend to any suit in law or equity, commenced or prosecuted against one of the United States by Citizens of another State, or by Citizens or Subjects of any Foreign State.

Amendment XII fn4 [Annotations]

The Electors shall meet in their respective states and vote by ballot for President and Vice-President, one of whom, at least, shall not be an inhabitant of the same state with themselves; they shall name in their ballots the person voted for as President, and in distinct ballots the person voted for as Vice- President, and they shall make distinct lists of all persons voted for as President, and of all persons voted for as Vice-President, and of the number of votes for each, which lists they shall sign and certify, and transmit sealed to the seat of the government of the United States, directed to the President of the Senate;--The President of the Senate shall, in the presence of the Senate and House of Representatives, open all the certificates and the votes shall then be counted;--The person having the greatest Number of votes for President, shall be the President, if such number be a majority of the whole number of Electors appointed; and if no person have such majority, then from the persons having the highest numbers not exceeding three on the list of those voted for as President, the House of Representatives shall choose immediately, by ballot, the President. But in choosing the President, the votes shall be taken by states, the representation from each state having one vote; a quorum for this purpose shall consist of a member or members from two-thirds of the states, and a majority of all the states shall be necessary to a choice. And if the House of Representatives shall not choose a President whenever the right of choice shall devolve upon them, before the fourth day of March next following, then the Vice- President shall act as President, as in the case of the death or other constitutional disability of the President--The person having the greatest number of votes as Vice-President, shall be the Vice-President, if such number be a majority of the whole number of Electors appointed, and if no person have a majority, then from the two highest numbers on the list, the Senate shall choose the Vice-President; a quorum for the purpose shall consist of two-thirds of the whole number of Senators, and a majority of the whole number shall be necessary to a choice. But no person constitutionally ineligible to the office of President shall be eligible to that of Vice-President of the United States.

Amendment XIII. fn5 [Annotations]

Section 1. Neither slavery nor involuntary servitude, except as a punishment for crime whereof the party shall have been duly convicted, shall exist within the United States, or any place subject to their jurisdiction.

Section 2. Congress shall have power to enforce this article by appropriate legislation.

Amendment XIV. fn6 [Annotations]

Section. 1. All persons born or naturalized in the United States and subject to the jurisdiction thereof, are citizens of the United States and of the State wherein they reside. No State shall make or enforce any law which shall abridge the privileges or immunities of citizens of the United States; nor shall any State deprive any person of life, liberty, or property, without due process of law; nor deny to any person within its jurisdiction the equal protection of the laws.

Section. 2. Representatives shall be apportioned among the several States according to their respective numbers, counting the whole number of persons in each State, excluding Indians not taxed. But when the right to vote at any election for the choice of electors for President and Vice President of the United States, Representatives in Congress, the Executive and Judicial officers of a State, or the members of the Legislature thereof, is denied to any of the male inhabitants of such State, being twenty-one years of age, and citizens of the United States, or in any way abridged, except for participation in rebellion, or other crime, the basis of representation therein shall be reduced in the proportion which the number of such male citizens shall bear to the whole number of male citizens twenty-one years of age in such State.

Section. 3. No person shall be a Senator or Representative in Congress, or elector of President and Vice President, or hold any office, civil or military, under the United States, or under any State, who, having previously taken an oath, as a member of Congress, or as an officer of the United States, or as a member of any State legislature, or as an executive or judicial officer of any State, to support the Constitution of the United States, shall have engaged in insurrection or rebellion against the same, or given aid or comfort to the enemies thereof. But Congress may by a vote of two-thirds of each House, remove such disability.

Section. 4. The validity of the public debt of the United States, authorized by law, including debts incurred for payment of pensions and bounties for services in suppressing insurrection or rebellion, shall not be questioned. But neither the United States nor any State shall assume or pay any debt or obligation incurred in aid of insurrection or rebellion against the United States, or any claim for the loss or emancipation of any slave; but all such debts, obligations and claims shall be held illegal and void.

Section. 5. The Congress shall have power to enforce, by appropriate legislation, the provisions of this article.

Amendment XV. fn7 [Annotations]

Section. 1. The right of citizens of the United States to vote shall not be denied or abridged by the United States or by any State on account of race, color, or previous condition of servitude.

Section. 2. The Congress shall have power to enforce this article by appropriate legislation.

Amendment XVI. fn8 [Annotations]

The Congress shall have power to lay and collect taxes on incomes, from whatever source derived, without apportionment among the several States, and without regard to any census or enumeration.

Amendment XVII fn9 [Annotations]

The Senate of the United States shall be composed of two Senators from each State, elected by the people thereof, for six years; and each Senator shall have one vote. The electors in each State shall have the qualifications requisite for electors of the most numerous branch of the State legislatures.

When vacancies happen in the representation of any State in the Senate, the executive authority of such State shall issue writs of election to fill such vacancies: Provided, That the legislature of any State may empower the executive thereof to make temporary appointments until the people fill the vacancies by election as the legislature may direct.

This amendment shall not be so construed as to affect the election or term of any Senator chosen before it becomes valid as part of the Constitution.

Amendment XVIII fn10 [Annotations]

Section. 1. After one year from the ratification of this article the manufacture, sale, or transportation of intoxicating liquors within, the importation thereof into, or the exportation thereof from the United States and all territory subject to the jurisdiction thereof for beverage purposes is hereby prohibited.

Sec. 2. The Congress and the several States shall have concurrent power to enforce this article by appropriate legislation.

Sec. 3. This article shall be inoperative unless it shall have been ratified as an amendment to the Constitution by the legislatures of the several States, as provided in the Constitution, within seven years from the date of the submission hereof to the States by the Congress.

Amendment XIX fn11 [Annotations]

The right of citizens of the United States to vote shall not be denied or abridged by the United States or by any State on account of sex. Congress shall have power to enforce this article by appropriate legislation.

Amendment XX fn12 [Annotations]

Section. 1. The terms of the President and Vice President shall end at noon on the 20th day of January, and the terms of Senators and Representatives at noon on the 3d day of January, of the years in which such terms would have ended if this article had not been ratified; and the terms of their successors shall then begin.

Sec. 2. The Congress shall assemble at least once in every year, and such meeting shall begin at noon on the 3d day of January, unless they shall by law appoint a different day.

Sec. 3. If, at the time fixed for the beginning of the term of the President, the President elect shall have died, the Vice President elect shall become President. If a President shall not have been chosen before the time fixed for the beginning of his term, or if the President elect shall have failed to qualify, then the Vice President elect shall act as President until a President shall have qualified; and the Congress may by law provide for the case wherein neither a President elect nor a Vice President elect shall have qualified, declaring who shall then act as President, or the manner in which one who is to act shall be selected, and such person shall act accordingly until a President or Vice President shall have qualified.

Sec. 4. The Congress may by law provide for the case of the death of any of the persons from whom the House of Representatives may choose a President whenever the right of choice shall have devolved upon them, and for the case of the death of any of the persons from whom the Senate may choose a Vice President whenever the right of choice shall have devolved upon them.

Sec. 5. Sections 1 and 2 shall take effect on the 15th day of October following the ratification of this article.

Sec. 6. This article shall be inoperative unless it shall have been ratified as an amendment to the Constitution by the legislatures of three-fourths of the several States within seven years from the date of its submission.

Amendment XXI fn13 [Annotations]

Section. 1. The eighteenth article of amendment to the Constitution of the United States is hereby repealed.

Sec. 2. The transportation or importation into any State, Territory, or possession of the United States for delivery or use therein of intoxicating liquors, in violation of the laws thereof, is hereby prohibited.

Sec. 3. This article shall be inoperative unless it shall have been ratified as an amendment to the Constitution by conventions in the several States, as provided in the Constitution, within seven years from the date of the submission hereof to the States by the Congress.

Amendment XXII fn14 [Annotations]

Section. 1. No person shall be elected to the office of the President more than twice, and no person who has held the office of President, or acted as President, for more than two years of a term to which some other person was elected President shall be elected to the office of the President more than once. But this Article shall not apply to any person holding the office of President, when this Article was proposed by the Congress, and shall not prevent any person who may be holding the office of President, or acting as President, during the term within which this Article becomes operative from holding the office of President or acting as President during the remainder of such term.

Sec. 2. This article shall be inoperative unless it shall have been ratified as an amendment to the Constitution by the legislatures of three-fourths of the several States within seven years from the date of its submission to the States by the Congress.

Amendment XXIII fn15 [Annotations]

Section. 1. The District constituting the seat of Government of the United States shall appoint in such manner as the Congress may direct: A number of electors of President and Vice President equal to the whole number of Senators and Representatives in Congress to which the District would be entitled if it were a State, but in no event more than the least populous State; they shall be in addition to those appointed by the States, but they shall be considered, for the purposes of the election of President and Vice President, to be electors appointed by a State; and they shall meet in the District and perform such duties as provided by the twelfth article of amendment.

Sec. 2. The Congress shall have power to enforce this article by appropriate legislation.

Amendment XXIV fn16 [Annotations]

Section. 1. The right of citizens of the United States to vote in any primary or other election for President or Vice President, for electors for President or Vice President, or for Senator or Representative in Congress, shall not be denied or abridged by the United States or any State by reason of failure to pay any poll tax or other tax.

Section. 2. The Congress shall have power to enforce this article by appropriate legislation.

Amendment XXV fn17 [Annotations]

Section. 1. In case of the removal of the President from office or of his death or resignation, the Vice President shall become President.

Section. 2. Whenever there is a vacancy in the office of the Vice President, the President shall nominate a Vice President who shall take office upon confirmation by a majority vote of both Houses of Congress.

Section. 3. Whenever the President transmits to the President pro tempore of the Senate and the Speaker of the House of Representatives has written declaration that he is unable to discharge the powers and duties of his office, and until he transmits to them a written declaration to the contrary, such powers and duties shall be discharged by the Vice President as Acting President.

Section. 4. Whenever the Vice President and a majority of either the principal officers of the executive departments or of such other body as Congress may by law provide, transmit to the President pro tempore of the Senate and the Speaker of the House of Representatives their written declaration that the President is unable to discharge the powers and duties of his office, the Vice President shall immediately assume the powers and duties of the office as Acting President.

Thereafter, when the President transmits to the President pro tempore of the Senate and the Speaker of the House of Representatives has written declaration that no inability exists, he shall resume the powers and duties of his office unless the Vice President and a majority of either the principal officers of the executive department or of such other body as Congress may by law provide, transmit within four days to the President pro tempore of the Senate and the Speaker of the House of Representatives their written declaration that the President is unable to discharge the powers and duties of his office. Thereupon Congress shall decide the issue, assembling within forty-eight hours for that purpose if not in session. If the Congress, within twenty-one days after receipt of the latter written declaration, or, if Congress is not in session, within twenty-one days after Congress is required to assemble, determines by two-thirds vote of both Houses that the President is unable to discharge the powers and duties of his office, the Vice President shall continue to discharge the same as Acting President; otherwise, the President shall resume the powers and duties of his office.

Amendment XXVI fn18 [Annotations]

Section. 1. The right of citizens of the United States, who are eighteen years of age or older, to vote shall not be denied or abridged by the United States or by any State on account of age.

Section. 2. The Congress shall have power to enforce this article by appropriate legislation.

Amendment XXVII fn19 [Annotations]

No law varying the compensation for the services of the Senators and Representatives shall take effect, until an election of Representatives shall have intervened.

This document is sponsored by the United States Senate on the United States Government Printing Office web site.

Footnotes

1 In Dillon v. Gloss, 256 U.S. 368 (1921), the Supreme Court stated that it would take judicial notice of the date on which a State ratified a proposed constitutional amendment. Accordingly the Court consulted the State journals to determine the dates on which each house of the legislature of certain States ratified the Eighteenth Amendment. It, therefore, follows that the date on which the governor approved the ratification, or the date on which the secretary of state of a given State certified the ratification, or the date on which the Secretary of State of the United States received a copy of said certificate, or the date on which he proclaimed that the amendment had been ratified are not controlling. Hence, the ratification date given in the following notes is the date on which the legislature of a given State approved the particular amendment (signature by the speaker or presiding officers of both houses being considered a part of the ratification of the "legislature"). When that date is not available, the date given is that on which it was approved by the governor or certified by the secretary of state of the particular State. In each case such fact has been noted. Except as otherwise indicated information as to ratification is based on data supplied by the Department of State.

2 Brackets enclosing an amendment number indicate that the number was not specifically assigned in the resolution proposing the amendment. It will be seen, accordingly, that only the Thirteenth, Fourteenth, Fifteenth, and Sixteenth Amendments were thus technically ratified by number. The first ten amendments along with two others that were not ratified were proposed by Congress on September 25, 1789, when they passed the Senate, having previously passed the House on September 24 (1 Annals of Congress 88, 913). They appear officially in 1 Stat. 97. Ratification was completed on December 15, 1791, when the eleventh State (Virginia) approved these amendments, there being then 14 States in the Union.

The several state legislatures ratified the first ten amendments to the Constitution on the following dates: New Jersey, November 20, 1789; Maryland, December 19, 1789; North Carolina, December 22, 1789; South Carolina, January 19, 1790; New Hampshire, January 25, 1790; Delaware, January 28, 1790; New York, February 27, 1790;

Pennsylvania, March 10, 1790; Rhode Island, June 7, 1790; Vermont, November 3, 1791; Virginia, December 15, 1791. The two amendments that then failed of ratification prescribed the ratio of representation to population in the House, and specified that no law varying the compensation of members of Congress should be effective until after an intervening election of Representatives. The first was ratified by ten States (one short of the requisite number) and the second, by six States; subsequently, this second proposal was taken up by the States in the period 1980-1992 and was proclaimed as ratified as of May 7, 1992. Connecticut, Georgia, and Massachusetts ratified the first ten amendments in 1939.

3 The Eleventh Amendment was proposed by Congress on March 4, 1794, when it passed the House, 4 Annals of Congress 477, 478, having previously passed the Senate on January 14, Id., 30, 31. It appears officially in 1 Stat. 402. Ratification was completed on February 7, 1795, when the twelfth State (North Carolina) approved the amendment, there being then 15 States in the Union. Official announcement of ratification was not made until January 8, 1798, when President John Adams in a message to Congress stated that the Eleventh Amendment had been adopted by three-fourths of the States and that it "may now be deemed to be a part of the Constitution." In the interim South Carolina had ratified, and Tennessee had been admitted into the Union as the sixteenth State.

The several state legislatures ratified the Eleventh Amendment on the following dates: New York, March 27, 1794; Rhode Island, March 31, 1794; Connecticut, May 8, 1794; New Hampshire, June 16, 1794; Massachusetts, June 26, 1794; Vermont, between October 9 and November 9, 1794; Virginia, November 18, 1794; Georgia, November 29, 1794; Kentucky, December 7, 1794; Maryland, December 26, 1794; Delaware, January 23, 1795; North Carolina, February 7, 1795; South Carolina, December 4, 1797.

4 The Twelfth Amendment was proposed by Congress on December 9, 1803, when it passed the House, 13 Annals of Congress 775, 776, having previously passed the Senate on December 2. Id., 209. It was not signed by the presiding officers of the House and Senate until December 12. It appears officially in 2 Stat. 306. Ratification was probably completed on June 15, 1804, when the legislature of the thirteenth State (New Hampshire) approved the amendment, there being then 17 States in the Union. The Governor of New Hampshire, however, vetoed this act of the legislature on June 20, and the act failed to pass again by two- thirds vote then required by the state constitution. Inasmuch as Article V of the Federal Constitution specifies that amendments shall become effective "when ratified by legislatures of three-fourths of the several States or by conventions in three-fourths thereof," it has been generally believed that an approval or veto by a governor is without significance. If the ratification by New Hampshire be deemed ineffective, then the amendment became operative by Tennessee's ratification on July 27, 1804. On September 25, 1804, in a circular letter to the Governors of the several

States, Secretary of State Madison declared the amendment ratified by three-fourths of the States.

The several state legislatures ratified the Twelfth Amendment on the following dates: North Carolina, December 22, 1803; Maryland, December 24, 1803; Kentucky, December 27, 1803; Ohio, between December 5 and December 30, 1803; Virginia, between December 20, 1803 and February 3, 1804; Pennsylvania, January 5, 1804; Vermont, January 30, 1804; New York, February 10, 1804; New Jersey, February 22, 1804; Rhode Island, between February 27 and March 12, 1804; South Carolina, May 15, 1804; Georgia, May 19, 1804; New Hampshire, June 15, 1804; and Tennessee, July 27, 1804. The amendment was rejected by Delaware on January 18, 1804, and by Connecticut at its session begun May 10, 1804. Massachusetts ratified this amendment in 1961.

5 The Thirteenth Amendment was proposed by Congress on January 31, 1865, when it passed the House, Cong. Globe (38th Cong., 2d Sess.) 531, having previously passed the Senate on April 8, 1964. Id. (38th cong., 1st Sess.), 1940. It appears officially in 13 Stat. 567 under the date of February 1, 1865. Ratification was completed on December 6, 1865, when the legislature of the twenty-seventh State (Georgia) approved the amendment, there being then 36 States in the Union. On December 18, 1865, Secretary of State Seward certified that the Thirteenth Amendment had become a part of the Constitution, 13 Stat. 774.

The several state legislatures ratified the Thirteenth Amendment on the following dates: Illinois, February 1, 1865; Rhode Island, February 2, 1865; Michigan, February 2, 1865; Maryland, February 3, 1865; New York, February 3, 1865; West Virginia, February 3, 1865; Missouri, February 6, 1865; Maine, February 7, 1865; Kansas, February 7, 1865; Massachusetts, February 7, 1865; Pennsylvania, February 8, 1865; Virginia, February 9, 1865; Ohio, February 10, 1865; Louisiana, February 15 or 16, 1865; Indiana, February 16, 1865; Nevada, February 16, 1865; Minnesota, February 23, 1865; Wisconsin, February 24, 1865; Vermont, March 9, 1865 (date on which it was "approved" by Governor); Tennessee, April 7, 1865; Arkansas, April 14, 1865; Connecticut, May 4, 1865; New Hampshire, June 30, 1865; South Carolina, November 13, 1865; Alabama, December 2, 1865 (date on which it was "approved" by Provisional Governor); North Carolina, December 4, 1865; Georgia, December 6, 1865; Oregon, December 11, 1865; California, December 15, 1865; Florida, December 28, 1865 (Florida again ratified this amendment on June 9, 1868, upon its adoption of a new constitution); Iowa, January 17, 1866; New Jersey, January 23, 1866 (after having rejected the amendment on March 16, 1865); Texas, February 17, 1870; Delaware, February 12, 1901 (after having rejected the amendment on February 8, 1865). The amendment was rejected by Kentucky on February 24, 1865, and by Mississippi on December 2, 1865.

<u>6</u> The Fourteenth Amendment was proposed by Congress on June 13, 1866, when it passed the House, Cong. Globe (39th Cong., 1st Sess.) 3148, 3149, having previously passed the Senate on June 8. Id., 3042. It appears officially in 14 Stat. 358 under date of June 16, 1866. Ratification was probably completed on July 9, 1868, when the legislature of the twenty-eighth State (South Carolina or Louisiana) approved the amendment, there being then 37 States in the Union. However, Ohio and New Jersey had prior to that date "withdrawn" their earlier assent to this amendment. Accordingly, Secretary of State Seward on July 20, 1868, certified that the amendment had become a part of the Constitution if the said withdrawals were ineffective. 15 Stat. 706-707. Congress on July 21, 1868, passed a joint resolution declaring the amendment a part of the Constitution and directing the Secretary to promulgate it as such. On July 28, 1868, Secretary Seward certified without reservation that the amendment was a part of the Constitution. In the interim, two other States, Alabama on July 13 and Georgia on July 21, 1868, had added their ratifications.

The several state legislatures ratified the Fourteenth Amendment on the following dates: Connecticut, June 30, 1866; New Hampshire, July 7, 1866; Tennessee, July 19, 1866; New Jersey, September 11, 1866 (the New Jersey Legislature on February 20, 1868 "withdrew" its consent to the ratification; the Governor vetoed that bill on March 5, 1868; and it was repassed over his veto on March 24, 1868); Oregon, September 19, 1866 (Oregon "withdrew" its consent on October 15, 1868); Vermont, October 30, 1866; New York, January 10, 1867; Ohio, January 11, 1867 (Ohio "withdrew" its consent on January 15, 1868); Illinois, January 15, 1867; West Virginia, January 16, 1867; Michigan, January 16, 1867; Kansas, January 17, 1867; Minnesota, January 17, 1867; Maine, January 19, 1867; Nevada, January 22, 1867; Indiana, January 23, 1867; Missouri, January 26, 1867 (date on which it was certified by the Missouri secretary of state); Rhode Island, February 7, 1867; Pennsylvania, February 12, 1867; Wisconsin, February 13, 1867 (actually passed February 7, but not signed by legislative officers until February 13); Massachusetts, March 20, 1867; Nebraska, June 15, 1867; Iowa, March 9, 1868; Arkansas, April 6, 1868; Florida, June 9, 1868; North Carolina, July 2, 1868 (after having rejected the amendment on December 13, 1866); Louisiana, July 9, 1868 (after having rejected the amendment on February 6, 1867); South Carolina, July 8, 1868 (after having rejected the amendment on December 20, 1866); Alabama, July 13, 1868 (date on which it was "approved" by the Governor); Georgia, July 21, 1868 (after having rejected the amendment on November 9, 1866--Georgia ratified again on February 2, 1870); Virginia, October 8, 1869 (after having rejected the amendment on January 9, 1867); Mississippi, January 17, 1870; Texas, February 18, 1870 (after having rejected the amendment on October 27, 1866); Delaware, February 12, 1901 (after having rejected the amendment on February 7, 1867). The amendment was rejected (and not subsequently ratified) by Kentucky on January 8, 1867. Maryland and California ratified this amendment in 1959.

<u>7</u> The Fifteenth Amendment was proposed by Congress on February 26, 1869, when it passed the Senate, Cong. Globe (40th Cong., 3rd Sess.) 1641, having previously passed the House on February 25. Id., 1563, 1564. It appears officially in 15 Stat. 346 under the date of February 27, 1869. Ratification was probably completed on February 3, 1870, when the legislature of the twenty-eighth State (Iowa) approved the amendment, there being then 37 States in the Union. However, New York had prior to that date "withdrawn" its earlier assent to this amendment. Even if this withdrawal were effective, Nebraska's ratification on February 17, 1870, authorized Secretary of State Fish's certification of March 30, 1870, that the Fifteenth Amendment had become a part of the Constitution. 16 Stat. 1131.

The several state legislatures ratified the Fifteenth Amendment on the following dates: Nevada, March 1, 1869; West Virginia, March 3, 1869; North Carolina, March 5, 1869; Louisiana, March 5, 1869 (date on which it was "approved" by the Governor); Illinois, March 5, 1869; Michigan, March 5, 1869; Wisconsin, March 5, 1869; Maine, March 11, 1869; Massachusetts, March 12, 1869; South Carolina, March 15, 1869; Arkansas, March 15, 1869; Pennsylvania, March 25, 1869; New York, April 14, 1869 (New York "withdrew" its consent to the ratification on January 5, 1870); Indiana, May 14, 1869; Connecticut, May 19, 1869; Florida, June 14, 1869; New Hampshire, July 1, 1869; Virginia, October 8, 1869; Vermont, October 20, 1869; Alabama, November 16, 1869; Missouri, January 7, 1870 (Missouri had ratified the first section of the 15th Amendment on March 1, 1869; it failed to include in its ratification the second section of the amendment); Minnesota, January 13, 1870; Mississippi, January 17, 1870; Rhode Island, January 18, 1870; Kansas, January 19, 1870 (Kansas had by a defectively worded resolution previously ratified this amendment on February 27, 1869); Ohio, January 27, 1870 (after having rejected the amendment on May 4, 1869); Georgia, February 2, 1870; Iowa, February 3, 1870; Nebraska, February 17, 1870; Texas, February 18, 1870; New Jersey, February 15, 1871 (after having rejected the amendment on February 7, 1870); Delaware, February 12, 1901 (date on which approved by Governor; Delaware had previously rejected the amendment on March 18, 1869). The amendment was rejected (and not subsequently ratified) by Kentucky, Maryland, and Tennessee. California ratified this amendment in 1962 and Oregon in 1959.

<u>8</u> The Sixteenth Amendment was proposed by Congress on July 12, 1909, when it passed the House, 44 Cong. Rec. (61st Cong., 1st Sess.) 4390, 4440, 4441, having previously passed the Senate on July 5. Id., 4121. It appears officially in 36 Stat. 184. Ratification was completed on February 3, 1913, when the legislature of the thirty-sixth State (Delaware, Wyoming, or New Mexico) approved the amendment, there being then 48 States in the Union. On February 25, 1913, Secretary of State Knox certified that this amendment had become a part of the Constitution. 37 Stat. 1785.

The several state legislatures ratified the Sixteenth Amendment on the following dates: Alabama, August 10, 1909; Kentucky, February 8, 1910; South Carolina, February 19, 1910; Illinois, March 1, 1910; Mississippi, March 7, 1910; Oklahoma, March 10, 1910; Maryland, April 8, 1910; Georgia, August 3, 1910; Texas, August 16, 1910; Ohio, January 19, 1911; Idaho, January 20, 1911; Oregon, January 23, 1911; Washington, January 26, 1911; Montana, January 27, 1911; Indiana, January 30, 1911; California, January 31, 1911; Nevada, January 31, 1911; South Dakota, February 1, 1911; Nebraska, February 9, 1911; North Carolina, February 11, 1911; Colorado, February 15, 1911; North Dakota, February 17, 1911; Michigan, February 23, 1911; Iowa, February 24, 1911; Kansas, March 2, 1911; Missouri, March 16, 1911; Maine, March 31, 1911; Tennessee, April 7, 1911; Arkansas, April 22, 1911 (after having rejected the amendment at the session begun January 9, 1911); Wisconsin, May 16, 1911; New York, July 12, 1911; Arizona, April 3, 1912; Minnesota, June 11, 1912; Louisiana, June 28, 1912; West Virginia, January 31, 1913; Delaware, February 3, 1913; Wyoming, February 3, 1913; New Mexico, February 3, 1913; New Jersey, February 4, 1913; Vermont, February 19, 1913; Massachusetts, March 4, 1913; New Hampshire, March 7, 1913 (after having rejected the amendment on March 2, 1911). The amendment was rejected (and not subsequently ratified) by Connecticut, Rhode Island, and Utah.

9 The Seventeenth Amendment was proposed by Congress on May 13, 1912, when it passed the House, 48 Cong. Rec. (62d Cong., 2d Sess.) 6367, having previously passed the Senate on June 12, 1911. 47 Cong. Rec. (62d Cong., 1st Sess.) 1925. It appears officially in 37 Stat. 646. Ratification was completed on April 8, 1913, when the thirty-sixth State (Connecticut) approved the amendment, there being then 48 States in the Union. On May 31, 1913, Secretary of State Bryan certified that it had become a part of the Constitution. 38 Stat 2049.

The several state legislatures ratified the Seventeenth Amendment on the following dates: Massachusetts, May 22, 1912; Arizona, June 3, 1912; Minnesota, June 10, 1912; New York, January 15, 1913; Kansas, January 17, 1913; Oregon, January 23, 1913; North Carolina, January 25, 1913; California, January 28, 1913; Michigan, January 28, 1913; Iowa, January 30, 1913; Montana, January 30, 1913; Idaho, January 31, 1913; West Virginia, February 4, 1913; Colorado, February 5, 1913; Nevada, February 6, 1913; Texas, February 7, 1913; Washington, February 7, 1913; Wyoming, February 8, 1913; Arkansas, February 11, 1913; Illinois, February 13, 1913; North Dakota, February 14, 1913; Wisconsin, February 18, 1913; Indiana, February 19, 1913; New Hampshire, February 19, 1913; Vermont, February 19, 1913; South Dakota, February 19, 1913; Maine, February 20, 1913; Oklahoma, February 24, 1913; Ohio, February 25, 1913; Missouri, March 7, 1913; New Mexico, March 13, 1913; Nebraska, March 14, 1913; New Jersey, March 17, 1913; Tennessee, April 1, 1913; Pennsylvania, April 2, 1913;

Connecticut, April 8, 1913; Louisiana, June 5, 1914. The amendment was rejected by Utah on February 26, 1913.

10 The Eighteenth Amendment was proposed by Congress on December 18, 1917, when it passed the Senate, Cong. Rec. (65th Cong. 2d Sess.) 478, having previously passed the House on December 17. Id., 470. It appears officially in 40 Stat. 1059. Ratification was completed on January 16, 1919, when the thirty-sixth State approved the amendment, there being then 48 States in the Union. On January 29, 1919, Acting Secretary of State Polk certified that this amendment had been adopted by the requisite number of States. 40 Stat. 1941. By its terms this amendment did not become effective until 1 year after ratification.

The several state legislatures ratified the Eighteenth Amendment on the following dates: Mississippi, January 8, 1918; Virginia, January 11, 1918; Kentucky, January 14, 1918; North Dakota, January 28, 1918 (date on which approved by Governor); South Carolina, January 29, 1918; Maryland, February 13, 1918; Montana, February 19, 1918; Texas, March 4, 1918; Delaware, March 18, 1918; South Dakota, March 20, 1918; Massachusetts, April 2, 1918; Arizona, May 24, 1918; Georgia, June 26, 1918; Louisiana, August 9, 1918 (date on which approved by Governor); Florida, November 27, 1918; Michigan, January 2, 1919; Ohio, January 7, 1919; Oklahoma, January 7, 1919; Idaho, January 8, 1919; Maine, January 8, 1919; West Virginia, January 9, 1919; California, January 13, 1919; Tennessee, January 13, 1919; Washington, January 13, 1919; Arkansas, January 14, 1919; Kansas, January 14, 1919; Illinois, January 14, 1919; Indiana, January 14, 1919; Alabama, January 15, 1919; Colorado, January 15, 1919; Iowa, January 15, 1919; New Hampshire, January 15, 1919; Oregon, January 15, 1919; Nebraska, January 16, 1919; North Carolina, January 16, 1919; Utah, January 16, 1919; Missouri, January 16, 1919; Wyoming, January 16, 1919; Minnesota, January 17, 1919; Wisconsin, January 17, 1919; New Mexico, January 20, 1919; Nevada, January 21, 1919; Pennsylvania, February 25, 1919; Connecticut, May 6, 1919; New Jersey, March 9, 1922; New York, January 29, 1919; Vermont, January 29, 1919.

11 The Nineteenth Amendment was proposed by Congress on June 4, 1919, when it passed the Senate, Cong. Rec. (66th Cong., 1st Sess.) 635, having previously passed the house on May 21. Id., 94. It appears officially in 41 Stat. 362. Ratification was completed on August 18, 1920, when the thirty-sixth State (Tennessee) approved the amendment, there being then 48 States in the Union. On August 26, 1920, Secretary of Colby certified that it had become a part of the Constitution. 41 Stat. 1823.

The several state legislatures ratified the Nineteenth Amendment on the following dates: Illinois, June 10, 1919 (readopted June 17, 1919); Michigan, June 10, 1919; Wisconsin, June 10, 1919; Kansas, June 16, 1919; New York, June 16, 1919; Ohio, June 16, 1919;

Pennsylvania, June 24, 1919; Massachusetts, June 25, 1919; Texas, June 28, 1919; Iowa, July 2, 1919 (date on which approved by Governor); Missouri, July 3, 1919; Arkansas, July 28, 1919; Montana, August 2, 1919 (date on which approved by governor); Nebraska, August 2, 1919; Minnesota, September 8, 1919; New Hampshire, September 10, 1919 (date on which approved by Governor); Utah, October 2, 1919; California, November 1, 1919; Maine, November 5, 1919; North Dakota, December 1, 1919; South Dakota, December 4, 1919 (date on which certified); Colorado, December 15, 1919 (date on which approved by Governor); Kentucky, January 6, 1920; Rhode Island, January 6, 1920; Oregon, January 13, 1920; Indiana, January 16, 1920; Wyoming, January 27, 1920; Nevada, February 7, 1920; New Jersey, February 9, 1920; Idaho, February 11, 1920; Arizona, February 12, 1920; New Mexico, February 21, 1920 (date on which approved by govrnor); Oklahoma, February 28, 1920; West Virginia, March 10, 1920 (confirmed September 21, 1920); Vermont, February 8, 1921. The amendment was rejected by Georgia on July 24, 1919; by Alabama on September 22, 1919; by South Carolina on January 29, 1920; by Virginia on February 12, 1920; by Maryland on February 24, 1920; by Mississippi on March 29, 1920; by Louisiana on July 1, 1920. This amendment was subsequently ratified by Virginia in 1952, Alabama in 1953, Florida in 1969, and Georgia and Louisiana in 1970.

12 The Twentieth Amendment was proposed by Congress on March 2, 1932, when it passed the Senate, Cong. Rec. (72d Cong., 1st Sess.) 5086, having previously passed the House on March 1. Id., 5027. It appears officially in 47 Stat. 745. Ratification was completed on January 23, 1933, when the thirty-sixth State approved the amendment, there being then 48 States in the Union. On February 6, 1933, Secretary of State Stimson certified that it had become a part of the Constitution. 47 Stat. 2569.

The several state legislatures ratified the Twentieth Amendment on the following dates: Virginia, March 4, 1932; New York, March 11, 1932; Mississippi, March 16, 1932; Arkansas March 17, 1932; Kentucky, March 17, 1932; New Jersey, March 21, 1932; South Carolina, March 25, 1932; Michigan, March 31, 1932; Maine, April 1, 1932; Rhode Island, April 14, 1932; Illinois, April 21, 1932; Louisiana, June 22, 1932; West Virginia, July 30, 1932; Pennsylvania, August 11, 1932; Indiana, August 15, 1932; Texas, September 7, 1932; Alabama, September 13, 1932; California, January 4, 1933; North Carolina, January 5, 1933; North Dakota, January 9, 1933; Minnesota, January 12, 1933; Arizona, January 13, 1933; Montana, January 13, 1933; Nebraska, January 13, 1933; Oklahoma, January 13, 1933; Kansas, January 16, 1933; Oregon, January 16, 1933; Delaware, January 19, 1933; Washington, January 19, 1933; Wyoming, January 19, 1933; Iowa, January 20, 1933; South Dakota, January 20, 1933; Tennessee, January 20, 1933; Idaho, January 21, 1933; New Mexico, January 21, 1933; Georgia, January 23, 1933; Missouri, January 23, 1933; Ohio, January 23, 1933; Utah, January 23, 1933; Colorado, January 24, 1933; Massachusetts, January 24, 1933; Wisconsin, January 24,

1933; Nevada, January 26, 1933; Connecticut, January 27, 1933; New Hampshire, January 31, 1933; Vermont, February 2, 1933; Maryland, March 24, 1933; Florida, April 26, 1933.

13 The Twenty-first Amendment was proposed by Congress on February 20, 1933, when it passed the House, Cong. Rec. (72d Cong., 2d Sess.) 4516, having previously passed the Senate on February 16. Id., 4231. It appears officially in 47 Stat. 1625. Ratification was completed on December 5, 1933, when the thirty-sixth State (Utah) approved the amendment, there being then 48 States in the Union. On December 5, 1933, Acting Secretary of State Phillips certified that it had been adopted by the requisite number of States. 48 Stat. 1749.

The several state conventions ratified the Twenty-first Amendment on the following dates: Michigan, April 10, 1933; Wisconsin, April 25, 1933; Rhode Island, May 8, 1933; Wyoming, May 25, 1933; New Jersey, June 1, 1933; Delaware, June 24, 1933; Indiana, June 26, 1933; Massachusetts, June 26, 1933; New York, June 27, 1933; Illinois, July 10, 1933; Iowa, July 10, 1933; Connecticut, July 11, 1933; New Hampshire, July 11, 1933; California, July 24, 1933; West Virginia, July 25, 1933; Arkansas, August 1, 1933; Oregon, August 7, 1933; Alabama, August 8, 1933; Tennessee, August 11, 1933; Missouri, August 29, 1933; Arizona, September 5, 1933; Nevada, September 5, 1933; Vermont, September 23, 1933; Colorado, September 26, 1933; Washington, October 3, 1933; Minnesota, October 10, 1933; Idaho, October 17, 1933; Maryland, October 18, 1933; Virginia, October 25, 1933; New Mexico, November 2, 1933; Florida, November 14, 1933; Texas, November 24, 1933; Kentucky, November 27, 1933; Ohio, December 5, 1933; Pennsylvania, December 5, 1933; Utah, December 5, 1933; Maine, December 6, 1933; Montana, August 6, 1934. The amendment was rejected by a convention in the State of South Carolina, on December 4, 1933. The electorate of the State of North Carolina voted against holding a convention at a general election held on November 7, 1933.

14 The Twenty-second Amendment was proposed by Congress on March 24, 1947, having passed the House on March 21, 1947, Cong. Rec. (80th Cong., 1st Sess.) 2392, and having previously passed the Senate on March 12, 1947. Id., 1978. It appears officially in 61 Stat. 959. Ratification was completed on February 27, 1951, when the thirty-sixth State (Minnesota) approved the amendment, there being then 48 States in the Union. On March 1, 1951, Jess Larson, Administrator of General Services, certified that it had been adopted by the requisite number of States. 16 Fed. Reg. 2019.

A total of 41 state legislatures ratified the Twenty-second Amendment on the following dates: Maine, March 31, 1947; Michigan, March 31, 1947; Iowa, April 1, 1947; Kansas, April 1, 1947; New Hampshire, April 1, 1947; Delaware, April 2, 1947; Illinois, April 3,

1947; Oregon, April 3, 1947; Colorado, April 12, 1947; California, April 15, 1947; New Jersey, April 15, 1947; Vermont, April 15, 1947; Ohio, April 16, 1947; Wisconsin, April 16, 1947; Pennsylvania, April 29, 1947; Connecticut, May 21, 1947; Missouri, May 22, 1947; Nebraska, May 23, 1947; Virginia, January 28, 1948; Mississippi, February 12, 1948; New York, March 9, 1948; South Dakota, January 21, 1949; North Dakota, February 25, 1949; Louisiana, May 17, 1950; Montana, January 25, 1951; Indiana, January 29, 1951; Idaho, January 30, 1951; New Mexico, February 12, 1951; Wyoming, February 12, 1951; Arkansas, February 15, 1951; Georgia, February 17, 1951; Tennessee, February 20, 1951; Texas, February 22, 1951; Utah, February 26, 1951; Nevada, February 26, 1951; Minnesota, February 27, 1951; North Carolina, February 28, 1951; South Carolina, March 13, 1951; Maryland, March 14, 1951; Florida, April 16, 1951; and Alabama, May 4, 1951.

15 The Twenty-third Amendment was proposed by Congress on June 16, 1960, when it passed the Senate, Cong. Rec. (86th Cong., 2d Sess.) 12858, having previously passed the House on June 14. Id., 12571. It appears officially in 74 Stat. 1057. Ratification was completed on March 29, 1961, when the thirty-eighth State (Ohio) approved the amendment, there being then 50 States in the Union. On April 3, 1961, John L. Moore, Administrator of General Services, certified that it had been adopted by the requisite number of States. 26 Fed. Reg. 2808.

The several state legislatures ratified the Twenty-third Amendment on the following dates: Hawaii, June 23, 1960; Massachusetts, August 22, 1960; New Jersey, December 19, 1960; New York, January 17, 1961; California, January 19, 1961; Oregon, January 27, 1961; Maryland, January 30, 1961; Idaho, January 31, 1961; Maine, January 31, 1961; Minnesota, January 31, 1961; New Mexico, February 1, 1961; Nevada, February 2, 1961; Montana, February 6, 1961; Colorado, February 8, 1961; Washington, February 9, 1961; West Virginia, February 9, 1961; Alaska, February 10, 1961; Wyoming, February 13, 1961; South Dakota, February 14, 1961; Delaware, February 20, 1961; Utah, February 21, 1961; Wisconsin, February 21, 1961; Pennsylvania, February 28, 1961; Indiana, March 3, 1961; North Dakota, March 3, 1961; Tennessee, March 6, 1961; Michigan, March 8, 1961; Connecticut, March 9, 1961; Arizona, March 10, 1961; Illinois, March 14, 1961; Nebraska, March 15, 1961; Vermont, March 15, 1961; Iowa, March 16, 1961; Missouri, March 20, 1961; Oklahoma, March 21, 1961; Rhode Island, March 22, 1961; Kansas, March 29, 1961; Ohio, March 29, 1961, and New Hampshire, March 30, 1961.

16 The Twenty-fourth Amendment was proposed by Congress on September 14, 1962, having passed the House on August 27, 1962. Cong. Rec. (87th Cong., 2d Sess.) 17670 and having previously passed the Senate on March 27, 1962. Id., 5105. It appears officially in 76 Stat. 1259. Ratification was completed on January 23, 1964, when the

thirty- eighth State (South Dakota) approved the Amendment, there being then 50 States in the Union. On February 4, 1964, Bernard L. Boutin, Administrator of General Services, certified that it had been adopted by the requisite number of States. 25 Fed. Reg. 1717. President Lyndon B. Johnson signed this certificate.

Thirty-eight state legislatures ratified the Twenty-fourth Amendment on the following dates: Illinois, November 14, 1962; New Jersey, December 3, 1962; Oregon, January 25, 1963; Montana, January 28, 1963; West Virginia, February 1, 1963; New York, February 4, 1963; Maryland, February 6, 1963; California, February 7, 1963; Alaska, February 11, 1963; Rhode Island, February 14, 1963; Indiana, February 19, 1963; Michigan, February 20, 1963; Utah, February 20, 1963; Colorado, February 21, 1963; Minnesota, February 27, 1963; Ohio, February 27, 1963; New Mexico, March 5, 1963; Hawaii, March 6, 1963; North Dakota, March 7, 1963; Idaho, March 8, 1963; Washington, March 14, 1963; Vermont, March 15, 1963; Nevada, March 19, 1963; Connecticut, March 20, 1963; Tennessee, March 21, 1963; Pennsylvania, March 25, 1963; Wisconsin, March 26, 1963; Kansas, March 28, 1963; Massachusetts, March 28, 1963; Nebraska, April 4, 1963; Florida, April 18, 1963; Iowa, April 24, 1963; Delaware, May 1, 1963; Missouri, May 13, 1963; New Hampshire, June 16, 1963; Kentucky, June 27, 1963; Maine, January 16, 1964; South Dakota, January 23, 1964.

17 This Amendment was proposed by the Eighty-ninth Congress by Senate Joint Resolution No. 1, which was approved by the Senate on February 19, 1965, and by the House of Representatives, in amended form, on April 13, 1965. The House of Representatives agreed to a Conference Report on June 30, 1965, and the Senate agreed to the Conference Report on July 6, 1965. It was declared by the Administrator of General Services, on February 23, 1967, to have been ratified.

This Amendment was ratified by the following States: Nebraska, July 12, 1965; Wisconsin, July 13, 1965; Oklahoma, July 16, 1965; Massachusetts, August 9, 1965; Pennsylvania, August 18, 1965; Kentucky, September 15, 1965; Arizona, September 22, 1965; Michigan, October 5, 1965; Indiana, October 20, 1965; California, October 21, 1965; Arkansas, November 4, 1965; New Jersey, November 29, 1965; Delaware, December 7, 1965; Utah, January 17, 1966; West Virginia, January 20, 1966; Maine, January 24, 1966; Rhode Island, January 28, 1966; Colorado, February 3, 1966; New Mexico, February 3, 1966; Kansas, February 8, 1966; Vermont, February 10, 1966; Alaska, February 18, 1966; Idaho, March 2, 1966; Hawaii, March 3, 1966; Virginia, March 8, 1966; Mississippi, March 10, 1966; New York, March 14, 1966; Maryland, March 23, 1966; Missouri, March 30, 1966; New Hampshire, June 13, 1966; Louisiana, July 5, 1966; Tennessee, January 12, 1967; Wyoming, January 25, 1967; Washington, January 26, 1967; Iowa, January 26, 1967; Oregon, February 2, 1967; Minnesota, February 10, 1967; Nevada, February 10, 1967; Connecticut, February 14, 1967;

Montana, February 15, 1967; South Dakota, March 6, 1967; Ohio, March 7, 1967; Alabama, March 14, 1967; North Carolina, March 22, 1967 Illinois, March 22, 1967; Texas, April 25, 1967; Florida, May 25, 1967.

Publication of the certifying statement of the Administrator of General Services that the Amendment had become valid was made on February 25, 1967, F.R. Doc. 67-2208, 32 Fed. Reg. 3287.

18 The Twenty-sixth Amendment was proposed by Congress on March 23, 1971, upon passage by the House of Representatives, the Senate having previously passed an identical resolution on March 10, 1971. It appears officially in 85 Stat. 825. Ratification was completed on July 1, 1971, when action by the legislature of the 38th State, North Carolina, was concluded, and the Administrator of the General Services Administration officially certified it to have been duly ratified on July 5, 1971. 36 Fed. Reg. 12725.

As of the publication of this volume, 42 States had ratified this Amendment: Connecticut, March 23, 1971; Delaware, March 23, 1971; Minnesota, March 23, 1971; Tennessee, March 23, 1971; Washington, March 23, 1971; Hawaii, March 24, 1971; Massachusetts, March 24, 1971; Montana, March 29, 1971; Arkansas, March 30, 1971; Idaho, March 30, 1971; Iowa, March 30, 1971; Nebraska, April 2, 1971; New Jersey, April 3, 1971; Kansas, April 7, 1971; Michigan, April 7, 1971; Alaska, April 8, 1971; Maryland, April 8, 1971; Indiana, April 8, 1971; Maine, April 9, 1971; Vermont, April 16, 1971; Louisiana, April 17, 1971; California, April 19, 1971; Colorado, April 27, 1971; Pennsylvania, April 27, 1971; Texas, April 27, 1971; South Carolina, April 28, 1971; West Virginia, April 28, 1971; New Hampshire, May 13, 1971; Arizona, May 14, 1971; Rhode Island, May 27, 1971; New York, June 2, 1971; Oregon, June 4, 1971; Missouri, June 14, 1971; Wisconsin, June 22, 1971; Illinois, June 29, 1971; Alabama, June 30, 1971; Ohio, June 30, 1971; North Carolina, July 1, 1971; Oklahoma, July 1, 1971; Virginia, July 8, 1971; Wyoming, July 8, 1971; Georgia, October 4, 1971.

19 This purported amendment was proposed by Congress on September 25, 1789, when it passed the Senate, having previously passed the House on September 24. (1 Annals of Congress 88, 913). It appears officially in 1 Stat. 97. Having received in 1789-1791 only six state ratifications, the proposal then failed of ratification while ten of the 12 sent to the States by Congress were ratified and proclaimed and became the Bill of Rights. The provision was proclaimed as having been ratified and having become the 27th Amendment, when Michigan ratified on May 7, 1992, there being 50 States in the Union. Proclamation was by the Archivist of the United States, pursuant to 1 U.S.C. Sec. 106b, on May 19, 1992. F.R.Doc. 92-11951, 57 Fed. Reg. 21187. It was also proclaimed by votes of the Senate and House of Representatives. 138 Cong. Rec. (daily ed) S 6948-49, H 3505-06.

The several state legislatures ratified the proposal on the following dates: Maryland, December 19, 1789; North Carolina, December 22, 1789; South Carolina, January 19, 1790; Delaware, January 28, 1790; Vermont, November 3, 1791; Virginia, December 15, 1791; Ohio, May 6, 1873; Wyoming, March 6, 1978; Maine, April 27, 1983; Colorado, April 22, 1984; South Dakota, February 1985; New Hampshire, March 7, 1985; Arizona, April 3, 1985; Tennessee, May 28, 1985; Oklahoma, July 10, 1985; New Mexico, February 14, 1986; Indiana, February 24, 1986; Utah, February 25, 1986; Arkansas, March 13, 1987; Montana, March 17, 1987; Connecticut, May 13, 1987; Wisconsin, July 15, 1987; Georgia, February 2, 1988; West Virginia, March 10, 1988; Louisiana, July 7, 1988; Iowa, February 9, 1989; Idaho, March 23, 1989; Nevada, April 26, 1989; Alaska, May 6, 1989; Oregon, May 19, 1989; Minnesota, May 22, 1989; Texas, May 25, 1989; Kansas, April 5, 1990; Florida, May 31, 1990; North Dakota, Mary 25, 1991; Alabama, May 5, 1992; Missouri, May 5, 1992; Michigan, May 7, 1992. New Jersey subsequently ratified on May 7, 1992.

The Avalon Project  *at Yale Law School*

Articles of Confederation

Annapolis Convention	Madison Debates	Federalist Papers	U. S. Constitution			
See Also Benjamin Franklin's Draft and John Dickinson's Draft						
See Discussion of The Articles of Confederation in Jefferson's Autobiography						
Art 1	Art 2	Art 3	Art 4	Art 5	Art 6	Art 7
Art 8	Art 9	Art 10	Art 11	Art 12	Art 13	

To all to whom these Presents shall come, we the undersigned Delegates of the States affixed to our Names send greeting.

Articles of Confederation and perpetual Union between the states of New Hampshire, Massachusetts-bay Rhode Island and Providence Plantations, Connecticut, New York, New Jersey, Pennsylvania, Delaware, Maryland, Virginia, North Carolina, South Carolina and Georgia.

I.

The Stile of this Confederacy shall be

"The United States of America".

II.

Each state retains its sovereignty, freedom, and independence, and every power, jurisdiction, and right, which is not by this Confederation expressly delegated to the United States, in Congress assembled.

III.

The said States hereby severally enter into a firm league of friendship with each other, for their common defense, the security of their liberties, and their mutual and general welfare, binding themselves to assist each other, against all force offered to, or attacks made upon them, or any of them, on account of religion, sovereignty, trade, or any other pretense whatever.

IV.

The better to secure and perpetuate mutual friendship and intercourse among the people of the different States in this Union, the free inhabitants of each of these States, paupers, vagabonds, and fugitives from justice excepted, shall be entitled to all privileges and immunities of free citizens in the several States; and the people of each State shall free ingress and regress to and from any other State, and shall enjoy therein all the privileges of trade and commerce, subject to the same duties, impositions, and restrictions as the inhabitants thereof respectively, provided that such restrictions shall not extend so far as to prevent the removal of property imported into any State, to any other State, of which the owner is an inhabitant; provided also that no imposition, duties or restriction shall be laid by any State, on the property of the United States, or either of them.

If any person guilty of, or charged with, treason, felony, or other high misdemeanor in any State, shall flee from justice, and be found in any of the United States, he shall, upon demand of the Governor or executive power of the State from which he fled, be delivered up and removed to the State having jurisdiction of his offense.

Full faith and credit shall be given in each of these States to the records, acts, and judicial proceedings of the courts and magistrates of every other State.

V.

For the most convenient management of the general interests of the United States, delegates shall be annually appointed in such manner as the legislatures of each State shall direct, to meet in Congress on the first Monday in November, in every year, with a powerreserved to each State to recall its delegates, or any of them, at any time within the year, and to send others in their stead for the remainder of the year.

No State shall be represented in Congress by less than two, nor more than seven members; and no person shall be capable of being a delegate for more than three years in any term of six years; nor shall any person, being a delegate, be capable of holding any office under the United States, for which he, or another for his benefit, receives any salary, fees or emolument of any kind.

Each State shall maintain its own delegates in a meeting of the States, and while they act as members of the committee of the States.

In determining questions in the United States in Congress assembled, each State shall have one vote.

Freedom of speech and debate in Congress shall not be impeached or questioned in any court or place out of Congress, and the members of Congress shall be protected in their persons from arrests or imprisonments, during the time of their going to and from, and attendence on Congress, except for treason, felony, or breach of the peace.

VI.

No State, without the consent of the United States in Congress assembled, shall send any embassy to, or receive any embassy from, or enter into any conference, agreement, alliance or treaty with any King, Prince or State; nor shall any person holding any office of profit or trust under the United States, or any of them, accept any present, emolument, office or title of any kind whatever from any King, Prince or foreign State; nor shall the United States in Congress assembled, or any of them, grant any title of nobility.

No two or more States shall enter into any treaty, confederation or alliance whatever between them, without the consent of the United States in Congress assembled, specifying accurately the purposes for which the same is to be entered into, and how long it shall continue.

No State shall lay any imposts or duties, which may interfere with any stipulations in treaties, entered into by the United States in Congress assembled, with any King, Prince or State, in pursuance of any treaties already proposed by Congress, to the courts of France and Spain.

No vessel of war shall be kept up in time of peace by any State, except such number only, as shall be deemed necessary by the United States in Congress assembled, for the defense of such State, or its trade; nor shall any body of forces be kept up by any State in time of peace, except such number only, as in the judgement of the United States in Congress assembled, shall be deemed requisite to garrison the forts necessary for the defense of such State; but every State shall always keep up a well-regulated and disciplined militia, sufficiently armed and accoutered, and shall provide and constantly have ready for use, in public stores, a due number of filed pieces and tents, and a proper quantity of arms, ammunition and camp equipage.

No State shall engage in any war without the consent of the United States in Congress assembled, unless such State be actually invaded by enemies, or shall have received certain advice of a resolution being formed by some nation of Indians to invade such State, and the danger is so imminent as not to admit of a delay till the United States in Congress assembled can be consulted; nor shall any State grant commissions to any ships or vessels of war, nor letters of marque or reprisal, except it be after a declaration of war by the United States in Congress assembled, and then only against the Kingdom or State and the subjects thereof, against which war has been so declared, and under such regulations as shall be established by the United States in Congress assembled, unless such State be infested by pirates, in which case vessels of war may be fitted out for that occasion, and kept so long as the danger shall continue, or until the United States in Congress assembled shall determine otherwise.

VII.

When land forces are raised by any State for the common defense, all officers of or under the rank of colonel, shall be appointed by the legislature of each State respectively, by whom such forces shall be raised, or in such manner as such State shall direct, and all vacancies shall be filled up by the State which first made the appointment.

VIII.

All charges of war, and all other expenses that shall be incurred for the common defense or general welfare, and allowed by the United States in Congress assembled, shall be defrayed out of a common treasury, which shall be supplied by the several States in proportion to the value of all land within each State, granted or surveyed for any person, as such land and the buildings and improvements thereon shall be estimated according to such mode as the United States in Congress assembled, shall from time to time direct and appoint.

The taxes for paying that proportion shall be laid and levied by the authority and direction of the legislatures of the several States within the time agreed upon by the United States in Congress assembled.

IX.

The United States in Congress assembled, shall have the sole and exclusive right and power of determining on peace and war, except in the cases mentioned in the sixth article -- of sending and receiving ambassadors -- entering into treaties and alliances, provided that no treaty of commerce shall be made whereby the legislative power of the respective States shall be restrained from imposing such imposts and duties on foreigners, as their own people are subjected to, or from prohibiting the exportation or importation of any species of goods or commodities whatsoever -- of establishing rules for deciding in all cases, what captures on land or water shall be legal, and in what manner prizes taken by land or naval forces in the service of the United States shall be divided or appropriated -- of granting letters of marque and reprisal in times of peace -- appointing courts for the trial of piracies and felonies commited on the high seas and establishing courts for receiving and determining finally appeals in all cases of captures, provided that no member of Congress shall be appointed a judge of any of the said courts.

The United States in Congress assembled shall also be the last resort on appeal in all disputes and differences now subsisting or that hereafter may arise between two or more States concerning boundary, jurisdiction or any other causes whatever; which authority shall always be exercised in the manner following. Whenever the legislative or executive authority or lawful agent of any State in controversy with another shall present a petition to Congress stating the matter in question and praying for a hearing, notice thereof shall be given by order of Congress to the legislative or executive authority of the other State in controversy, and a day assigned for the appearance of the parties by their lawful agents, who shall then be directed to appoint by joint consent, commissioners or judges to constitute a court for hearing and determining the matter in question: but if they cannot agree, Congress shall name three persons out of each of the United States, and from the list of such persons each party shall alternately strike out one, the petitioners beginning, until the number shall be reduced to thirteen; and from that number not less than seven, nor more than nine names as Congress shall direct, shall in the presence of Congress be drawn out by lot, and the persons whose names shall be so drawn or any five of them, shall be commissioners or judges, to hear and finally determine the controversy, so always as a major part of the judges who shall hear the cause shall agree in the determination: and if either party shall neglect to attend at the day appointed, without showing reasons, which Congress shall judge sufficient, or being present shall refuse to strike, the Congress shall proceed to nominate three persons out of each State, and the secretary of Congress shall strike in behalf of such party absent or refusing; and the judgement and sentence of the court to be appointed, in the manner before prescribed, shall be final and conclusive; and if any of the parties shall refuse to submit to the authority of such court, or to appear or defend their claim or cause, the court shall nevertheless proceed to pronounce sentence, or judgement, which shall in like manner be final and decisive, the judgement or sentence and other proceedings being in either case transmitted to Congress, and lodged among the acts of Congress for the security of the parties concerned: provided that every commissioner, before he sits in judgement, shall take an oath to be administered by one of the judges of the supreme or superior court of the State, where the cause shall be tried, 'well and truly to hear and determine the matter in question, according to the best of his judgement, without favor, affection or hope of reward': provided also, that no State shall be deprived of territory for the benefit of the United States.

All controversies concerning the private right of soil claimed under different grants of two or more States, whose jurisdictions as they may respect such lands, and the States which passed such grants are adjusted, the said grants or either of them being at the same time claimed to have originated antecedent to such settlement of jurisdiction, shall on the petition of either party to the Congress of the United States, be finally determined as near as may be in the same manner as is before presecribed for deciding disputes respecting territorial jurisdiction between different States.

The United States in Congress assembled shall also have the sole and exclusive right and power of regulating the alloy and value of coin struck by their own authority, or by that of the respective States -- fixing the standards of weights and measures throughout the United States -- regulating the trade and managing all affairs with the Indians, not members of any of the States, provided that the legislative right of any State within its own limits be not infringed or violated -- establishing or regulating post offices from one State to another, throughout all the United States, and exacting such postage on the papers passing through the same as may be requisite to defray the expenses of the said office -- appointing all officers of the land forces, in the service of the United States, excepting regimental officers -- appointing all the officers of the naval forces, and commissioning all officers whatever in the service of the United States -- making rules for the government and regulation of the said land and naval forces, and directing their operations.

The United States in Congress assembled shall have authority to appoint a committee, to sit in the recess of Congress, to be denominated 'A Committee of the States', and to consist of one delegate from each State; and to appoint such other committees and civil officers as may be necessary for managing the general affairs of the United States under their direction -- to appoint one of their members to preside, provided that no person be allowed to serve in the office of president more than one year in any term of three years; to ascertain the necessary sums of money to be raised for the service of the United States, and to appropriate and apply the same for defraying the public expenses -- to borrow money, or emit bills on the credit of the United States, transmitting every half-year to the respective States an account of the sums of money so borrowed or emitted -- to build and equip a navy -- to agree upon the number of land forces, and to make requisitions from each State for its quota, in proportion to the number of white inhabitants in such State; which requisition shall be binding, and thereupon the legislature of each State shall appoint the regimental officers, raise the men and cloath, arm and equip them in a solid-like manner, at the expense of the United States; and the officers and men so cloathed, armed and equipped shall march to the place appointed, and within the time agreed on by the United States in Congress assembled. But if the United States in Congress assembled shall, on consideration of circumstances judge proper that any State should not raise men, or should raise a smaller number of men than the quota thereof, such extra number shall be raised, officered, cloathed, armed and equipped in the same manner as the quota of each State, unless the legislature of such State shall judge that such extra number cannot be safely spread out in the same, in which case they shall raise, officer, cloath, arm and equip as many of such extra number as they judeg can be safely spared. And the officers and men so cloathed, armed, and equipped, shall march to the place appointed, and within the time agreed on by the United States in Congress assembled.

The United States in Congress assembled shall never engage in a war, nor grant letters of marque or reprisal in time of peace, nor enter into any treaties or alliances, nor coin money, nor regulate the value thereof, nor ascertain the sums and expenses necessary for the defense and welfare of the United States, or any of them, nor emit bills, nor borrow money on the credit of the United States, nor appropriate money, nor agree upon the number of vessels of war, to be built or purchased, or the number of land or sea forces to be raised, nor appoint a commander in chief of the army or navy, unless nine States assent to the same: nor shall a question on any other point, except for adjourning from day to day be determined, unless by the votes of the majority of the United States in Congress assembled.

The Congress of the United States shall have power to adjourn to any time within the year, and to any place within the United States, so that no period of adjournment be for a longer duration than the space of six months, and shall publish the journal of their proceedings monthly, except such parts thereof relating to treaties, alliances or military operations, as in their judgement require secrecy; and the yeas and nays of the delegates of each State on any question shall be entered on the journal, when it is desired by any delegates of a State, or any of them, at his or their request shall be furnished with a transcript of the said journal, except such parts as are above excepted, to lay before the legislatures of the several States.

X.

The Committee of the States, or any nine of them, shall be authorized to execute, in the recess of Congress, such of the powers of Congress as the United States in Congress assembled, by the consent of the nine States, shall from time to time think expedient to vest them with; provided that no power be delegated to the said Committee, for the exercise of which, by the Articles of Confederation, the voice of nine States in the Congress of the United States assembled be requisite.

XI.

Canada acceding to this confederation, and adjoining in the measures of the United States, shall be admitted into, and entitled to all the advantages of this Union; but no other colony shall be admitted into the same, unless such admission be agreed to by nine States.

XII.

All bills of credit emitted, monies borrowed, and debts contracted by, or under the authority of Congress, before the assembling of the United States, in pursuance of the present confederation, shall be deemed and considered as a charge against the United States, for payment and satisfaction whereof the said United States, and the public faith are hereby solemnly pleged.

XIII.

Every State shall abide by the determination of the United States in Congress assembled, on all questions which by this confederation are submitted to them. And the Articles of this Confederation shall be inviolably observed by every State, and the Union shall be perpetual; nor shall any alteration at any time hereafter be made in any of them; unless such alteration be agreed to in a Congress of the United States, and be afterwards confirmed by the legislatures of every State.

And Whereas it hath pleased the Great Governor of the World to incline the hearts of the legislatures we respectively represent in Congress, to approve of, and to authorize us to ratify the said Articles of Confederation and perpetual Union. Know Ye that we the undersigned delegates, by virtue of the power and authority to us given for that purpose, do by these presents, in the name and in behalf of our respective constituents, fully and entirely ratify and confirm each and every of the said Articles of Confederation and perpetual Union, and all and singular the matters and things therein contained: And we do further solemnly plight and engage the faith of our respective constituents, that they shall abide by the determinations of the United States in Congress assembled, on all questions, which by the said Confederation are submitted to them. And that the Articles thereof shall be inviolably observed by the States we respectively represent, and that the Union shall be perpetual.

In Witness whereof we have hereunto set our hands in Congress. Done at Philadelphia in the State of Pennsylvania the ninth day of July in the Year of our Lord One Thousand Seven Hundred and Seventy-Eight, and in the Third Year of the independence of America.

Agreed to by Congress 15 November 1777 In force after ratification by Maryland, 1 March 1781

Source:
Documents Illustrative of the Formation of the Union of the American States.
Government Printing Office, 1927.
House Document No. 398.
Selected, Arranged and Indexed by Charles C. Tansill

The Federalist Papers/No. 39

From Wikisource

The Conformity of the Plan to Republican Principles

To the People of the State of New York:

THE last paper having concluded the observations which were meant to introduce a candid survey of the plan of government reported by the convention, we now proceed to the execution of that part of our undertaking.

The first question that offers itself is, whether the general form and aspect of the government be strictly republican. It is evident that no other form would be reconcilable with the genius of the people of America; with the fundamental principles of the Revolution; or with that honorable determination which animates every votary of freedom, to rest all our political experiments on the capacity of mankind for self-government. If the plan of the convention, therefore, be found to depart from the republican character, its advocates must abandon it as no longer defensible.

What, then, are the distinctive characters of the republican form? Were an answer to this question to be sought, not by recurring to principles, but in the application of the term by political writers, to the constitution of different States, no satisfactory one would ever be found. Holland, in which no particle of the supreme authority is derived from the people, has passed almost universally under the denomination of a republic. The same title has been bestowed on Venice, where absolute power over the great body of the people is exercised, in the most absolute manner, by a small body of hereditary nobles. Poland, which is a mixture of aristocracy and of monarchy in their worst forms, has been dignified with the same appellation. The government of England, which has one republican branch only, combined with an hereditary aristocracy and monarchy, has, with equal impropriety, been frequently placed on the list of republics. These examples, which are nearly as dissimilar to each other as to a genuine republic, show the extreme inaccuracy with which the term has been used in political disquisitions.

If we resort for a criterion to the different principles on which different forms of government are established, we may define a republic to be, or at least may bestow that name on, a government which derives all its powers directly or indirectly from the great body of the people, and is administered by persons holding their offices during pleasure, for a limited period, or during good behavior. It is ESSENTIAL to such a government that it be derived from the great body of the society, not from an inconsiderable proportion, or a favored class of it; otherwise a handful of tyrannical nobles, exercising their oppressions by a delegation of their powers, might aspire to the rank of republicans, and claim for their government the honorable title of republic. It is SUFFICIENT for such a government that the persons administering it be appointed, either directly or indirectly, by the people; and that they hold their appointments by either of the tenures just specified; otherwise every government in the United States, as well as every other popular government that has been or can be well organized or well executed, would be degraded from the republican character. According to the constitution of every State in the Union, some or other of the officers of government are appointed indirectly only by the people. According to most of them, the chief magistrate himself is so appointed. And according to one, this mode of appointment is extended to one of the co-ordinate branches of the legislature. According to all the constitutions, also, the tenure of the highest offices is extended to a definite period, and in many instances, both within the legislative and executive departments, to a period of years. According to the provisions of most of the constitutions, again, as well as according to the most respectable and received opinions on the subject, the members of the judiciary department are to retain their offices by the firm tenure of good behavior.

On comparing the Constitution planned by the convention with the standard here fixed, we perceive at once that it is, in the most rigid sense, conformable to it. The House of Representatives, like that of one branch at least of all the State legislatures, is elected immediately by the great body of the people. The Senate, like the present Congress, and the Senate of Maryland, derives its appointment indirectly from the people. The President is indirectly derived from the choice of the people, according to the example in most of the States. Even the judges, with all other officers of the Union, will, as in the several States, be the choice, though a remote choice, of the people themselves, the duration of the appointments is equally conformable to the republican standard, and to the model of State constitutions The House of Representatives is periodically elective, as in all the States; and for the period of two years, as in the State of South Carolina. The Senate is elective, for the period of six years; which is but one year more than the period of the Senate of Maryland, and but two more than that of the Senates of New York and Virginia. The President is to continue in office for the period of four years; as in New York and Delaware, the chief magistrate is elected for three years, and in South Carolina for two years. In the other States the election is annual. In several of the States, however, no constitutional provision is made for the impeachment of the chief magistrate. And in Delaware and Virginia he is not impeachable till out of office. The President of the United States is impeachable at any time during his continuance in office. The tenure by which the judges are to hold their places, is, as it unquestionably ought to be, that of good behavior. The tenure of the ministerial offices generally, will be a subject of legal regulation, conformably to the reason of the case and the example of the State constitutions.

Could any further proof be required of the republican complexion of this system, the most decisive one might be found in its absolute prohibition of titles of nobility, both under the federal and the State governments; and in its express guaranty of the republican form to each of the latter.

"But it was not sufficient," say the adversaries of the proposed Constitution, "for the convention to adhere to the republican form. They ought, with equal care, to have preserved the FEDERAL form, which regards the Union as a CONFEDERACY of sovereign states; instead of which, they have framed a NATIONAL government, which regards the Union as a CONSOLIDATION of the States." And it is asked by what authority this bold and radical innovation was undertaken? The handle which has been made of this objection requires that it should be examined with some precision.

Without inquiring into the accuracy of the distinction on which the objection is founded, it will be necessary to a just estimate of its force, first, to ascertain the real character of the government in question; secondly, to inquire how far the convention were authorized to propose such a government; and thirdly, how far the duty they owed to their country could supply any defect of regular authority.

First. In order to ascertain the real character of the government, it may be considered in relation to the foundation on which it is to be established; to the sources from which its ordinary powers are to be drawn; to the operation of those powers; to the extent of them; and to the authority by which future changes in the government are to be introduced.

On examining the first relation, it appears, on one hand, that the Constitution is to be founded on the assent and ratification of the people of America, given by deputies elected for the special purpose; but, on the other, that this assent and ratification is to be given by the people, not as individuals composing one entire nation, but as composing the distinct and independent States to which they respectively belong. It is to be the assent and ratification of the several States, derived from the supreme authority in each State, the authority of the people themselves. The act, therefore, establishing the Constitution, will not be a NATIONAL, but a FEDERAL act.

That it will be a federal and not a national act, as these terms are understood by the objectors; the act of the people, as forming so many independent States, not as forming one aggregate nation, is obvious from this single consideration, that it is to result neither from the decision of a MAJORITY of the people of the Union, nor from that of a MAJORITY of the States. It must result from the UNANIMOUS assent of the several States that are parties to it, differing no otherwise from their ordinary assent than in its being expressed, not by the legislative authority, but by that of the people themselves. Were the people regarded in this transaction as forming one nation, the will of the majority of the whole people of the United States would bind the minority, in the same manner as the majority in each State must bind the minority; and the will of the majority must be determined either by a comparison of the individual votes, or by considering the will of the majority of the States as evidence of the will of a majority of the people of the United States. Neither of these rules have been adopted. Each State, in ratifying the Constitution, is considered as a sovereign body, independent of all others, and only to be bound by its own voluntary act. In this relation, then, the new Constitution will, if established, be a FEDERAL, and not a NATIONAL constitution.

The next relation is, to the sources from which the ordinary powers of government are to be derived. The House of Representatives will derive its powers from the people of America; and the people will be represented in the same proportion, and on the same principle, as they are in the legislature of a particular State. So far the government is NATIONAL, not FEDERAL. The Senate, on the other hand, will derive its powers from the States, as political and coequal societies; and these will be represented on the principle of equality in the Senate, as they now are in the existing Congress. So far the government is FEDERAL, not NATIONAL. The executive power will be derived from a very compound source. The immediate election of the President is to be made by the States in their political characters. The votes allotted to them are in a compound ratio, which considers them partly as distinct and coequal societies, partly as unequal members of the same society. The eventual election, again, is to be made by that branch of the legislature which consists of the national representatives; but in this particular act they are to be thrown into the form of individual delegations, from so many distinct and coequal bodies politic. From this aspect of the government it appears to be of a mixed character, presenting at least as many FEDERAL as NATIONAL features.

The difference between a federal and national government, as it relates to the OPERATION OF THE GOVERNMENT, is supposed to consist in this, that in the former the powers operate on the political bodies composing the Confederacy, in their political capacities; in the latter, on the individual citizens composing the nation, in their individual capacities. On trying the Constitution by this criterion, it falls under the NATIONAL, not the FEDERAL character; though perhaps not so completely as has been understood. In several cases, and particularly in the trial of controversies to which States may be parties, they must be viewed and proceeded against in their collective and political capacities only. So far the national countenance of the government on this side seems to be disfigured by a few federal features. But this blemish is perhaps unavoidable in any plan; and the operation of the government on the people, in their individual capacities, in its ordinary and most essential proceedings, may, on the whole, designate it, in this relation, a NATIONAL government.

But if the government be national with regard to the OPERATION of its powers, it changes its aspect again when we contemplate it in relation to the EXTENT of its powers. The idea of a national government involves in it, not only an authority over the individual citizens, but an indefinite supremacy over all persons and things, so far as they are objects of lawful government. Among a people consolidated into one nation, this supremacy is completely vested in the national legislature. Among communities united for particular purposes, it is vested partly in the general and partly in the municipal legislatures. In the former case, all local authorities are subordinate to the supreme; and may be controlled, directed, or abolished by it at pleasure. In the latter, the local or municipal authorities form distinct and independent portions of the supremacy, no more subject, within their respective spheres, to the general authority, than the general authority is subject to them, within its own sphere. In this relation, then, the proposed government cannot be deemed a NATIONAL one; since its jurisdiction extends to certain enumerated objects only, and leaves to the several States a residuary and inviolable sovereignty over all other objects. It is true that in controversies relating to the boundary between the two jurisdictions, the tribunal which is ultimately to decide, is to be established under the general government. But this does not change the principle of the case. The decision is to be impartially made, according to the rules of the Constitution; and all the usual and most effectual precautions are taken to secure this impartiality. Some such tribunal is clearly essential to prevent an appeal to the sword and a dissolution of the compact; and that it ought to be established under the general rather than under the local governments, or, to speak more properly, that it could be safely established under the first alone, is a position not likely to be combated.

If we try the Constitution by its last relation to the authority by which amendments are to be made, we find it neither wholly NATIONAL nor wholly FEDERAL. Were it wholly national, the supreme and ultimate authority would reside in the MAJORITY of the people of the Union; and this authority would be competent at all times, like that of a majority of every national society, to alter or abolish its established government. Were it wholly federal, on the other hand, the concurrence of each State in the Union would be essential to every alteration that would be binding on all. The mode provided by the plan of the convention is not founded on either of these principles. In requiring more than a majority, and principles. In requiring more than a majority, and particularly in computing the proportion by STATES, not by CITIZENS, it departs from the NATIONAL and advances towards the FEDERAL character; in rendering the concurrence of less than the whole number of States sufficient, it loses again the FEDERAL and partakes of the NATIONAL character.

The proposed Constitution, therefore, is, in strictness, neither a national nor a federal Constitution, but a composition of both. In its foundation it is federal, not national; in the sources from which the ordinary powers of the government are drawn, it is partly federal and partly national; in the operation of these powers, it is national, not federal; in the extent of them, again, it is federal, not national; and, finally, in the authoritative mode of introducing amendments, it is neither wholly federal nor wholly national.

PUBLIUS.

The Federalist Papers/No. 10

From Wikisource

The Same Subject Continued: The Union as a Safeguard Against Domestic Faction and Insurrection

To the People of the State of New York:

AMONG the numerous advantages promised by a well constructed Union, none deserves to be more accurately developed than its tendency to break and control the violence of faction. The friend of popular governments never finds himself so much alarmed for their character and fate, as when he contemplates their propensity to this dangerous vice. He will not fail, therefore, to set a due value on any plan which, without violating the principles to which he is attached, provides a proper cure for it. The instability, injustice, and confusion introduced into the public councils, have, in truth, been the mortal diseases under which popular governments have everywhere perished; as they continue to be the favorite and fruitful topics from which the adversaries to liberty derive their most specious declamations. The valuable improvements made by the American constitutions on the popular models, both ancient and modern, cannot certainly be too much admired; but it would be an unwarrantable partiality, to contend that they have as effectually obviated the danger on this side, as was wished and expected. Complaints are everywhere heard from our most considerate and virtuous citizens, equally the friends of public and private faith, and of public and personal liberty, that our governments are too unstable, that the public good is disregarded in the conflicts of rival parties, and that measures are too often decided, not according to the rules of justice and the rights of the minor party, but by the superior force of an interested and overbearing majority. However anxiously we may wish that these complaints had no foundation, the evidence, of known facts will not permit us to deny that they are in some degree true. It will be found, indeed, on a candid review of our situation, that some of the distresses under which we labor have been erroneously charged on the operation of our governments; but it will be found, at the same time, that other causes will not alone account for many of our heaviest misfortunes; and, particularly, for that prevailing and increasing distrust of public engagements, and alarm for private rights, which are echoed from one end of the continent to the other. These must be chiefly, if not wholly, effects of the unsteadiness and injustice with which a factious spirit has tainted our public administrations.

By a faction, I understand a number of citizens, whether amounting to a majority or a minority of the whole, who are united and actuated by some common impulse of passion, or of interest, adversed to the rights of other citizens, or to the permanent and aggregate interests of the community.

There are two methods of curing the mischiefs of faction: the one, by removing its causes; the other, by controlling its effects.

There are again two methods of removing the causes of faction: the one, by destroying the liberty which is essential to its existence; the other, by giving to every citizen the same opinions, the same passions, and the same interests.

It could never be more truly said than of the first remedy, that it was worse than the disease. Liberty is to faction what air is to fire, an aliment without which it instantly expires. But it could not be less folly to abolish liberty, which is essential to political life, because it nourishes faction, than it would be to wish the annihilation of air, which is essential to animal life, because it imparts to fire its destructive agency.

The second expedient is as impracticable as the first would be unwise. As long as the reason of man continues fallible, and he is at liberty to exercise it, different opinions will be formed. As long as the connection subsists between his reason and his self-love, his opinions and his passions will have a reciprocal influence on each other; and the former will be objects to which the latter will attach themselves. The diversity in the faculties of men, from which the rights of property originate, is not less an insuperable obstacle to a uniformity of interests. The protection of these faculties is the first object of government. From the protection of different and unequal faculties of acquiring property, the possession of different degrees and kinds of property immediately results; and from the influence of these on the sentiments and views of the respective proprietors, ensues a division of the society into different interests and parties.

The latent causes of faction are thus sown in the nature of man; and we see them everywhere brought into different degrees of activity, according to the different circumstances of civil society. A zeal for different opinions concerning religion, concerning government, and many other points, as well of speculation as of practice; an attachment to different leaders ambitiously contending for pre-eminence and power; or to persons of other descriptions whose fortunes have been interesting to the human passions, have, in turn, divided mankind into parties, inflamed them with mutual animosity, and rendered them much more disposed to vex and oppress each other than to co-operate for their common good. So strong is this propensity of mankind to fall into mutual animosities, that where no substantial occasion presents itself, the most frivolous and fanciful distinctions have been sufficient to kindle their unfriendly passions and excite their most violent conflicts. But the most common and durable source of factions has been the various and unequal distribution of property. Those who hold and those who are without property have ever formed distinct interests in society. Those who are creditors, and those who are debtors, fall under a like discrimination. A landed interest, a manufacturing interest, a mercantile interest, a moneyed interest, with many lesser interests, grow up of necessity in civilized nations, and divide them into different classes, actuated by different sentiments and views. The regulation of these various and interfering interests forms the principal task of modern legislation, and involves the spirit of party and faction in the necessary and ordinary operations of the government.

No man is allowed to be a judge in his own cause, because his interest would certainly bias his judgment, and, not improbably, corrupt his integrity. With equal, nay with greater reason, a body of men are unfit to be both judges and parties at the same time; yet what are many of the most important acts of legislation, but so many judicial determinations, not indeed concerning the rights of single persons, but concerning the rights of large bodies of citizens? And what are the different classes of legislators but advocates and parties to the causes which they determine? Is a law proposed concerning private debts? It is a question to which the creditors are parties on one side and the debtors on the other. Justice ought to hold the balance between them. Yet the parties are, and must be, themselves the judges; and the most numerous party, or, in other words, the most powerful faction must be expected to prevail. Shall domestic manufactures be encouraged, and in what degree, by restrictions on foreign manufactures? are questions which would be differently decided by the landed and the manufacturing classes, and probably by neither with a sole regard to justice and the public good. The apportionment of taxes on the various descriptions of property is an act which seems to require the most exact impartiality; yet there is, perhaps, no legislative act in which greater opportunity and temptation are given to a predominant party to trample on the rules of justice. Every shilling with which they overburden the inferior number, is a shilling saved to their own pockets.

It is in vain to say that enlightened statesmen will be able to adjust these clashing interests, and render them all subservient to the public good. Enlightened statesmen will not always be at the helm. Nor, in many cases, can such an adjustment be made at all without taking into view indirect and remote considerations, which will rarely prevail over the immediate interest which one party may find in disregarding the rights of another or the good of the whole.

The inference to which we are brought is, that the CAUSES of faction cannot be removed, and that relief is only to be sought in the means of controlling its EFFECTS.

If a faction consists of less than a majority, relief is supplied by the republican principle, which enables the majority to defeat its sinister views by regular vote. It may clog the administration, it may convulse the society; but it will be unable to execute and mask its violence under the forms of the Constitution. When a majority is included in a faction, the form of popular government, on the other hand, enables it to sacrifice to its ruling passion or interest both the public good and the rights of other citizens. To secure the public good and private rights against the danger of such a faction, and at the same time to preserve the spirit and the form of popular government, is then the great object to which our inquiries are directed. Let me add that it is the great desideratum by which this form of government can be rescued from the opprobrium under which it has so long labored, and be recommended to the esteem and adoption of mankind.

By what means is this object attainable? Evidently by one of two only. Either the existence of the same passion or interest in a majority at the same time must be prevented, or the majority, having such coexistent passion or interest, must be rendered, by their number and local situation, unable to concert and carry into effect schemes of oppression. If the impulse and the opportunity be suffered to coincide, we well know that neither moral nor religious motives can be relied on as an adequate control. They are not found to be such on the injustice and violence of individuals, and lose their efficacy in proportion to the number combined together, that is, in proportion as their efficacy becomes needful.

From this view of the subject it may be concluded that a pure democracy, by which I mean a society consisting of a small number of citizens, who assemble and administer the government in person, can admit of no cure for the mischiefs of faction. A common passion or interest will, in almost every case, be felt by a majority of the whole; a communication and concert result from the form of government itself; and there is nothing to check the inducements to sacrifice the weaker party or an obnoxious individual. Hence it is that such democracies have ever been spectacles of turbulence and contention; have ever been found incompatible with personal security or the rights of property; and have in general been as short in their lives as they have been violent in their deaths. Theoretic politicians, who have patronized this species of government, have erroneously supposed that by reducing mankind to a perfect equality in their political rights, they would, at the same time, be perfectly equalized and assimilated in their possessions, their opinions, and their passions.

A republic, by which I mean a government in which the scheme of representation takes place, opens a different prospect, and promises the cure for which we are seeking. Let us examine the points in which it varies from pure democracy, and we shall comprehend both the nature of the cure and the efficacy which it must derive from the Union.

The two great points of difference between a democracy and a republic are: first, the delegation of the government, in the latter, to a small number of citizens elected by the rest; secondly, the greater number of citizens, and greater sphere of country, over which the latter may be extended.

The effect of the first difference is, on the one hand, to refine and enlarge the public views, by passing them through the medium of a chosen body of citizens, whose wisdom may best discern the true interest of their country, and whose patriotism and love of justice will be least likely to sacrifice it to temporary or partial considerations. Under such a regulation, it may well happen that the public voice, pronounced by the representatives of the people, will be more consonant to the public good than if pronounced by the people themselves, convened for the purpose. On the other hand, the effect may be inverted. Men of factious tempers, of local prejudices, or of sinister designs, may, by intrigue, by corruption, or by other means, first obtain the suffrages, and then betray the interests, of the people. The question resulting is, whether small or extensive republics are more favorable to the election of proper guardians of the public weal; and it is clearly decided in favor of the latter by two obvious considerations:

In the first place, it is to be remarked that, however small the republic may be, the representatives must be raised to a certain number, in order to guard against the cabals of a few; and that, however large it may be, they must be limited to a certain number, in order to guard against the confusion of a multitude. Hence, the number of representatives in the two cases not being in proportion to that of the two constituents, and being proportionally greater in the small republic, it follows that, if the proportion of fit characters be not less in the large than in the small republic, the former will present a greater option, and consequently a greater probability of a fit choice.

In the next place, as each representative will be chosen by a greater number of citizens in the large than in the small republic, it will be more difficult for unworthy candidates to practice with success the vicious arts by which elections are too often carried; and the suffrages of the people being more free, will be more likely to centre in men who possess the most attractive merit and the most diffusive and established characters.

It must be confessed that in this, as in most other cases, there is a mean, on both sides of which inconveniences will be found to lie. By enlarging too much the number of electors, you render the representatives too little acquainted with all their local circumstances and lesser interests; as by reducing it too much, you render him unduly attached to these, and too little fit to comprehend and pursue great and national objects. The federal Constitution forms a happy combination in this respect; the great and aggregate interests being referred to the national, the local and particular to the State legislatures.

The other point of difference is, the greater number of citizens and extent of territory which may be brought within the compass of republican than of democratic government; and it is this circumstance principally which renders factious combinations less to be dreaded in the former than in the latter. The smaller the society, the fewer probably will be the distinct parties and interests composing it; the fewer the distinct parties and interests, the more frequently will a majority be found of the same party; and the smaller the number of individuals composing a majority, and the smaller the compass within which they are placed, the more easily will they concert and execute their plans of oppression. Extend the sphere, and you take in a greater variety of parties and interests; you make it less probable that a majority of the whole will have a common motive to invade the rights of other citizens; or if such a common motive exists, it will be more difficult for all who feel it to discover their own strength, and to act in unison with each other. Besides other impediments, it may be remarked that, where there is a consciousness of unjust or dishonorable purposes, communication is always checked by distrust in proportion to the number whose concurrence is necessary.

Hence, it clearly appears, that the same advantage which a republic has over a democracy, in controlling the effects of faction, is enjoyed by a large over a small republic,--is enjoyed by the Union over the States composing it. Does the advantage consist in the substitution of representatives whose enlightened views and virtuous sentiments render them superior to local prejudices and schemes of injustice? It will not be denied that the representation of the Union will be most likely to possess these requisite endowments. Does it consist in the greater security afforded by a greater variety of parties, against the event of any one party being able to outnumber and oppress the rest? In an equal degree does the increased variety of parties comprised within the Union, increase this security. Does it, in fine, consist in the greater obstacles opposed to the concert and accomplishment of the secret wishes of an unjust and interested majority? Here, again, the extent of the Union gives it the most palpable advantage.

The influence of factious leaders may kindle a flame within their particular States, but will be unable to spread a general conflagration through the other States. A religious sect may degenerate into a political faction in a part of the Confederacy; but the variety of sects dispersed over the entire face of it must secure the national councils against any danger from that source. A rage for paper money, for an abolition of debts, for an equal division of property, or for any other improper or wicked project, will be less apt to pervade the whole body of the Union than a particular member of it; in the same proportion as such a malady is more likely to taint a particular county or district, than an entire State.

In the extent and proper structure of the Union, therefore, we behold a republican remedy for the diseases most incident to republican government. And according to the degree of pleasure and pride we feel in being republicans, ought to be our zeal in cherishing the spirit and supporting the character of Federalists.

PUBLIUS.

AMERICAN INTERGOVERNMENTAL RELATIONS

FOUNDATIONS, PERSPECTIVES, AND ISSUES

Fourth Edition

Laurence J. O'Toole Jr., Editor
University of Georgia

CQ PRESS

A Division of Congressional Quarterly Inc.
Washington, D.C.

Puppy Federalism and the Blessings of America

Edward L. Rubin

The United States is a nation that enjoys many blessings. We have vast reserves of petroleum (although we are using them up), magnificent forests (although we are cutting them down), spacious skies, amber waves of grain, lots of coal, and the world's leading supply of molybdenum. We also have wonderful political resources: the English tradition of liberty, well-established representative institutions, a willingness to channel political commitments into two major parties, a deep understanding of law, and a long-standing ability to solve civil conflicts through adjudication.

Perhaps the most valuable of these political resources, however, is our sense of national unity, our belief that we constitute a single people and a single polity. One of the reasons why this is such a great blessing is that it allows us to dispense with federalism. A subsidiary blessing is that it allows us to ignore the political questions that underlie federalism, issues that we would like to ignore because they point to the autocratic origins of all governments, and the impossibility of using democratic principles to constitute a polity.

This fortunate situation did not obtain at the beginning of our history, and we feel a bit guilty about basking in its glow today. Consequently, we have fashioned something for ourselves that can be described as puppy federalism; like puppy love, it looks somewhat authentic but does not reflect the intense desires that give the real thing its inherent meaning. The main purpose of puppy federalism is to convince ourselves that we have not altered the conception of the government that the Framers maintained, when, of course, we have; that we are not a bureaucratized administrative state, when, of course, we are;

From Edward L. Rubin, *Annals of the American Academy of Political and Social Science* (571/March 2001) pp. 37–51, Copyright © 2001 by Sage Publications. Reprinted by permission of Sage Publications, Inc.

and that we are a geographically diverse nation, whose regions exhibit interesting differences, when, of course, we are a highly homogenized, commercial, media-driven culture smeared across the width of an entire continent.

. . . The reason nations opt for federalism is that it is an alternative to dissolution, civil war, or other manifestations of a basic unwillingness of the people in some geographic area to live under the central government (Buchanan 1991; Sunstein 1991). Conversely, the reason groups of nations or other polities that want to combine opt to create a federal system, as opposed to a unified one, is that the people in the separate polities are unwilling to submit to unified, central control (Bartkus 1999). In either case, the motivation is a basic lack of national unity, an unwillingness of some groups to submit themselves to centralized control, to regard themselves as members of a single polity that must, for better or worse, reach collective decisions. They may feel that they will be discriminated against in the larger unit; that resources within the geographic region they inhabit will not be used for their benefit; that policies will be imposed on them that they find intolerable; or simply that they want to retain their own identity (Dikshit 1975; Duchacek 1970; Hannum 1990). Federalism is a solution to this problem, a compromise between unity and independence.

Decentralization is not sufficient in a situation where one or several groups are unwilling to submit to central control. The compromise that these groups want is federalism; they want the autonomy of their subunit's government to be protected as a right, not merely recognized as a desirable policy (Friedrich 1968, 188–227). By virtue of this recognition, the autonomy they have secured is placed outside the realm of ordinary politics. The king cannot eliminate it by an ordinary royal order; the voters, or their representatives, cannot do so by a simple majority. In our system, this means that the courts, acting in response to a claim of right, will invalidate normal legislation that trenches on the agreed-upon autonomy of the subunits (Choper 1980). That autonomy can be altered only by a constitutional amendment. . . .

The Blessings of National Unity

From the national perspective, a sense of unity among its citizens, a willingness to act as part of a single polity, is a political resource of enormous value, more valuable than petroleum, molybdenum, or rutabaga. It means that sectional disagreements or rivalries will be resolved within the context of the nation's political process and that a decision, having been reached, will be obeyed. Other disagreements will, of course, remain; there may be conflicts between social classes, ethnic groups, religious groups, or purely ideological alliances, and these conflicts may lead to violence. But the disagreements between groups of people who live in different geographic regions of the nation will not rise to this intensity; people will value their membership in the nation over their sectionally specific views and will compromise those views, or even abandon them, in conflictual situations.

Not only does a sense of national unity remove one major source of political conflict, but it removes the most dangerous source of such conflict. While it is possible for two contending groups that are geographically intermixed to rip a nation and themselves apart, as has occurred in Lebanon, Rwanda, and (at a regional level) Northern Ireland, most intense conflicts tend to be sectional, as Kosovo, Chechnya, Nagorno-Karabakh (Armenia-Azerbaijan), Kurdistan, Eritrea, the Ogaden (Ethiopia-Somalia), Western Sahara, Sudan, Kurdistan, Sri Lanka, and East Timor attest in recent history alone (Buchanan 1991; Cassese 1995). In part, this may be because a geographically defined group lacks the cross-cutting ties with others that racially or religiously defined groups often possess (Hannum 1990). In part, it may be that secession is a viable option only for geographically defined groups and that this extreme solution is an inducement to political extremism (Buchanan 1991; Dikshit 1975). Whatever the reason, a nation is not only fortunate—it is blessed—if it does not have any such groups, if the people in every region feel a greater loyalty to the nation as a whole than they do to their particular region.

In a democracy, national unity, and the resulting lack of sectional divisions, confers a further, if somewhat more abstract advantage. It conceals from the nation's citizens, and perhaps even from its political theorists, the awkward fact that democratic mechanisms cannot be used to constitute the nation. Creating a nation requires some form of autocracy. The reason is that the defining feature of democracy, in either its direct or representative varieties, is that major decisions are reached by the people themselves or by their elected representatives (Birch 1993, 45–68; Held 1996, 70–120). In practical terms, this means that the decisions are reached by having the people vote, either for the policy itself or for the representatives who in turn select the policy. Before a vote is taken, however, someone must decide who is eligible to vote and what the rules for conducting that vote will be.

That decision obviously cannot be determined by a vote; it requires an autocrat of some sort, an individual or an elite, who can establish the initial rules. Thus the principle of democracy, although it may be a perfectly good way to run the ordinary business of government, cannot stand on its own. If we start, either in reality or as a thought experiment, with people in a pregovernmental condition, no government can be established by purely democratic means.

. . . This is not an abstract matter; it is a crucial feature of national politics that implicates the precise issues to which federalism is addressed. From a national perspective, a proponent of representative democracy believes that a constitution should be established, and leaders should be chosen, by a majority of the electorate. But those whose primary loyalty is to a geographic region of this nation will object. "We do not want to be governed by strangers," they will say, "and the fact that those strangers are more numerous than us only makes the situation worse. We too believe in democracy, and we want a majority of the people—our people—to decide whether we want to join your nation, and on what terms. If a majority of our people want to have an independent nation, rather than being part of a larger one, that majority should not be overridden by outsiders." A sense of national unity that is shared by every region of a nation conceals this awkward difficulty in the theory and practice of democracy by making it essentially irrelevant.

Federalism in American History

For most of its history, the United States was a nation that needed federalism. The sense of national unity that would have led the voting populace to choose a unified, national regime did not prevail among the 13 American states at the time the Constitution was ratified and the United States was formed (Rakove 1979). People's loyalty to their own state was stronger than their loyalty to the nascent national regime, and thus they opted for a federal system, where the constituent states retained large areas of autonomy as a matter of right (Lutz 1988; Rakove 1996, 161–202). Nor was there sufficient unanimity about the federalist solution to mask the authoritarian origins of the government. While a majority of the people, when considered as a totality, probably favored a federal union, a majority of each state's population did not. In at least two states, North Carolina and Rhode Island, the majority was opposed, so that the autocratic manner in which the ratification process was established made a difference (Main 1961, 249; Van Doren 1948). In fact, these two states joined the Union only because they were compelled by further autocratic means. The same autocratic compulsion was applied to those regions within and beyond the established states with a Native American majority. It may also be assumed that, in any state, or section of a state, where the majority of the people were slaves, that majority would have preferred to establish an independent regime where they were free, rather than joining a nation that continued to enslave them.

During the first half of the nineteenth century, the new, federally organized nation was subject to two conflicting trends. On the one hand, the success of the central government, its general respect for white people's rights, its acquisition of vast territories, and the dramatic increase in national wealth that it seemed to engender all contributed to a growing sense of national unity. People began to think of themselves as Americans, rather than Georgians or New Yorkers (Ackerman 1991, 3–33; Beer 1993, 360–77). At the same time, however, the rejection of slavery in the North (Hildreth 1854; Olmstead 1953) and its enthusiastic continuation in the South (Fitzhugh 1854 [1965]) created an ever widening division. To the people of the North, slavery was a violation of the nation's true norms, and the people of the southern states were disruptive members of the polity who were violating those norms. But the white people of the southern states, the only people in those states with a political voice, were more committed to the institution of slavery than they were to the Union; despite their growing commitment to the nation in other areas, enough of their identification with their states remained that this identification could be reasserted, and become primary, when they found themselves unwilling to abide by the decisions of the majority regarding slavery. Consequently, they decided to secede (Stampp 1959).

At this point, of course, the democratic process and every other process of ordinary government broke down. The people of the North could no longer use voting, persuasion, or an appeal to national unity to convince the white people of the South to rejoin the Union because the southerners no longer regarded themselves as part of the same polity. The only remaining approach was to start killing them and devastating their lands until they decided that the amount of misery that was being inflicted on them exceeded their commitment to slavery. At that point, they rejoined the Union on the central government's terms.

Despite this unpromising beginning, the nation was restored and a sense of national unity gradually developed. Slavery was the principal thing that had distinguished the South from the North; the other characteristic features of southern culture had been products of that basic difference. With the military defeat of the South, and the subsequent recognition that slavery was beyond restoration, white southerners began to see themselves once more as members of the United States. Within that general framework, however, they still wanted to retain their familiar social hierarchy and so proceeded, through the Ku Klux Klan, the crop lien system, the Jim Crow laws, and a variety of other mechanisms, to deprive the freed slaves of their newly won rights and the opportunity to improve their political, economic, or social status (Gillette 1979; Litwack 1979; Woodward 1951). As the North's centralizing impulse, fueled by moral outrage at the southern treatment of the slaves, gradually waned, the southern states were allowed to maintain the distinctive institutions that continued African American subjugation. In every other major area—language, religion, culture, race, ethnicity, and political ideology—white southerners and northerners were largely identical, and federalism served no function. Its only purpose, in the period that followed the Civil War, was to allow the southern states to maintain their system of apartheid.

This system, and thus the role of federalism in the United States, lasted for about a century. Beginning in the 1950s, white people in the parts of the United States outside the South began to perceive the southern treatment of African Americans as morally unacceptable. The result was a series of actions by national institutions, which were dominated by these white nonsoutherners, to abolish southern apartheid; they included Brown v. Board of Education[1] and other Supreme Court decisions, the Civil Rights Act of 1964, and the executive policies of the Kennedy, Johnson, and Nixon administrations (Harvey 1971; Martin 1979). These actions were perceived, quite correctly, as an abrogation of America's remaining federalist commitment to allow distinctly different normative systems to prevail in different states. The success of the effort eliminated the major difference between the South and the rest of the United States. It contributed, moreover, to the elimination of the more subtle, incremental differences such as the South's lower levels of wealth, industrial development, and education. The New South that emerged during the 1970s and 1980s shared the highly uniform, homogenized commercial culture of the United States as a whole. Any further need for federalism was thus eliminated.

Puppy Federalism in Modern America

At present, the United States is a socially homogenized and politically centralized nation. Regional differences between different parts of the nation are minimal, and those that exist are based on inevitable economic variations, rather than any historical or cultural distinctions. . . . There are also variations in the concentration of various religious and ethnic groups throughout the country. The low salience of religious differences in the United States, however, makes these differences virtually irrelevant. Ethnic divisions are, of course, more salient, and the concentration of African Americans in the South prior to the 1950s was one of the bases of the South's distinctive culture and the continued relevance of federalism. The massive migration of African Americans to other sections of the nation has largely eliminated this regional distinction; race relations remain a major problem in America, but it is a problem that now exists in virtually every region, where it is played out in similar terms. Hispanic and Asian ethnicity is also salient, but these groups have also become widely diffused during the postwar era.

With the minor exceptions of Utah and Hawaii, there is no American state with a truly distinctive social profile. Those differences that do exist may loom large to us, but that is because of our insularity; once we compare our differences with the linguistic, religious, cultural, and historical differences that exist in large nations such as India, Indonesia, and Nigeria, or even smaller ones such as Spain, Cameroon, and itsy-bitsy Belgium, ours shrink to insignificance.

Our political culture is more uniform still. The overwhelming majority of Americans identify with one of two major political parties, whose differences, while again salient to us, are minuscule by international standards. Our states, supposedly free to establish their own regimes, have opted for highly similar structures with minor variations (Gardner 1992). No state has instituted a parliamentary system, for example, although that is the dominant pattern for democratic regimes in the world today; only one state, Nebraska, dispenses with the peculiarly American feature of a bicameral legislature; no state denies its courts the power of judicial review. Certainly, no American state has even attempted to establish a theocratic or autocratic regime; thus, under the current reading of the guarantee clause that restricts it to such matters (but see Merritt 1988), there has been no felt need to invoke the clause, or otherwise intervene in the political process of any state, during the entire course of the twentieth century (Bonfield 1962;

Chemerinsky 1994; Choper 1994). Most important, the primary political loyalty of the vast majority of Americans is to the nation. . . .

Despite this high level of national unity, there remains a certain nostalgia for our bygone federalist system. This nostalgia arises from at least three sources, and probably more. The first is that the Framers are correctly perceived as having established a federalist regime, for reasons described above, and we incorrectly fear that some horrible consequences will ensue if we admit that we no longer abide by their intentions. Second, the yearning of many Americans for the simplicity of the premodern era, and the more sinister yearning of some Americans for the moonlight, magnolia, and mint-julep era of the antebellum South, slides over to the federalism that prevailed at that time. Third, we dislike the centralized administrative state and see federalism as a welcome antidote to the government that we have created and that we need but do not like.

The result of all this yearning is that we continue to insist that we have a federalist system, even though we neither have it nor need it. The dangerous, debilitating problems that federalism is designed to resolve—the lack of national unity, the persistence of separatism, the underlying social and political differences that are cemented in place by centuries of history and hatred—are mercifully absent in the modern United States. Consequently, we no longer recognize federalism as an unfortunate expedient. . . . Thus we can enjoy the idea of federalism because we have forgotten the grave problems associated with its actuality. What we have instead is puppy federalism, a thin patina of rights talk draped across the areas where we have opted for decentralization as an administrative strategy.

The actions of the Republican-dominated Congress of the last six years illustrates the superficiality of American federalism. In general, the Republicans have declared a stronger commitment to federalism than the Democrats, yet recent Republican Congresses have continued the policies of their Democratic predecessors, enacting statutes that federalize areas previously reserved to state law and contradict the federalism decisions of a Supreme Court with which they supposedly agree. For example, the 104th Congress enacted the Church Arson Prevention Act of 1996, making destructive acts against religious institutions a federal crime. The act's basis of federal jurisdiction is the one that proponents of federalism often dismiss as a pretext and that was used in the statute struck down by *United States v. Lopez*[2]—interstate commerce. That same Republican Congress also enacted Megan's Law, requiring certain offenders to register with state law enforcement officers—apparently a case of the outrageous, Framer-ignoring, states'-rights-crushing commandeering of state officers that was struck down in *United States v. Printz.*[3] The 104th Congress also enacted the Drug-Induced Rape Prevention and Punishment Act of 1996, which makes the use of "date rape" drugs a federal offense. In spirit, this act is an extension of the Violence Against Women Act, which was passed just before the Republicans took control of Congress and was struck down in *United States v. Morrison*[4] on an interpretation of the interstate commerce clause. Technically, the act extends the Controlled Substances Act and will probably be invulnerable to judicial attack, but this only leads one to wonder why the Republican Congress feels comfortable endorsing and extending a statute drafted in 1970 by one of the most Democratic, nationalizing Congresses in history and taking away the states' police power authority to decide which substances they will forbid their own citizens to ingest. This is, incidentally, a live issue, as indicated by the various states that have tried to modify their prohibitions against marijuana, only to run afoul of federal authorities.

The reason a Republican Congress would enact statutes of this sort is that our federalism is puppy federalism. When state policies correspond to national norms in a given area, or when there is no national norm, that area can be left to state authority. As soon as a national norm emerges, and some states diverge from that norm, federal authorities will act, as they did against the southern states once racial equality became a general goal. In the last two decades, crime has become a matter of grave concern, and the result has been a steady federalization of the criminal law that continues regardless of the party in control of Congress. When the crunch comes, the crunch being a political demand for action, federalism counts for nothing.

The 104th Congress's most significant legislative action, the Personal Responsibility and Work Opportunity Reconciliation Act, might appear to reflect a commitment to genuine federalism, but it does not; rather, it only underscores the absence of any such commitment. It is true that this act changes prior law in providing block grants of federal funds to the states, rather than channeling federal grants to individuals through state administrators as had been the case under the prior Aid to Families with Dependent Children (AFDC) program. But the main reason for this, despite the federalist rhetoric that accompanied its enactment, was that the federal purpose and federal methodology had changed. The purpose is now to discourage the creation of out-of-wedlock children, not to

provide these children with support; as the very first sentence of the act declares, "Marriage is the foundation of a successful society." The methodology is to compel the states to achieve specified results in accordance with the stated purposes, rather than compelling them to follow specified procedures. Thus the statute gives block grants and does not specify procedures. This undoubtedly gives the states more latitude in the procedural area, but it imposes much greater demands regarding the results. It defines criteria for an "eligible state" (two different sets of criteria, actually), a "qualifying state," a "high performing state," and a "needy state" (42 U.S.C. §403(a)). In accordance with these various criteria, it demands that each state submit a plan to show how it will achieve the statutory purpose, sets specific guidelines for rates of out-of-wedlock births and work participation, places numerous prohibitions and limitations on the use of the block grants, provides bonuses to high-performing states, imposes penalties on states that fail to abide by the limits on fund use or fail to achieve specified levels of results, and requires frequent and detailed reports (id. §§404–11).

Is this really federalism; is it really the way one sovereign treats another sovereign? It seems to bear a closer resemblance to the way a superior treats a subordinate administrator, and not a very trusted subordinate at that. There is a tone in all these provisions, and particularly in the bonuses and penalties, that is much more demeaning to the states than the AFDC idea that they should administer federal funds in a specified manner. The reason for this apparent breach of federalist etiquette by a Republican Congress is not difficult to discern. Because we have only puppy federalism, the national government will give states control over policy only in areas that are not of national concern. It will retain control over any policy that it regards as truly important. When AFDC was enacted, child poverty was the predominant concern, and the political subtext was that southern states could not be relied upon to treat their African American citizens fairly. With the rise of the New South, and the decline in Congress's commitment to racial justice, this concern no longer predominates. Instead, we have the new moralism, with public policy directed to preventing out-of-wedlock births and ensuring that no one but the severely disabled receive welfare payments without working. The new law reflects those concerns. It does not represent a decrease in federal control but a new methodology for control, a new political subtext that the methodology is intended to achieve, and a new public policy that seeks to discipline licentious New York and indulgent California, rather than racist Georgia and Louisiana.

Conclusion

There is no major law reform conclusion to be derived from this discussion. The United States possesses the blessing of national unity, and thus its national government will continue to legislate on any issue that it and the nation in general deem important. One possible conclusion is that the Supreme Court's recent federalism decisions are incorrect—which they are—but as long as the ideology of the justices is not overly divergent from that of the nation as a whole, they are not likely to hand down any decisions with significant impact. The real message of this discussion is for scholars. It is time to stop being fooled by political rhetoric and mistaking puppy federalism for the real thing. Real federalism is gone; America is a centralized administrative state. Rather than mourning its demise, we should feel grateful that our nation no longer needs this unfortunate expedient, and we should focus our attention on complex and important issues, such as decentralization. Instead of a theory of federalism, we need a theory about what policies should be centralized, what policies should be decentralized, and, in both cases, the optimal way for a national government to supervise the regional subordinates that we continue to describe as states.

References

Ackerman, Bruce. 1991. *We the People.* Vol. 1, *Foundations.* Cambridge, Mass: Belknap Press.

Bartkus, Viva. 1999. *The Dynamic of Secession.* New York: Cambridge University Press.

Beer, Samuel. 1993. *To Make a Nation.* Cambridge, MA: Belknap Press.

Birch, Anthony. 1993. *The Concepts and Theories of Modern Democracy.* London: Routledge.

Bonfield, Arthur. 1962. The Guarantee Clause of Article IV, Section 4: A Study in Constitutional Desuetude. *Minnesota Law Review* 46:513–72.

Buchanan, Allen. 1991. *Secession: The Morality of Political Divorce from Fort Sumpter to Lithuania and Quebec.* Boulder, CO: Westview Press.

Cassese, Antonio. 1995. *Self-Determination of Peoples.* New York: Cambridge University Press.

Chemerinsky, Erwin. 1994. Cases Under the Guarantee Clause Should Be Justiciable. *University of Colorado Law Review* 65:849–80.

Choper, Jesse. 1994. Observations on the Guarantee Clause. *University of Colorado Law Review* 65:741–47.

Dikshit, Ramesh. 1975. *The Political Geography of Federalism.* Delhi: Macmillan Co. of India.

Duchacek, Ivo. 1970. *Comparative Federalism: The Territorial Dimension of Politics.* New York: Holt, Rinehart & Winston.

Fitzhugh, George. 1854 [1965]. *Sociology for the South: Or, The Failure of a Free Society.* New York: B. Franklin.

Friedrich, Carl. 1968. *Constitutional Government and Democracy.* 4th ed. Waltham, MA: Blaisdell.

Gardner, James. 1992. The Failed Discourse of State Constitutionalism. *Michigan Law Review* 90:761–837.

Gillette, William. 1979. *Retreat from Reconstruction, 1869–1879.* Baton Rouge: Louisiana State University Press.

Hannum, Hurst. 1990. *Autonomy, Sovereignty, and Self-Determination.* Philadelphia: University of Pennsylvania Press.

Harvey, James. 1971. *Black Civil Rights During the Johnson Administration.* Jackson, MS: University & College Press of Mississippi.

Held, David. 1996. *Models of Democracy.* 2d ed. Stanford, CA: Stanford University Press.

Hildreth, Richard. 1854. *Despotism in America.* New York: Negro University Press.

Litwack, Leon. 1979. *Been in the Storm So Long: The Aftermath of Slavery.* New York: Knopf.

Lutz, David. 1988. *The Origins of American Constitutionalism.* Baton Rouge: Louisiana State University Press.

Main, Jackson Turner. 1961. *The Antifederalists: Critics of the Constitution 1781–1788.* Chapel Hill: University of North Carolina Press.

Martin, John. 1979. *Civil Rights and the Crisis of Liberalism: The Democratic Party, 1945–76.* Boulder, CO: Westview Press.

Merritt, Deborah. 1988. The Guarantee Clause and State Autonomy: Federalism for a Third Century. *Columbia Law Review* 88:1–78.

Olmstead, Frederick Law. 1953. *The Cotton Kingdom,* ed. Arthur Schlesinger. New York: Knopf.

Rakove, Jack. 1979. *The Beginnings of National Politics: An Interpretive History of the Constitutional Congress.* New York: Knopf.

——— 1996. *Original Meanings: Politics and Ideas in the Making of the Constitution.* New York: Knopf.

Stampp, Kenneth. 1959. *The Causes of the Civil War.* Englewood Cliffs, NJ: Prentice-Hall.

Sunstein, Cass. 1991. Constitutionalism and Secession. *University of Chicago Law Review* 58:633–70.

Van Doren, Carl. 1948. *The Great Rehearsal.* New York: Times Reading.

Woodward, C. Van. 1951. *The Origins of the New South, 1877–1913.* Baton Rouge: Louisiana State University Press.

Notes

1. 347 U.S. 483 (1954).
2. 514 U.S. 549 (1995).
3. 521 U.S. 898 (1997).
4. 120 S. Ct. 1740 (2000).

25

The Katrina Breakdown

Jonathan Walters and Donald F. Kettl

When Hurricane Katrina hit New Orleans, only one thing disintegrated as fast as the earthen levees that were supposed to protect the city, and that was the intergovernmental relationship that is supposed to connect local, state and federal officials before, during and after such a catastrophe.

In sifting through the debris of the disaster response, the first question is why intergovernmental cooperation broke down so completely. While it's hard even at this point to get an official accounting of exactly what happened, clearly there were significant communication and coordination problems at all levels of government. At the moment, much time and effort is being spent assigning culpability—for a lack of preparation, delayed decision making, bureaucratic tie-ups and political infighting—to individuals and agencies. But in the end, all such investigations may produce little that is of widespread practical use.

What is more critical, and has significant implications for the future of emergency management in the United States, is the need to explicitly and thoroughly define governments' roles and responsibilities so that officials in other jurisdictions don't suffer the same sort of meltdown in the next natural or man-made disaster. The lurching tactical responses to the terrorist attacks of 2001 and [2005's] rash of major hurricanes only underline the truly fundamental issue: how to sort out who should do what—and how to make sure the public sector is ready to act when the unexpected but inevitable happens.

It won't be easy. Some in the federal government clearly feel that if they're going to be blamed for failures—failures that they ascribe at least in part to state and local officials—then they'd prefer a system where the federal government has the option of being much more preemptive in

handling large-scale domestic disasters. States as a whole, though, are not going to go along with any emergency management plan that involves the feds declaring something like martial law. They would much prefer that existing protocols be continued and the Federal Emergency Management Agency regain its independence from the Department of Homeland Security and be led by experienced professionals rather than political appointees.

A Growing Federal Role

In fact, the history of disaster response and recovery in the United States has witnessed an ever-increasing federal role. On April 22, 1927, President Calvin Coolidge named a special cabinet-level committee headed by Commerce Secretary Herbert Hoover to deal with the massive flooding that was ravaging communities up and down the Mississippi River Valley that year. The scene, described in John M. Barry's highly topical chronicle, "Rising Tide: The Great Mississippi Flood of 1927 and How It Changed America," arguably represents the beginning of the modern era of intergovernmental disaster response. (It also represents the first clear attempt to politicize federal disaster response, with Hoover consciously riding his performance during the disaster all the way to the White House.)

In 1950, the federal government began trying to formalize intergovernmental roles and responsibilities through the Federal Civil Defense Act, which defined the scope and type of assistance that the federal government would extend to states and localities after certain kinds of disasters or emergencies (although Congress had been offering financial aid to states and localities in a piecemeal fashion since the early 1800s). In 1979, President Jimmy Carter created the Federal Emergency Management Agency, largely in response to governors' complaints about the fragmented nature of federal disaster planning and assistance. And in 1988, Congress passed the Robert T. Stafford Disaster Relief Act, which outlined the protocols for disaster declaration and what sort of intergovernmental response would follow.

From 1989 to 1992, a succession of disasters, including the Loma Prieta earthquake in California and hurricanes Hugo in South Carolina and Andrew in Florida, put the whole issue of intergovernmental emergency response in the public hot seat, notes Tom Birkland, director of the Center for Policy Research at the Rockefeller College of Public Affairs and Policy. In particular, the disasters highlighted the federal

From *Governing*, December 2005, 20–25. Reprinted with the permission of the authors.

government's slow-footed and bureaucratic response in the wake of such catastrophic events. (To be sure, such events were also teaching state and local governments plenty about *their* emergency response capabilities.) That, in turn, led to a major turnaround at FEMA, with the appointment of James Lee Witt, the first FEMA director to arrive on the job with actual state emergency management experience.

In general, two things were going on around the increasing federal role in emergency readiness and response, Birkland says. States and localities were getting hooked on federal money—especially for recovery. But American presidents were also discovering the political benefits of declaring disasters, which allowed them to liberally sprinkle significant amounts of cash around various states and localities in distress. "That spending grew considerably under the Clinton administration," says Birkland. "And it created the expectation of federal government largesse. Federal spending, however, was always meant to supplement and not supplant state and local spending."

Local Response

But if the federal role in disaster response and recovery has increased—along with expectations of federal help—emergency management experts at all levels still agree on the basics of existing emergency response protocol: All emergencies are, initially at least, local—or local and state—events. "For the first 48 to 72 hours, it's understood that local and state first responders are principally responsible," says Bill Jenkins, director of the Homeland Security and Justice Issues Group, which is currently looking into the intergovernmental response to Katrina. "The feds come in as requested after that."

The extent to which the local-state-federal response ramps up depends on a host of factors, including the size of the incident and what plans and agreements are in place prior to any event. It also very much depends on the capacity of the governments involved. Some local and state governments have the ability to deal with disasters on their own and seem less inclined to ask for outside help. Others seem to hit the intergovernmental panic button more quickly. But whichever it is, say those on the front line of emergency response, how various governmental partners in emergency response and recovery are going to respond shouldn't be a surprise-filled adventure. Key players at every level of government should have a very good idea of what each will be expected to do or provide when a particular disaster hits.

Most important to the strength of the intergovernmental chain are solid relationships among those who might be called upon to work closely together in times of high stress. "You don't want to meet someone for the first time while you're standing around in the rubble," says Jarrod Bernstein, spokesman for the New York City Office of Emergency Management. "You want to meet them during drills and exercises." In New York, says Bernstein, the city has very tight relationships with state and federal officials in a variety of agencies. "They're involved in all our planning and all our drills. They have a seat at all the tabletop exercises we do."

During those exercises, says Bernstein, federal, state and local officials establish and agree on what their respective jobs will be when a "big one" hits. Last summer, for example, the city worked with FEMA, the U.S. Department of Health and Human Services, the Federal Bureau of Investigation and New York State health and emergency response officials on an exercise aimed at collecting 8 million doses of medicine and distributing them throughout the city in a 48-hour window. "What we were looking at is how we'd receive medical stockpiles from the federal government, break them down and push them out citywide. There is a built-in federal component to that plan," Bernstein says.

No Plan B

While pre-plans and dry runs are all well and good, they're not much use if not taken seriously, however. In 2004, FEMA and Louisiana's Office of Homeland Security and Emergency Preparedness conducted a tabletop exercise, called Hurricane Pam, that simulated a Category 3 storm hitting and flooding New Orleans. It identified a huge gap in disaster planning: An estimated 100,000 people wouldn't be able to get out of the city without assistance. As is standard in emergency management practice, it is the locality's responsibility—at least initially—to evacuate residents, unless other partners are identified beforehand.

Critics of Mayor Ray Nagin say he failed to follow up aggressively on the finding. Last spring, the city floated the notion that it would rely primarily on the faith-based community to organize and mobilize caravans for those without cars or who needed special assistance getting out of the city. The faith-based community balked, however, citing liability issues. The city never came up with a Plan B.

Meanwhile, the Department of Homeland Security had great confidence in its 426-page "all-hazards" National Response Plan. Unveiled last January, it "establishes standardized training, organization and communications procedures for multi-jurisdictional interaction; clearly identifies authority and leadership responsibilities; enables incident response to be handled at the lowest possible organizational and jurisdictional level; ensures the seamless integration of the federal government when an incident exceeds state or local capabilities; and provides the means to swiftly deliver federal support in response to catastrophic incidents."

Katrina was its first test. And in the wake of the Category 4 storm and subsequent flooding, the city's vital resources—communications, transportation, supplies and manpower—were quickly overwhelmed. But DHS Secretary Michael Chertoff waited until 24 hours after the levees were breached to designate the hurricane as an "incident of national significance"—requiring an extensive and well-coordinated response by federal, state, local, tribal and nongovernmental authorities to save lives, minimize damage and provide the basis for long-term community and economic recovery."

The nation—indeed the world—bore painful witness to its failure.

"There are mechanisms and protocols set up as part of the National Response Plan, and those were not followed," says John R. Harrald, director of the Institute for Crisis, Disaster and Risk Management at George Washington University. Harrald notes that under the response plan, one of the first things that's supposed to happen is the rapid activation of a joint operations center to coordinate the intergovernmental response. In Louisiana, that didn't happen quickly enough, he says.

Calling in the Troops

As a result of Katrina, and to a lesser extent hurricanes Rita and Wilma, the general citizenry and elected leaders at all levels of government, as well as emergency responders up and down the chain of command, are demanding a comprehensive review of how local, state and federal governments work (or don't work) together.

Part of that discussion has to include what to do when a state or local government's ability to prepare, respond or to ask for help is either impaired or wiped out altogether. "The question is what do you do when state and local capacity fails for one reason or another, either because they're overwhelmed or they're incompetent," says GWU's

Harrald. "Do we have a system that allows us to scale up adequately or do we need a system where we can bring the military in sooner but that doesn't give away state and local control?"

Bill Leighty, Virginia Governor Mark Warner's chief of staff, who volunteered to spend two weeks in Louisiana helping manage the state response to Katrina, says he thinks there needs to be a serious intergovernmental discussion about when, for example, it might be appropriate to involve the military more directly in a domestic crisis. It is a position born of watching FEMA in action, versus what he saw of the military while he was in New Orleans. FEMA's bureaucratic approach to every item it provided or action it took was, at times, brutally exasperating, says Leighty. "But when you tell the 82nd Airborne, 'Secure New Orleans,' they come in and they know exactly what to do and it gets done."

Even some long-time New Orleans residents, who watched helplessly as looters rampaged through parts of the city, say they wouldn't have minded at all if the military had stepped in to restore order. "There are times when people are overwhelmed," says Frank Cilluffo, director of the Homeland Security Policy Institute at George Washington University, "and they don't care what color uniform is involved in coming to the rescue—red, blue or green."

However, both Kathleen Babineaux Blanco, the Democratic governor of Louisiana, and Haley Barbour, the Republican governor of Mississippi, strenuously objected to requests from the White House to give the Pentagon command over their states' National Guard troops. And President George W. Bush's suggestion of a quick resort to the military in future disasters stunned many observers, including those in his own party. In a television address from New Orleans, he argued that only the armed forces were "capable of massive logistical operations on a moment's notice."

But governors were aghast at the idea that the military would become America's first responders. In a USA Today poll, 36 of 38 governors (including brother Jeb Bush) opposed the plan. Michigan Governor Jennifer Granholm put it bluntly: "Whether a governor is a Republican or Democrat, I would expect the response would be, 'Hell no.'" For one blogger, the worry was "How long before a creek flooding in a small town in Idaho will activate the 82d Airborne Division?"

Bush grabbed the military option in part because of the poor performance of state and local governments. Indeed, everyone breathed a sigh of relief when Coast Guard Admiral Thad Allen arrived to assume command.

Part of the explanation also lies in public opinion polls. A Pew Research Center survey just after the storm revealed that nearly half of those surveyed believed state and local governments had done a fair or poor job—and there was no partisan difference on that conclusion. That meant the smart political play for Bush, although he didn't fare much better in the poll, was to suggest that the military might have to do what state and local governments could not.

That idea, of course, could scarcely be further from the strategy the Republicans had spent a generation building. The Richard Nixon–Ronald Reagan model of new federalism revolved around giving the states more autonomy and less money. But faced with the need to do something—and lacking any alternative—Bush reached back to Lyndon Johnson's Great Society philosophy of an expanded role for the federal government.

But Bush's plan to push the military into a first-response role was clearly less a broad policy strategy than a tactic to find a safe haven in the post-Katrina blame game. That became clear in November, when he announced his avian flu initiative. In that plan, he penciled in a heavy role for state and local public health officials.

Control and Contention

Some believe there is a middle ground when it comes to issues of authority and autonomy. James A. Stever, director of the Center for Integrated Homeland Security and Crisis Management at the University of Cincinnati, says he and colleagues had forwarded a paper to the former head of Homeland Security, Tom Ridge, outlining the concept of "homeland restoration districts." The idea is to have established criteria for when a more robust federal disaster response might be appropriate. Recovery districts would allow for ad hoc federal takeovers of specific geographic areas when appropriate, says Stever, rather than creating some new, overriding national response protocol that calls for broad federal preemption of local and state authority.

But sifting through such ideas—and the others that are sure to surface—is going to mean rekindling the sort of conversation about intergovernmental coordination and cooperation that Washington hasn't seen in a long time. Whether the current Congress and administration will be willing to conduct that conversation isn't clear. State and local officials, for their part, have been called in by Congress to testify on how the intergovernmental response to disasters ought to go.

But such sessions have frequently had the familiar ring of both state and local tensions over who controls federal funding, as well as a little tin-cup rattling.

For example, in testimony before the House Homeland Security Committee, David Wallace, mayor of Sugar Land, Texas, argued that the first lesson learned in the wake of Katrina is that local governments should have more control over how federal homeland security first-responder money should be spent. "There was a real concern from the beginning that an over-reliance by the federal government on a state-based distribution system for first responder resources and training would be slow and result in serious delays in funding reaching high-threat, high-risk population areas." Wallace concluded his testimony with a request for federal funding for what he describes as Regional Logistics Centers, designed to bring local regional resources to bear in the immediate aftermath of disasters.

Nor is it only touchy issues of funding and control related to readiness and response that need discussing, points out Paul Posner, who spent years as a GAO intergovernmental affairs analyst. "There's other knotty issues that cause a lot of intergovernmental friction, like federal insurance policies, local building codes and state land use policies." These are key issues that Posner points out all influence how vulnerable certain places are to disasters in the first place.

From hurricanes and pandemics to earthquakes and terrorism, the United States is grappling with the prospect of a host of cataclysmic events. Taken individually, most communities face a small chance of being hit, but experts agree that it's not a matter of "if" but "when" another large-scale disaster will occur somewhere in the United States. As Katrina so powerfully illustrated, a fragmented intergovernmental response can be disastrous.

The Six Suburban Eras
of the United States

ROBERT LANG, JENNIFER LEFURGY, AND ARTHUR C. NELSON

Introduction

The Metropolitan Institute at Virginia Tech (MI) proposes a timeline to show the flow of suburban eras and types. The timeline defines six periods of U.S. suburban development in order to establish more common base years for historical data analysis. As the field of suburban studies matures into a formal academic sub-discipline, these suggested eras can help guide research projects.

The current standard split in suburban history, proposed by New Urbanists such as Andres Duany, offers a rather crude division into pre- and post-World War II periods (Duany, Plater-Zyberk, and Speck 2000). But this simple pre/post-war dichotomy is a caricature of suburban history. It can be argued that one suburban era actually spans the immediate pre- and post-war decades, which are labeled "Mid-Century Suburbs" (or the years 1930 to 1970) in this note. In addition, the post-war period is now so long, at 60 plus years, that it too can be divided into eras. Consider, for example an article by Robert Lang, Edward Blakely, and Meghan Gough (2005) that looks at the "new suburban metropolis" period from 1970 to 2010.

This timeline is not meant to be definitive. There are no clean breaks in history. Thus the timeline is depicted as a meandering river to indicate the continuous flow of events. The dates show stops along the way where the river course shifts, implying a directional change in history.

This note divides American suburban history into six eras. It finds that the United States is now in the fifth era and will soon enter a sixth one. The timeline also indicates some exemplar suburbs of each period and touches on key political changes and technological innovations. However, this argument does not subscribe to the notion of technological or economic determinism. Previous efforts to categorize historic eras focused especially on advances in transit technology (Stern and Massengale 1981), but multiple forces propel suburban change, and this proposed timeline also considers how cultural influences shaped the course of evolution.

The timeline reflects current thinking on the suburbs and incorporates the work of many historians including James

Borchert (1996), Robert Fishman (1987, 1990), Dolores Hayden (2003), Kenneth Jackson (1985), Chester Liebs (1985), Richard Longstreth (1998, 1999), and Sam Bass Warner, Jr. (1962, 1972). The understanding of the three later eras is driven mostly by the current work of researchers at MI and the Brookings Institution's Metropolitan Policy Program. The labels attached to these eras were developed by MI and reflect its conceptualization of how the suburbs have evolved since the mid-19th century.

Before 1850: Proto Suburbs

Prior to 1850, U.S. suburbs were mostly extensions of cities (Jackson 1985, Warner 1972). They featured street plans and housing that closely resembled the urban core. In this era, the urban fringe featured dense row houses that abruptly give way to open fields and farms. However, some historians have documented the fact that the residents of early U.S. suburbs such as Brooklyn already had a different demographic character than residents of the central city (Jackson 1985). At first, these borderlands were poorer than the core. But with the introduction of ferry service around New York harbor, neighborhoods such as Brooklyn Heights emerged that catered to middle-income commuters. Henry Binford (1988) finds a similar development pattern at the fringe of Boston in the first half of the 19th century.

The earliest distinctly non–urban looking suburbs began in the United Kingdom in the early 19th century (Fishman 1987). They appeared first in London (Clapham Common—1800) and later Manchester (Victoria Park—1830s). These same kinds of "picturesque" suburbs did not emerge in the United States until the second half of the 19th century.

1850 to 1890: Town and Country Suburbs

The notion of suburbs as distinct physical places from cities became evident in the United States by the 1850s (Fishman 1987). The earliest documented English-style American suburb was Llewellyn Park, NJ, designed by Frederick Law Olmsted in 1857. Olmsted's work captured in design and spirit an entire mid-19th century U.S. movement that elevated domesticity and the nuclear family. This movement, along with the picturesque landscape architecture, had its roots in England.

But note that we do not refer to this suburban era as "picturesque" as some others have (Hayden 2003). That is because these suburbs are only part of the suburban story of the period. The flip side of the affluent picturesque places was a more moderate-income and city-like suburb based on horse-drawn streetcars (Hayden 2003). These streetcars were a big improvement over horse-drawn omnibuses because they were faster and carried more load (Warner 1962). They helped change the course of urban development in places such as New York, where suburbs now spread north on Manhattan Island instead of only crossing the East River to Brooklyn (Jackson 1985).

The horse-drawn streetcar suburbs were much denser and more traditionally urban that their picturesque counterparts—thus they were the "town" in the "town and country suburbs." But they also were now distinct from the urban core. In places such as the Jamaica Plains neighborhood of Boston, the architecture began to shift in the 1850s from the tight row houses such as those found on Beacon Hill to a looser configuration with side alleys (Warner 1962). In many cases, the houses were fully detached but remained on small narrow lots. To a modern eye, this does not seem as important a distinction, but it signaled a much larger change. Also note that many of the "town" suburbs had been annexed by the central city and appeared for all intents and purposes to be "urban neighborhoods" (Rusk 1993). Yet in the context of the mid-to-late 19th century American metropolis, these places were suburbs. The best example of a neighborhood built in this style was Gross Park in Chicago, dating from the 1880s (Hayden 2003).

1890 to 1930: Streetcar Suburbs

By the late 1880s, the first electric streetcars—or trolleys—were in use. The trolleys were a turbo version of the horse-drawn streetcars (Warner 1962). They were much bigger and faster and helped spread development for miles past the old urban core. Many of the trends that began in the horse-drawn era were greatly accentuated and extended by trolleys—the suburban houses spread out more (especially in places such as Los Angeles) and differences between the look and feel of the edge and the core grew (Fishman 1987). The streetcars so dominated the construction and speculation of this period that many historians use them to label this suburban era (Warner 1962). Suburban diversity, which began in earlier eras, continues and intensifies with the emergence of large-scale residential "city suburbs" (Borchert 1996).

Suburban retail and commercial districts also began to change radically in the streetcar suburbs (Liebs 1985). The old, dense form of Main Street now took on an elongated appearance. Storefronts stretched to reflect the fact that people might now window shop from a fast-moving trolley. These extended main streets, also referred to as "taxpayer strips," were the forerunner of the auto-based strip (Liebs 1985; Lang, LeFurgy, and Hornburg 2005). Many of these places exist today, threading through the edges of central cities and older suburbs, and are to the modern eye "traditional looking." But in their era, these strips represented a sharp break with commercial districts in the urban core.

Automobiles were invented around the same time as trolleys, but had much less immediate impact on urban development in the early years of the 20th century. They were expensive, hard to store, and poorly accommodated in urban places. Yet the streetcars began to loosen up the American metropolis so effectively that cars began to find navigating suburbs easier with each passing year. The first commercial districts to begin building parking lots were the trolley-based taxpayer strips. By the 1920s, the west side of Los Angeles began to develop fully auto-based shopping (Longstreth 1998, 1999).

1930 to 1970: Mid-Century Suburbs

Key developments during this era include the creation of Federal Housing Administration loans in the 1930s, which greatly improved middle-income access to suburban housing, and the beginning of the interstate highways in 1956 (Jackson 1985). Suburban architecture grew even more distinct from both traditional urban and even earlier suburbs (Hayden 2003). The dominant housing type was the one-story ranch-style home with a minimally classic exterior and a modern open floor plan. The scale of development expanded, especially after World War II in projects such as Levittown and Lakewood (Hayden 2003). The modest suburban shopping centers of the early 20th century exploded into massive malls that, beginning in 1956, were mostly enclosed and climate-controlled (Liebs 1985).

The New Urbanists, such as Andres Duany (Duany, Plater-Zyberk, and Speck 2000) and James Kunstler (1993), argue that a clean break in history exists between the pre- and post-World War II eras. In their view, all development before the war was pedestrian-oriented and traditional in form. After the war came an auto-dominated environment of subdivisions and shopping malls. However, the historical literature does not support this simplistic view (Harris 1988) and instead indicates that many early 20th century suburbs began a slow, decades-long adoption of automobiles (Liebs 1985). By the 1930s, cars were poised to significantly remake the American metropolis, but first a depression and then war greatly slowed the pace of urban change (Jackson 1985). Yet in the few places that still grew during the depression and war, such as the Los Angeles and Washington, DC, regions, the car made its mark (Longstreth 1998, 1999). These places, along with select parts of suburban New York, contain many examples of 1930s auto suburbs complete with proto tract-style subdivisions and early auto-oriented shopping centers.

Thus, a new suburban style emerged at the mid-20th century. This style existed both immediately before and after the war. There is just so much more development occurring after the war, that Mid-Century Suburbs were said to have a "post-war" style.

1970 to 2010: New Metropolis Suburbs

The interstate beltways, constructed mostly in the 1960s, paved the way for a boom in suburban commercial development by the 1970s. A new suburban-dominated metropolis emerged during this period (Fishman 1990; Sharpe and Wallock 1994). The amount of suburban office space surpassed that of central cities, giving rise to Edge Cities and even more commonly Edgeless Cites (Lang 2003)—a more sprawling style of commercial development. Suburbs now typically had the region's balance of people, shopping, and business, yet they maintained a distinct non-urban look (Lang, Blakely and Gough 2005). They became cities in function, but not in form (Fishman 1990; Lang 2003).

The suburbs also grew diverse (Lang and LeFurgy 2006). The 1965 reform in immigration law led to a surge in the foreign-born population of the United States by the 1980s. The cities no longer had a monopoly on attracting immigrants. By the first decade of the 21st century, the suburbs equaled cities as immigrant magnets (Frey 2003). The suburbs also attracted growing numbers of nontraditional households, including single and even gay residents (Brekhus 2003; Frey and Berube 2003). In fact, the suburbs grow so diverse in this era that a whole new language was needed to describe the multiple types of communities and their complicated forms of development.

The suburban split between upscale and more modest development, detectable even in the 19th century, intensified in this era (Orfield 1997, 2002). Many older suburbs from the streetcar, and even mid-century, periods were in decline (most town and country era suburbs have been annexed by central cities). The amount of suburban poverty dramatically increased in places that fall outside the "favored quarter" (Leinberger 1997), or the most affluent wedge of the metropolis. Places in the favored quarter boomed. Newer suburbs at the edge of the region featured "McMansions" as the average house size in new construction nearly doubled from 1970 to the end of the century (Lang and Danielsen 2002). Closer-in suburbs within this quarter became cosmopolitan and competed directly with fashionable urban neighborhoods for the region's arts and intellectual communities (Lang, Hughes, and Danielsen 1997).

2010 and beyond: Megapolitan Suburbs

A new suburban era may emerge after 2010. It likely will be characterized by an enlarging exurban belt that stretches so far from the original urban core that its residents may have a choice of directions in which to commute. For example, people living around Fredericksburg, VA, 50 miles south of Washington, DC, now have the option of commuting south to Richmond or north to the District of Columbia or booming Northern Virginia. The commuter sheds in the "Megapolitan Suburbs" will link up vast networks of cities (Carbonell and Yaro 2005). The scale of the building also will be enormous as the nation adds at least 30 million new residents each decade until mid-century (Nelson 2004).

Lang and Dhavale (2005) developed a new trans-metropolitan geography that labels vast urban zones "Megapolitan Areas." The first one emerged in the Northeast between Maine and Virginia (Gottmann 1961), but now nine others reach into all regions of the United States. By 2005, Megapolitans captured more than two in three Americans, and the share will grow significantly by 2050 (Lang and Dhavale 2005).

A wave of suburban gentrification will occur post-2010, especially in the favored quarter. Many of the new developments will intensify the urban look and feel of many suburbs. A new urbanity will sweep the suburbs—they will still not look like traditional cities, but may incorporate more urban elements than Edge Cities of the past. Many first-generation Edge Cities will lose their edge as traditional cores revive and more distant suburbs explode with new development (Lang 2003). The scale of urbanity may shift away from mega projects in the suburbs—like Edge Cities—and into smaller scale town centers. The new town centers will have less concentrated office space than Edge Cities, but will be more mixed-use and pedestrian-oriented than the current form of suburban commercial development.

References

Binford, Henry, C. 1988. *The First Suburbs: Residential Communities on the Boston Periphery, 1815–1860.* Chicago: University of Chicago Press.

Borchert, James. 1996. Residential City Suburbs: The Emergence of a New Suburban Type, 1880–1930. *Journal of Urban History* 22: 283–307.

Brekhus, Wayne. 2003. *Peacocks, Chameleons, Centaurs: Gay Suburbia and the Grammar of Social Identity.* Chicago: University of Chicago Press.

Carbonell, Armando and Robert Yaro. 2005. American Spatial Development and the New Megalopolis. *Landlines* 17(2): 2–5.

Duany, Andres, Elizabeth Plater-Zyberk, and Jeff Speck. 2000. *Suburban Nation.* New York: North Point Press.

Fishman, Robert. 1987. *Bourgeois Utopias: The Rise and Fall of Suburbia.* New York: Basic Books.

Fishman, Robert. 1990. America's New City: Megalopolis Unbound. *Wilson Quarterly* 14(1): 24–45.

Frey, William. 2003. Melting Post Suburbs: A Study of Suburban Diversity. In Bruce Katz and Robert E. Lang (eds.), *Redefining Cities and Suburbs: Evidence from Census 2000,* Volume I, pp. 155–180. Washington, DC: Brookings Institution Press.

Frey, William and Alan Berube. 2003. City Families and Suburban Singles: An Emerging Household Story. In Bruce Katz and Robert E. Lang (eds.), *Redefining Cities and Suburbs: Evidence from Census 2000,* Volume I, pp. 257–288. Washington, DC: Brookings Institution Press.

Gottmann, Jean. 1961. *Megalopolis: The Urbanized Northeastern Seaboard of the United States.* New York: Twentieth-Century Fund.

Harris, Richard. 1988. American Suburbs: A Sketch of a New Interpretation. *Journal of Urban History* 15: 98–103.

Hayden, Dolores. 2003. *Building Suburbia: Green Fields and Urban Growth, 1820.* New York: Vintage Books.

Jackson, Kenneth. 1985. *Crabgrass Frontier: The Suburbanization of the United States.* New York: Oxford University Press.

Kunstler, James H. 1993. *Geography of No-where: The Rise and Decline of America's Man-made Landscape.* New York: Free Press.

Lang, Robert. 2003. *Edgeless Cities: Exploring the Elusive Metropolis.* Washington, DC: Brookings Institution.

Lang, Robert E. and Karen A. Danielsen. 2002. Monster Homes. *Planning* (5): 2–7.

Lang, Robert and Dawn Dhavale. 2005. "Beyond Megalopolis: Exploring America's New "Megapolitan" Geography." Census Report Series: 05:01. Alexandria, VA: Metropolitan Institute at Virginia Tech.

Lang, Robert E. and Jennifer LeFurgy. 2006. *Boomburbs: The Rise of America's Accidental Cities.* Washington, DC: Brookings Institution Press.

Lang, Robert E., Edward J. Blakely, and Meghan Z. Gough. 2005. Keys to the New Metropolis: America's Big, Fast-Growing Suburban Counties. *Journal of the American Planning Association* 71(4): 381–391.

Lang, Robert E., James W. Hughes, and Karen A. Danielsen. 1997. Targeting the Suburban Urbanites: Marketing Central City Housing. *Housing Policy Debate* 8(2): 437–470.

Lang, Robert, Jennifer LeFurgy, and Steven Hornburg. 2005. From Wall Street to Your Street: New Solutions for Smart Growth Finance. Coral Gables, FL: Funders' Network for Smart Growth and Livable Communities.

Leinberger, Christopher. 1997. The Favored Quarter; Where the Bosses Live, Jobs and Development Follow. *Atlanta Journal Constitution,* June 8.

Liebs, Chester. 1985. *Main Street to Miracle Mile: American Roadside Architecture.* Boston: Little, Brown.

Longstreth, Richard. 1998. *City Center to Regional Mall: Architecture, the Automobile, and Retailing in Los Angeles, 1920–1950.* Cambridge, MA: MIT Press.

Longstreth, Richard. 1999. *The Drive-In, the Supermarket, and the Transformation of Commercial Space in Los Angeles, 1914–1941.* Cambridge, MA: MIT Press.

Nelson, Arthur C. 2004. Toward a New Metropolis: The Opportunity to Rebuild America. Washington, DC: Brookings Institution Metropolitan Policy Program Survey Series (December).

Orfield, Myron. 1997. *Metro Politics: A Regional Agenda for Community and Stability.* Washington, DC: The Brookings Institution Press.

Orfield, Myron. 2002. *American Metropolitics.* Washington, DC: The Brookings Institution Press.

Rusk, David. 1993. *Cities Without Suburbs.* Washington, DC: Woodrow Wilson Center Press.

Sharpe, William and Leonard Wallock. 1994. Bold New City or Built-Up 'Burb? Redefining Contemporary Suburbia. *American Quarterly* 46(1): 1–30.

Stern, Robert A.M. and John M. Massengale. 1981. The Anglo-American Suburb, Architectural Design Profile 37, Vol. 51, No. 10/11. New York: St. Martin's Press.

Warner, Sam Bass, Jr. 1962. *Streetcar Suburbs: The Process of Growth in Boston, 1870–1900.* Cambridge, MA: Harvard University Press.

ROBERT E. LANG is the Director of the Metropolitan Institute at Virginia Tech and is an Associate Professor in the school's Urban Affairs and Planning Program. He is also co-editor of *Opolis.* **JENNIFER LEFURGY** is the Deputy Director of the Metropolitan Institute at Virginia Tech. Along with Robert Lang, she is authoring *Boomburbs: The Rise of America's Accidental Cities* for the Brookings Institution Press. She is also doctoral candidate in Virginia Tech's Urban Affairs and Planning program. **ARTHUR C. NELSON** is professor and founding director of Virginia Tech's Urban Affairs and Planning Program at the Alexandria Center. He was formerly professor of city and regional planning, and public policy at Georgia Tech and adjunct professor of law at Georgia State University.

From *Opolis: An International Journal of Suburban and Metropolitan Studies,* Vol. 2, No. 1, 2006, pp. 65–72. Copyright © 2006 by Opolis. Reprinted by permission.

Return to Center

States that moved offices and jobs out to the suburbs are moving them back downtown.

CHRISTOPHER D. RINGWALD

Last spring, New York's Department of Environmental Conservation moved back where it started out: downtown Albany. After 30 years in a headquarters just off Interstate 87, in the suburb of Colonie, the agency and its 1,900 employees packed up and relocated to 625 Broadway, a few blocks from the state capitol.

Not every employee is happy—most had grown accustomed to off-ramp freeway access, massive parking lots and other accoutrements of a suburban location. On the other hand, there are compensations. "I like having sidewalks to walk on," says Franz Litz, a DEC attorney, standing outside his new 14-story office building after strolling back from lunch at a nearby restaurant. "I can walk to some meetings," says one of his colleagues. "Before, I used to have to drive to all of them."

Whether they approve of it or not, however, the return to downtown Albany is a change that thousands of New York State employees will need to get used to. The DEC is only one of the agencies involved. The state's Dormitory Authority, which finances and constructs major public facilities, has moved to a five-story glass-and-granite box at 515 Broadway, down the street from DEC. The state Comptroller's office is consolidating its workforce a few blocks away. In the past five years, more than 4,500 state employees have relocated into the city's center.

None of this is a coincidence. New York's General Services Commissioner, Kenneth Ringler, puts it succinctly. "The governor," he says, "has a downtown policy."

This is not the first time that major efforts have been launched to rescue downtown Albany. During the 1960s and 1970s, Governor Nelson Rockefeller—with the strong support of Democratic Mayor Erastus Corning II—cleared 80 acres in the center of the city and built the Empire State Plaza, nine giant buildings arrayed on a marble mall with vast reflecting pools. Grandiose, windswept and impersonal, the project has always generated more critics than admirers. Still, it did serve the purpose of concentrating thousands of state workers in the vicinity of the capitol.

But as the workforce ballooned in the 1980s, little effort was made to accommodate the new growth in the center of the city. Many agencies located in the suburbs. By the early 1990s, downtown Albany was again forlorn, Empire State Plaza notwithstanding. The new governor, George Pataki, decided it was time to try again.

That in itself might seem a little surprising. Pataki did not come into office with a reputation as an urbanist—all of his prior experience had been in Peekskill, a small village in northern Westchester County, where he was mayor and served as a state legislator. But Peekskill underwent its own miniature revival in the 1990s as artists from New York were enticed by cheap studio space and old houses.

This hometown experience had its effect on Pataki. In 1998, he proposed and the legislature approved a $240 million "Albany plan," built around returning the central city to its former role as the nerve center of state government. "By moving state facilities into downtown areas and neighborhoods," Pataki said, "we can revitalize the cities that are so important to the state, and particularly the city of Albany. We are committed to Albany being not just the capital, but being a revitalized capital."

The Pataki administration is trying not to repeat the mistakes of the previous era. "It is important how we locate in downtowns," Ringler says, "and not just that we do so." Instead of bulldozing vast sections of town to build a massive complex, the state has built at modest scale at various locations within the existing downtown grid. The buildings line up along the sidewalk; the new architecture blends reasonably well with historic appearances.

No state government is currently attempting anything as ambitious as New York's, but a surprising number of them have a similar idea. In New Jersey, where much of the state workforce moved to leased suburban space during the 1980s, the departments of Human Services and Education have both moved back to downtown Trenton. Former Governor Christine Todd Whitman halted construction of a Revenue Division building in suburban Hamilton Township "because it was going to move jobs out of the city," according to Robert Runciano, the state's former director of Property Management and Construction.

Two years ago, Kentucky was ready to build a new office for its Transportation Cabinet. Many state legislators favored moving it out of the capital area in central Frankfort. The business community wanted to keep it there. Business won. Construction started last month on the new Transportation center, a five-story, $113 million downtown building that will house several hundred workers. "The construction of it has spurred a lot of other developments, new water and sewer lines and also private development," says Don Speer, commissioner of the state Department of Administration. Meanwhile, a nearby public-private project, the Sullivan Square Office Building, has consolidated state workers from scattered spots and attracted a graphics firm with 50 employees.

Alabama's capital, Montgomery, lost so many state offices to the suburbs that, as one visitor put it, the city presented the image "of these gleaming alabaster government buildings up on a hill and down below it was a desperate scene" of urban decay. It was the state pension fund for civil servants and teachers that turned the tide by building six prime office buildings, one of them 26 stories, to lease to state agencies along Commerce Street, in the heart of downtown, and on Dexter Avenue, which leads up to the capitol. "It stabilized a deteriorating and dying central business district," says Tommy Tyson, the city's director of planning. The influx of money and workers has generated new restaurants and led to the opening of two hotels.

The phenomenon exists in even the smallest state capitals. In Montpelier, Vermont (population 8,000), rented state offices on the outskirts are being moved to retrofitted state-owned buildings downtown. And a $10 million state office project is on the drawing board. "The policy is to invest in downtowns whenever renovating or building state office space," says Thomas Torti, Vermont's Building and General Services commissioner. "If you're coming to see the tax people, drop something off at motor vehicles and then check on personnel, those are all near each other now." The new facilities in Montpelier aim to stimulate other development through multi-use buildings with room for retail and commerce. A new state parking complex is slated to include offices and housing.

I n New York's case, the Albany plan is more complicated than just a one-way return to the city. It is actually a game of musical buildings. While some agencies head back downtown, others are being shuffled around to take advantage of the space being vacated. The Transportation Department will occupy the offices that the Department of Environmental Protection has given up. The Depression-era Alfred E. Smith building, an ornate downtown landmark badly in need of renovation, is being fixed up to house workers coming in from the 350-acre Harriman campus, built in the 1960s on the outskirts of the city. The state has yet to decide whether the 16 Harriman buildings will be sold to private developers. By preliminary estimates, the plan could save at least $86 million in renovation costs and recoup millions more from sales.

Albany is not the only city in the area benefiting from the urban commitment. Across the Hudson, in tiny, blue-collar Rensselaer, the state's Office of Children and Family Services consolidated its workers, previously spread across various sites, into a renovated felt factory. Ten miles upriver in Troy, the state restored two historic structures and a defunct mall and moved

in more than 1,000 workers from the Health, Labor and Law departments. About 20 miles west, Schenectady, already home to the headquarters of the state lottery, is gaining 450 Department of Transportation workers and a new office building. In distant Buffalo, an old windshield wiper factory was remodeled to create 60,000 square feet of space for the New York State Office of Temporary Disability Assistance and other tenants. "The local mayors are ecstatic," says Ringler, the General Services administrator.

Not everyone is on board. Critics trace the Troy moves to log-rolling, saying that these came at the behest of Joseph Bruno, the Senate majority leader who represents Troy. Others challenge the deal between Pataki and Jerry Jennings, the Democratic mayor of Albany, that led to the ongoing $11 million reconstruction of Pearl Street, the city's downtown backbone.

And there are those who complain that the Albany Plan relies too heavily on the buildings themselves, rather than on the less tangible investments needed for urban recovery. "State workers are downtown, and that's more people downtown," says Paul Bray, a local planning and environmental attorney and founder of a monthly civic forum, the Albany Roundtable. "But building a city is a much more nuanced, complex thing than moving offices."

Bray wants the state to provide incentives for its employees to live downtown, as well as work there, so that the city's core no longer will empty out after the work day. Critics also say the money spent on construction of bulky parking garages for each new building—a feature demanded by public employee unions—could have been used for improved bus lines or other alternatives to the automobile. "Cities make poor suburbs," Bray says. "You really need to concentrate on mass transit more than parking garages."

I n truth, no one can guarantee that the return of state government to any downtown will generate a local economic revival. The sidewalks of downtown Troy, a treasure-trove of 19th-century buildings, are busier since the civil servants began arriving in 1995. But Mayor Mark Pattison warns his counterparts in New York and elsewhere not to expect new government offices to work miracles. "They are not causing the economic boom that people thought they might," Pattison told a local newspaper reporter earlier this year. "The myth of the state worker is that they don't work hard. In fact, they have just a half-hour for lunch, and when they're done working, they go back home to the family and kids just like we all do. They bring a little bit of additional business but not quite the amount we expected."

Meanwhile, at the Stagecoach coffee and sandwich shop in downtown Albany, just across the park from the new Environmental Conservation building, a longtime employee concedes it is taking a while for the relocated workers to reorient themselves to city life. "It's been good for business, but not as great as we expected," she said last fall. "They complain because there's no mall to go to, they don't have enough shops to go to. A lot of them get an hour for lunch, and they don't know what to do with themselves."

But some of the restaurant's employees have been working longer hours since the Environmental Conservation building opened. And a couple of blocks away, the owners of Lodge's, a small department store dating back to the 1800s, are renovating four long-empty storefronts for interested retail and commercial tenants.

Whatever the economic impact turns out to be, long-suffering downtown Albany seems convinced that the plan will have been worth the effort, and the cost—if only for reasons of simple logic. "It's the capital," says Chungchin Chen, executive director of the Capital District Regional Planning Commission. "The agencies are supposed to be there—instead of dispersed in the suburbs."

From *Governing*, April 2002, pp. 34–36. Copyright © 2002 by *Congressional Quarterly*, Inc. Reprinted by permission.

The Sprawl Debate:
Let Markets Plan

Peter Gordon
University of Southern California

Harry W. Richardson
University of Southern California

Sprawl issues ought not be a federal issue because land-use control is local. Americans have been moving to both suburban and private communities for many years, an expression of the constitutional right to travel. They seek more direct control over their personal property rights. Both trends are at odds with the desire of planners to impose more controls via land-use and growth controls. Planners base their arguments on the need to control urban sprawl. Examining their arguments one-by-one shows that they are empirically weak. The controls are ineffective and will do little to slow these shifts in residential location. The logic of the planners' position would be to control development everywhere via state and even federal legislation, but this is undesirable, unattainable, and probably unconstitutional. Sprawl will remain an issue over which state and local jurisdictions will either continue to fight or find an uneasy accommodation.

In the presidential election campaign of 2000, both candidates responded to a request from an environmental group for a written statement of their position on sprawl. Al Gore's statement was more than double the length of that of George W. Bush, but both took a strong anti-sprawl position. Nevertheless, the sprawl issue never took fire in the campaign, despite the obviously great interest in the issue among the American public. The reason is not difficult to find. Land use is a local policy problem as demonstrated from constitutional decisions tracing back to the 1920s. The federal government, moreover, cannot address land use directly. This explains why the Clinton administration's initiatives in this sphere (e.g., the Communities Reinvestment Act) focused on the revival of central cities as an indirect approach to controlling sprawl. In the case of land-use controls, the central intergovernmental issue is the role of state versus local governments. The federal system gives priority to state rights, but local governments do not give up their police power of controlling land use lightly. In several states that have passed mandatory statewide growth-management legislation, some local jurisdictions (counties or municipalities) have been very recalcitrant.

Another point about the U.S. presidential election of 2000 is that it confirmed the long-term trend of declining voter participation. Turnouts in 2000 and 1996 were among the lowest in U.S. history.[1] The rational

---

[1]Susan Schmidt and John Mintz, "Voter Turnout Up Only Slightly Despite Big Drive," *The Washington Post*, 9 November 2000, p. A35.

© Publius: The Journal of Federalism 31:3 (Summer 2001)

131

economic explanation emphasizes the fact that growing affluence raises opportunity costs, which make voting and other forms of political participation less attractive and less likely. An elaboration of this view comes from both Charles Tiebout's classic concept of "voting with your feet"[2] and Albert Hirschman's *Exit, Voice, and Loyalty.*[3] As exit options become affordable for more people, there will be less voice and less interest in conventional politics. Current and past trends in residential location echo this point. Planners proposing tougher land-use regulations in the name of preventing urban sprawl should take note.

Affluence makes mobility an option for increasing numbers of people. Social, occupational, and geographic mobility are usually intertwined. People often move into new careers, different income strata, and new locations simultaneously. For many years, Americans have moved into the suburbs as they have moved up in life. The importance of either the exercise of voice or the cultivation of loyalty in communities where people have few ties and few reasons to nurture ties may be less compelling.

Debates over the pervasiveness of these phenomena have recently surfaced in discussions of whether more Americans than ever are now *Bowling Alone.*[4] Although Robert Putnam cites considerable evidence for a noticeable decline in community and social capital, his critics suggest that he has been looking in all the wrong places; the Kiwanis Club's membership may be down but the Sierra Club's membership is way up.[5] Others suggest that it is entirely reasonable for people to "substitute freedom of choice for the binding power of custom and tradition."[6] We live in a world of trade-offs.

In the next section, we discuss the federal role in land-use planning. We then briefly discuss what we call the two migrations in the United States. Large numbers of people are engaged in two forms of exit, moving into private communities and/or into suburban/exurban locations where they expect more direct and personal control over their property. Afterwards, we revisit the sprawl debate to reiterate our position that the arguments used by planners and others for vastly enhanced public land-use controls are weak. In the concluding section, we discuss the irony of proposals for stronger state controls at a time when people are looking for property-rights assurances that they find more attractive.

[2]Charles M. Tiebout, "A Pure Theory of Public Expenditures," *Journal of Political Economy* 64 (October 1956): 416-424.

[3]Albert O. Hirschman, *Exit, Voice and Loyalty: Responses to Decline in Firms, Organizations and States* (Cambridge: Harvard University Press, 1970).

[4]Robert D. Putnam, *Bowling Alone: The Collapse and Revival of American Community* (New York: Simon and Shuster, 2000).

[5]Lynne L. Kiesling, "Book Review," *The Cato Journal* 20 (Spring/Summer 2000): 131-133.

[6]Paul Heyne, *A Students' Guide to Economics* (New York: Prentice Hall, 2000), p. 28.

THE FEDERAL ROLE IN LAND-USE PLANNING

In recent years, there have been many state, county, and local ballot initiatives about growth management, "smart growth," and sprawl. In the past two elections (1998 and 2000), the majority of the initiatives to control sprawl passed.[7] Yet, there remain many jurisdictions that refused to accept a growth-management agenda, and an even larger number that did not get involved in the debate and were willing to accept development, even remaining enthusiastic about it. The result is that, regardless of how fast the sprawl-containment strategy spreads, there are always cities and counties where development can take place. Thus, the anti-sprawl movement recognized that the way to control this was to press for state legislation. This explains Washington's Growth Management Act of 1990 and the abortive Citizen's Growth Management Initiative in Arizona in 2000 (Proposition 202). Even with a state-mandated growth-management strategy, it is difficult to control development in all jurisdictions because most statutes cannot avoid leaving some wiggle-room for pro-development cities and counties. Furthermore, even if a state program is watertight, developers can always find other states in which to develop, often just across the border. For example, when Portland Metro adopted its restrictive urban growth boundaries in 1979, much of the focus of development shifted to the contiguous Clark County in Washington State. This has continued even after Washington passed its own Growth Management Act in 1990.[8] Hence, the logic of the argument is to develop a federal land-use policy controlling development in all states.

Such an evolution is almost unthinkable. Local jurisdictions have retained controls over local land-use under the principle of the police power ever since the U.S. Supreme Court case of *Village of Euclid v. Ambler Realty Co.* in 1926. The federal government has indirect influence on land-use decisions under other public interest legislation, especially in the environmental area such as the 1970 Clean Air Act, the 1972 Clean Water Act (originally called the Water Pollution Control Act Amendments), and the 1973 Endangered Species Act. Nevertheless, the federal courts have recently shown a strong interest in the "takings" issue[9] with cases such as *Nollan v. California Coastal Commission,*[10] *Lucas v. South Carolina Coastal Council,*[11] and *Dolan v. City of Tigard.*[12] But this is a far cry from a takeover by the federal government of

[7]Samuel R. Staley and Gerald C.S. Mildner, "The Price of Managing Growth," *Urban Land* 59 (February 2000): 18-22, cites a source that reports 1,000 such bills were introduced in 1999 alone, with 20 percent of them passing. Others cite 240 similar measures introduced between 1996 and 1998 with 75 percent passing.

[8]Chang-Hee Christine Bae, "The Cross-Border Impacts of Growth Management Controls: Portland, Oregon, and Clark County, Washington," (paper presented at the Pacific Regional Science Conference, Portland, Oregon, July 2001).

[9]Robert Meltz, Dwight H. Merriam, and Richard M. Frank, *The Takings Issue: Constitutional Limits on Land-use Control and Environmental Regulation* (Washington, DC: Island Press, 1999).

[10]*Nollan v. California Coastal Commission*, 483 U.S. 825 (1987).

[11]*Lucas v. South Carolina Coastal Council*, 112 S. Ct. 2886 (1992).

[12]*Dolan v. The City of Tigard*, 114 S. Ct. 2309 (1994)

land-use controls. Some other countries with unitary rather than federal political systems (such as South Korea and the United Kingdom) have not hesitated to adopt national land-use policies with strong anti-sprawl elements, but it is difficult to conceive of this happening in the United States, given the principle of states' rights and the long tradition of local land-use and zoning powers.

The two migrations discussed in the next section reassert the important constitutional principle of the right to travel, while (less obviously) some of the discussions about spatial equity that frequently crop up in the sprawl discussions raise the similarly important constitutional issue of equal protection.

THE TWO MIGRATIONS

Increasing mobility reinforces the claim of urban economists that people choose their local government (and local school district)[13] at the same time as they choose their place of residence. However, the decision is more complex than simply shopping for local public goods. Because most Americans own their residence (66 percent of occupied housing units were owner occupied in 1997; the homeownership rate in 1999 was 67 percent; both proportions are historic highs),[14] and because their home is their largest tangible asset, it is understandable that choice of residence is often influenced by how property rights are secured. Such rights include the very important "collective neighborhood property rights" that assure that neighboring properties are well maintained.[15] Buyers understandably look for credible commitments by cities and/or developers. These motives underlie the demand for land-use controls and zoning rules.

There are two ways in which people get such rules, either in the market or from local government. Not surprisingly, private zoning predates public zoning in America. The landmark *Euclid* case,[16] which led to widespread zoning by cities, was decided in 1926, while private communities such as Gramercy Park in New York and Louisbourg Square in Boston have been private associations since 1831 and 1844 respectively. Evan McKenzie provides some of the relevant history:

> These and other subdivisions pioneered what was to become one of the most significant trends in American urban history; the use by developers of common ownership plans and deed restrictions as private land-planning devices. Similar methods were used by 19th century St. Louis subdividers who provided such services as street maintenance, snow removal, mowing,

[13]Caroline M. Hoxby, "Does Competition Among Public Schools Benefit Students and Taxpayers?" *The American Economic Review* 90:5 (December 2000): 1209-1238, reports that the more such choices parents have, the higher are student achievement scores and the lower is school spending.
[14]United States Census Bureau, *Statistical Abstract of the United States: 2000* 120th ed. (Washington, DC: U.S. Government Printing Office, 2000), Tables 1212 and 1213.
[15]Robert H. Nelson, "A Private Property Right Theory of Zoning," *The Urban Lawyer* 11 (1979): 713-732.
[16]*Village of Euclid v. Ambler Realty Co.*, 272 U.S. 365 (1926).

tree trimming, and street lighting to private neighborhoods through hundreds of private street associations. By 1928 scores of luxury subdivisions across the country were using deed restrictions–inclding racially sensitive covenants–as their legal architecture. To guarantee enforcement of these covenants, developers were organizing 'homeowner associations' so that residents could sue those who violated the rules.[17]

Racial restrictions were outlawed in 1948, but private zoning is now making a spectacular comeback with the rise of property owners' associations. Common Interest Developments (CIDs) are essentially run by private governments set in motion by the developer. They exist at the pleasure of local governments and supply and manage the public goods used by the residents. Each resident holds title to his or her own home plus a share in all of the common areas. The governing covenants are usually much more detailed than zoning codes, but the conditions of enforcement allow some flexibility (via specified rules and often requiring supermajorities) if circumstances require it.[18]

Several writers have linked these phenomena to the seminal work of Charles Tiebout[19] who suggested that choice among local governments amounted to a market for local public goods with different people able to express diverse preferences for such goods by "voting with their feet." Yet, the CID phenomenon is more than that. Because the benefits that people get from consuming public goods available within some community (more accurately, "territorial goods")[20] are capitalized in the value of residential land, the supply side can be described in terms of standard optimizing entrepreneurial market behavior; developers are intent on creating packages of residential amenities that maximize the value of their properties. This suggests that both territorial goods and the rules of governance are formed via a market test. No public official in a traditional municipality has similar incentives. Donald Boudreaux and Randall Holcombe[21] also point out that markets for constitutional rules are particularly important because moving is costly: "[c]onstitutions and intergovernmental competition are substitutes for each other."[22] Further, optimal constitutional arrangements are most likely to be executed before the residents move in, before bargaining between large numbers of homeowners becomes too complicated and too expensive.

[17]Evan McKenzie, *Privatopia: Homeowner Associations and the Rise of Residential Private Government* (New Haven: Yale University Press, 1994).

[18]Robert H. Nelson, "Privatizing the Neighborhood: A Proposal to Replace Zoning with Private Collective Property Rights to Existing Neighborhoods," *George Mason Law Review* 7 (Summer 1999): 1-54, enumerates the legal differences between condominium ownership and planned unit development (PUD), which make up about two-thirds of CIDs.

[19]Tiebout, "A Pure Theory of Public Expenditures," 416-424.

[20]Fred Foldvary, *Public Goods and Private Communities* (Aldershot, Hants, U.K. and Brookfield, VT: Edward Elgar Publishing Co, 1994).

[21]Donald J. Boudreaux and Randall G. Holcombe, "Contractual Governments in Theory and Practice," *The Voluntary City*, eds. D. Beito, et al. (Ann Arbor: University of Michigan Press, forthcoming).

[22]Ibid., 14.

These innovations in local governance are part of a long history of
institutions developed to make transactions cheaper and, thereby, facilitate
commerce and prosperity.[23] This is a more reasonable explanation than
the critics' view, exemplified by McKenzie's assertion that "growing numbers
of Americans who wish to purchase new houses are going to be living in
CIDs, and under the rule of private governments, regardless of their
preferences."[24] On the contrary, there are thousands of independent
homebuilders who succeed only if they meet consumers' demands. They
have little choice but to be responsive to people's preferences for local
public goods and to their demand for assurances of neighborhood quality
and good governance. This is the key to economic efficiency.

In *Zoning and Property Rights*, Robert Nelson argues that the current
interest in private zoning can also be explained by the inherent problems
of conventional politicized zoning. Zoning rights (to be more precise,
neighborhood collective-property rights) are routinely, if informally,
transacted. Developers usually gain development rights if they agree to
certain payments (usually for infrastructure improvements) and related
concessions. It is not surprising that many of them also make substantial
political contributions, treated as a cost of doing business. Nelson points
out that these transactions are to be expected but that they are inefficient.
Greater efficiency is available if communities could bargain directly with
developers without the involvement of a third-party zoning board. In fact,
he suggests that widespread NIMBY attitudes are the result of the property
owners' mistrust of the zoning board's ability to adequately represent owners'
interests (economists refer to this as an "agency" problem). If third-party
zoning boards cannot be trusted, then the best deal is no deal.

Similarly, Robert Ellickson[25] suggests changes in state laws that would
make it easier to form Block Improvement Districts, making the advantages
of private government available to many who are less mobile in older
neighborhoods.[26] He proposes this as a way to strengthen social cohesion
and civic society in the inner city.

Developers' commitments are often more credible than those of
politicians.[27] This is not surprising. The rise of environmentalism is one of
the major reasons for the current political recognition of many more
stakeholders' interests (usually at the expense of property owners' interests).

[23]Bruce L. Benson, "Economic Freedom and the Evolution of Law," *The Cato Journal* 18 (1998): 209-232.

[24]McKenzie, *Privatopia*, p. 12. Critics also confuse CIDs with gated communities. The overwhelming number of CID communities are not gated with estimates ranging from 10 - 20 percent. (Timothy Egan, "Many Seek Security in Private Communities," *New York Times*, 3 September 1995, pp. A1, A22.)

[25]Robert C. Ellickson, "New Institutions for Old Neighborhoods," *Duke Law Review* 48 (1998): 75-110.

[26]Similar proposals are suggested by Nelson. (Robert H. Nelson, "Privatizing the Neighborhood: A Proposal to Replace Zoning with Private Collective Property Rights to Existing Neighborhoods," *George Mason Law Review* 7 (1999): 1-54.)

[27]Jerell Richer, "Urban Congestion and Developer Precommitments: Unilateral Solutions to Dynamic Inconsistency," *Urban Studies* 32 (October 1995): 1279-1291; Boudreaux and Holcombe, "Contractual Governments in Theory and Practice," *The Voluntary City*, eds. D. Beito, et al.

This has resulted in the proliferation of the number of commissions with many types of discretionary powers over new development that must be satisfied in many established jurisdictions. In many U.S. cities, substantial proportions (often as much as one-half) of the value added of new development is from the efforts in getting all of the necessary approvals in place - before any ground is broken. Property owners increasingly surrender rights to a "common pool"; "[i]ll-defined rights replace well-defined ones."[28] While the courts debate the extent to which these events might constitute a "taking" of property in violation of the U.S. Constitution's Fifth Amendment, people and markets are providing clearer remedies.

None of this should be surprising. Even where private zoning is not available, private services appear where public provision is problematic. Jitneys (though often illegal) supplement public transit in most large U.S. cities; many families now avail themselves of private schools or home-schooling (which is facilitated by a growing number of websites designed to help them); and more is now spent on private security services than on federal, state, and local police.[29]

Current discussions of "urban sprawl" almost inevitably lead to recommendations of ways in which public zoning and regulation can be strengthened (often via proposals to make it a statewide or "regional" function)[30] at a time when people, voting with their feet and with their pocketbooks, are engaging in two types of exit, embracing the private alternatives and/or moving to communities in more peripheral places with fewer controls. The two major current migrations in the United States, into the suburbs (and beyond, into the exurbs) as well as into private communities, are the antithesis of (and undermine) the regulatory trends. In 1998, almost 42 million Americans lived in private communities. Between 1975 and 1998, the share of housing units in CIDs grew from 2.6 percent to 14.8 percent; in the same interval, the suburban share of the housing stock increased by from 36.4 percent to 46.1 percent (the suburban housing stock grew by 80.2 percent while population increased by 25.1 percent).[31] Both moves involve high stakes, including the search for more favorable property-rights arrangements.

[28]Richard A. Epstein, *Takings: Private Property and the Power of Eminent Domain* (Cambridge: Harvard University Press, 1985), p. 265.

[29]Bruce L. Benson, "Why Crime Declines," *Ideas on Liberty* 50 (January 2000): 22-25.

[30]For a brief history of the problems created by regional governments in the U.S., see, Fred Siegel, "Is Regional Government the Answer?" *The Public Interest* 137 (Fall 1999): 85-98.

[31]Clifford J. Treese, *Community Associations Factbook* (Alexandria, VA: Community Associations Institute, 1999). Consistent employment time series from the Bureau of Economic Analysis are available for counties. These show that most 1975-98 private sector job growth was in the fringe counties of the largest metro areas (1 million or more pop.), where job growth was 1.5 times the U.S. rate. Recently released census population data show that of the top ten 1990 central cities (New York, Los Angeles, Chicago, Houston, Philadelphia, San Diego, Detroit, Dallas, Phoenix, San Antonio), four grew faster in the 1990-2000 interval than the U.S. while six did not. Of the latter, two (Philadelphia and Detroit) continued to shrink. Only two of the top ten central cities (New York and San Antonio) grew faster than their metro areas. It is hard to see a "back to the city" movement. Gentrification exists but is a minor phenomenon.

Both migrations also have their critics. Yet, such criticism is reminiscent of a much older debate over what respect we accord the choices made by individuals over how they wish to live and work.[32] Do we progress via a "spontaneous order"[33] that is essentially "bottom-up," or is "top-down" better? About the time when the latter appeared permanently discredited, it was revived in the guise of growth controls, New Urbanism, and "smart growth" plans for "sustainable development."

THE SPRAWL DEBATE

If regulators are no match for the market, then continuing attempts to implement their agenda will be wasteful. Even as communications and transportation costs continue to fall, cities will thrive because there are always strong social and economic reasons for people to interact. Today, this interaction can take place as effectively in Silicon Valley as in traditional dense urban environments.[34] No planner can anticipate or fine-tune these changes in residential location, but markets sort them out efficiently. The new spatial arrangements then breed the innovations (both social and technological) that enable society to grow and prosper.

New Urbanism

This is the polar opposite of the anti-sprawl position. Smart-growth advocates see "a growing sense that the suburban paradigm, which has dominated since the 1940s and 1950s, cannot sustain another generation of growth."[35] Peter Calthorpe[36] is specific when he suggests a New Urbanism where "there should be defined edges (i.e., Urban Growth Boundaries), the circulation system should function for the pedestrian (i.e., supported by regional transit systems), public space should be formative rather than residual (i.e., preservation of major open-space networks), civic and private domains should form a complementary hierarchy (i.e., related cultural centers, commercial districts and residential neighborhoods) and population and use should be diverse (i.e., created by adequate affordable housing and a jobs/housing balance)." There is little analysis or discussion of the costs, the implied trade-offs, the consistency between the various proposals, or even the consumer's desire for such forms. There is no anxiety over the loss of property rights, nor over their politicization. The repetitive use of the word "should" means do what I tell you: I know better. Even the New Urbanist fall-back position that "building walkable neighborhoods may not get people out of their cars and building front porches may not create

[32]Joel Garreau, *Edge City: Life on the New Frontier* (New York: Anchor Books, 1991).

[33]Friedrich A. Hayek, *The Fatal Conceit: The Errors of Socialism* (Chicago: The University of Chicago Press, 1978).

[34]Silicon Valley office rents were recently reported to be $70 per square foot while Manhattan's were slightly less than $58. San Francisco's $76 rates are attributed by many to the Silicon Valley boom.

[35]Peter Katz, *The New Urbanism: Toward an Architecture of Community* (New York: McGraw-Hill, 1994), p. ix.

[36]Ibid., xiii.

an integrated convivial communities, [but] people should be given a choice,"[37] is not plausible; there is no acknowledgment of the fact that markets regularly generate the more feasible choices while discarding the infeasible ones, based on how opportunity costs compare to consumers' willingness to pay.

Among the key principles of public policy espoused by the New Urbanists are the following: promoting neighborhoods that are diverse in terms of use (e.g., mixed use developments) and populations (mixed in terms of age, race, and income); designing communities with transportation alternatives (especially walking, cycling, and public transit) to reduce automobile dependence, implying a strong emphasis on compactness; preferring infill development rather than peripheral expansion; giving some priority to accessible public spaces, community institutions, and a variety of parks and other open spaces to foster communitarian behavior; providing affordable housing distributed throughout the metropolitan region as part of a jobs-housing balance strategy; stressing the importance of farmland preservation and environmental conservation, combined with architectural and landscape design principles that pay attention to local history and cultural heritage, climate, and ecology; and recognizing the metropolitan region as the functional economic region coupled with revenue sharing among its municipalities to finance the alleviation of region-wide problems.

Market Realities

What is wrong with this approach? Most important, it embraces unrealistic social engineering based on a false diagnosis of society's urban problems, an excessive faith in the ability to change the world, and the prescription of policies that are implementable only under very special circumstances. We will illustrate this claim with some examples.

Durability of Capital

Even if the New Urbanists could capture both political and popular support for their physical planning prescriptions, the results would do little to change the metropolitan landscape.[38] The reason is that the urban capital stock is already largely in place and changes very slowly. As for the residential capital stock, much of it has been built in the last 40 years, and the time of its physical obsolescence is far off. Hence, the practical consequences of New Urbanism continue to be a small number of relatively small communities accommodating a minuscule proportion of metropolitan population growth. Demonstration projects, the object of international study tours; a pleasant living environment for a few thousand households; and well-paid lecture tours for a small number of somewhat immodest architects, the New Urbanist communities amount to little more.

[37]Peter Calthorpe, *The Next American Metropolis* (New York: Princeton Architectural Press, 1993).
[38]Anthony Downs, *A New Vision for Metropolitan America* (Washington, DC: Brookings Institution, 1994).

Residential Preferences

Fannie Mae has been conducting surveys about housing preferences for years. The findings have changed little. Regardless of income, race, or current tenure status, 75-80 percent of households would prefer to live in a single-family home with a private yard. Whereas it may be possible via creative architectural and landscape design to produce high-density single-family home developments in the suburbs that are compatible with these preferences, it is probably impossible at the close-in infill sites promoted by the New Urbanists. Developers are not stupid, large ones have extensive marketing expertise, and in general they produce the housing that buyers want so as to guarantee their profitability. If New Urbanist-type developments were demanded by consumers, they would be built. Obviously, we have no objection in principle to the idea that producers should offer consumers what they want, and we favor experiments by builders that provide a market test to see whether households are open to a change in residential lifestyles. An interesting question, especially with regard to infill projects, is whether these alternatives are acceptable to the community at large, as opposed to the prospective purchasers. There are many examples of broader community objections to high-density projects, usually on traffic-generation grounds.

Farmland Preservation

A favorite argument of the New Urbanists and other anti-sprawl protagonists is that low-density suburban residential development is eating up prime agricultural land. Agricultural productivity has risen sharply because of a shift to profitable land-intensive crops. Urban development still absorbs less than 5 percent of the continental landmass. The argument that this is adversely affecting the world food supply is nonsense. Starvation is a problem of distribution and inefficient food policies, not of aggregate supply.[39] Finally, the environmental argument for preserving agricultural land is undercut by the fact that agriculture is, by far, the country's largest polluting sector, generating $173 billion of pollution damages in water pollution alone.

Mixed Land Uses

New Urbanist communities are intended to be more than residential subdivisions. The plans are to have shops, a wide array of personal and consumer services, and workplace sites. Only by developing a broad mix of land uses can the goals of walking to work and to shop be met. This is one of the plans for Kentlands, Maryland, perhaps the most successful of the New Urbanist communities; yet commercial development there lags far behind. Apart from the pedestrian-opportunities objective, however, there

[39] Joyce Burnette and Joel Mokyr, "The Standard of Living through the Ages," *The State of Humanity*, ed. Julian L. Simon (Oxford: Blackwell, 1995).

is no particular reason why these communities need to create an employment base. The idea of "selfcontainment" was one of the principles behind the creation of the British New Towns. Certainly, with the freestanding New Towns on green-field sites (less clearly with the modified Expanding Town concept), it never worked well.[40] Employment centers emerged, but they did not cater to the local population. For skill mismatch and other reasons, the overwhelming tendency was for New Town residents to work elsewhere while the jobs in the New Towns were filled by commuters from outside. As a result, the strategy probably resulted in more commuting rather than less. This would be more true today than it was then because of ubiquitous accessibility by automobile. There is a stronger argument for having retail and other consumer services provided locally, but even in this case, facilities have developed slowly as shoppers are attracted to major malls and other large-scale clusters.

Social Equity Issues

New Urbanist rhetoric gives substantial attention to promoting equity, fostering residential mixing, providing affordable housing, and reducing income differentials between central cities and suburbs via middle-class infill development. Yet there is little evidence that New Urbanist communities have achieved these goals. Instead, they are turning out to be rather elitist settlements with average income levels much higher than in the surrounding areas. The Laguna West area, for example, has a household income two-thirds higher than Sacramento County, where it is located. At Seaside, Florida, the 1996 average sales price reached $503,500.[41] New Urbanist communities command a price premium of up to 25 percent.[42] Offering variety in the housing stock does result in some income mixing, but there are few signs of racial mixing, and supplying a range of housing products is typical of many standard residential subdivisions and is not restricted to New Urbanist communities.

As for the idea that New Urbanism can contribute to the stability, if not revival, of the central city, it remains just that- an idea. There is very little to show for it in practice. Despite the call for an integrated metropolitan unity, most New Urbanist communities are being built on green-field sites some distance away from the central city. Infill development has been limited –probably of necessity because of land scarcity–to tiny pockets. Hence, there is no identifiable relationship between New Urbanist communities and the fate of central cities and those who live there. If there is some consensus for tackling the social problems found in the central cities (and it is by no

[40]Peter Hall, *Cities of Tomorrow* (Oxford: Blackwell, 1988); Colin Ward, *New Town, Home Town, the Lessons of Experience* (London: Calouste Gulbenkian Foundation, 1993).

[41]Alexander Garvin, "Is the New Urbanism Passe?" *Lusk Review* 4 (1998): 12-32.

[42]Mark J. Eppli and Charles C. Tu, *Valuing The New Urbanism: The Impact of the New Urbanism On Prices of Single-Family Homes* (Washington, DC: The Urban Land Institute, 1999).

means clear that this consensus exists), it would be far better to deal with these problems by direct, tightly targeted measures rather than by land-use controls and social experiments on the metropolitan fringe. As David Harvey states: New Urbanism "builds an image of community and a rhetoric of place-based civic pride and consciousness for those who do not need it, while abandoning those that do to their 'underclass' fate."[43]

Communitarianism

Although the New Urbanists are regarded by some as very conservative, reactionary, and even stodgy, from an architectural point of view, they adhere to a very old architectural tradition, that design affects social behavior, and they radicalize it to the extent that they argue that incorporating specific design elements not only in buildings but also in street layouts and neighborhood patterns can generate a communitarian spirit and dramatically increase social interaction. Although there are precedents for this view (in the writings of Jane Jacobs,[44] for example), and most people would accept that our behavior is sensitive to, and affected by, the surrounding physical environment, the New Urbanists take the argument to extremes. A major problem with their argument is that, on the ground rather than in their proposals, New Urbanist communities look little different than standard suburban areas. Even if one accepts the communitarian argument, it is difficult to believe that such subtle changes in the built environment could have more than minuscule social interaction effects. A more fundamental problem is that many New Urbanist projects are so influenced by the nostalgic longing for the archetypical small town of the past that they fall into the trap of believing that recreating its physical structure (at least to some degree) can simultaneously recreate its social and civic behavior. But society, culture, and behavior have changed so much that this is a false dream. Harvey makes the point very well: "The New Urbanism assembles much of its rhetorical and political power through a nostalgic appeal to 'community' as a panacea for our social and economic as well as urban ills. . . . (H)arking back to a mythological past carries its own dangerous freight."[45]

Andres Duany himself argues that New Urbanist communities make American society and human behavior better in three ways: (1) making life richer for children; (2) allowing one to age in place (not so much by creating nearby housing opportunities for empty nesters but by making pedestrian mobility possible); and (3) eliminating the need for more than one car.[46] But the first two goals are attainable in a wide variety of urban and suburban residential environments, while the third has not been achieved because

---

[43]David Harvey, "The New Urbanism and the Communitarian Trap," *Harvard Design Magazine* 6 (Winter/Spring 1997).

[44]Jane Jacobs, *The Death and Life of Great American Cities* (New York: Prentice-Hall, 1961).

[45]Harvey, "The New Urbanism and the Communitarian Trap," 68-69.

[46]Harvey, "New Urbanism: Urban or Suburban?" 47-63.

New Urbanist community residents have similar automobiles-per-household ratios to households elsewhere. The explanation of this last point is obvious; the accessibility and mobility needs of individuals cannot be satisfied by constraining them to inside the community, at least within walking distance.

Tripmaking

A major claim of the New Urbanists is that their proposals will lead to major changes in travel behavior: reduced automobile dependence, more transit use, increased bicycling, and a pedestrian-friendly development. Unfortunately, there is little justification for these claims. A high proportion of trips is external to the community (for instance, almost all jobs are outside), and cars remain necessary for mobility. No significant transit services have been developed to link New Urbanist communities to nearby centers; for example, the plans for a transit system to link Laguna West with Sacramento (about 10 miles away) never materialized. The majority opinion is that the New Urbanist communities will never be dense enough or large enough to justify significant (i.e., frequent) transit service.[47] Duany admits that market preferences, heterogeneous housing demands, and the open-space provisions that drastically reduce gross densities compared with net residential densities result in relatively low densities compared with transit-oriented neighborhoods. Careful analysis of the tripmaking impacts[48] suggests that it is unclear whether higher density communities will result in more auto trips or less. The limited scope of retail and other consumer services in New Urbanist communities (typically, one shopping center) means that even within these communities, most services are beyond the average American's tolerance for service-oriented walking (i.e., between one-quarter and one-half mile). The New Urbanist communities often lend themselves to comfortable cycling, but bicycles remain a niche travel mode, at least for Americans.

NEGLECTED FACTS

Analysts arguing for stronger land-use controls continue to promote their agenda regardless of the weight of evidence that conflicts with their views. The arguments for stronger land-use controls remain weak, for the following reasons:[49]

1. *The air is getting cleaner in spite of more people, more automobiles, and more vehicle miles driven.* In the years 1979-1996, U.S. population grew by 29 percent, vehicles by 98 percent, and vehicle miles traveled (VMT) by 125 percent; yet, in the same interval, all four on-road vehicle emissions (VOC, NOx, PM_{10} and CO) declined.[50]

[47]Downs, *A New Vision for Metropolitan America*.

[48]Randall Crane, "Cars and Drivers in the New Suburbs: Linking Access to Travel in Neo-traditional Planning," *Journal of the American Planning Association* 62 (Winter 1996): 51-65.

[49]Peter Gordon and Harry W. Richardson, "Prove It," *The Brookings Review* 16 (Fall 1998): 23-25.

[50]*http://www.fhwa.dot.gov/environment/AIR_ABS.HTM*, 1997; Table on page 8.

2. *Reductions in most air pollutants began well before the onset of federal environmental regulation.* In developed countries, market pressures account for responsiveness to the demand for a cleaner environment and have caused technological improvements to be implemented as long as common-law protections and incentives were not preempted.[51]

3. *Much more food is being grown on much less land.* Cropland use in the United States peaked in 1930.[52] Reforestation in America is the result of greater agricultural efficiencies leading farmers to farm only their best land.[53] The amount of farmland would be even less in the absence of federal programs that pay handsomely for "farmlands" not farmed.

4. *Suburb-to-suburb commuting and low-density settlement ease traffic congestion.* Average commuting speeds increased between 1983 and 1990 and again between 1990 and 1995.[54] Although trip distances have increased, trip times have increased only modestly. There is inevitable congestion because access is almost everywhere free (a problem) and continues to be widely seen as an entitlement (the source of the problem). Given all of this, it is surprising how little congestion there is. Flexible land markets (e.g., the "suburbanization of commuting") provide the traffic safety valve; "impending gridlock" remains forever impending. The casual observation that the worst traffic conditions occur in the densest cities is backed by careful research. Donald Pickrell and Paul Schmieck[55] demonstrate that, after controlling for income and other household characteristics, the elasticity of household VMT with respect to residential density is approximately -0.1. A doubling of densities would decrease VMT per household by 10 percent, but with twice as many households, there would be many more trips.

The Nationwide Personal Transportation Survey journey-to-work trip times correlate positively (significantly) with urbanized

---

[51]Roger Meiners and Bruce Yandle, "Common Law and the Conceit of Modern Environmental Policy," *George Mason Law Review* 7 (1999): 923-963. Indur M. Goklany, "Empirical Evidence Regarding the Role of Nationalization in Improving U.S. Air Quality," *The Common Law and the Environment: Rethinking the Statutory Basis for Modern Environmental Law*, eds. Roger E. Meiners and Andrew P. Morriss (New York: Rowman & Littlefield Publishers, 2000).

[52]The U.S. Department of Agriculture recently revised its 1997 National Resources Inventory (*www.nhq.nrcs.usda.gov/NRI/*), admitting that its widely cited earlier warnings about the loss of farmland was due to a "statistical software" error.

[53]Thomas H. Frey, "Trends in Land Use in the United States," *The State of Humanity*, ed. Julian L. Simon (Oxford: Blackwell, 1995).

[54]Patricia S. Hu and Jennifer R. Young, *Summary of Travel Trends: 1995 Nationwide Personal Transportation Survey* (Washington, DC: U.S. Department of Transportation, Federal Highway Administration, 1999), p. 44.

[55]Donald Pickrell and Paul Schmiek, "Trends in Motor Vehicle Ownership and use: Evidence from the Nationwide Personal Transportation Survey," *Journal of Transportation and Statistics* 2 (1999): 1-17.

area population densities. Other cross-sectional studies corroborate the intuition that high development densities are associated with high congestion.[56] Kenneth Orski reports that "(t)he Ballston rail transit station in Northern Virginia, often cited as a national model of a compact transit-oriented 'village' that is supposed to encourage walking and reduce car use, is a case in point. With density five times higher than their neighboring spread-out Fairfax City/Oakton area, Ballston creates more than four times as many daily vehicle trips than its low-density neighbor."[57]

Even where everything is within walking distance and everyone rides bicycles, people continue to drive their automobiles, and often. Household trip frequencies are often the wild card. It is by no means clear that these remain unchanged when access is improved. It is more likely that Americans will buy more as the price drops.[58] The federal Clean Air Act mandates higher densities, and federal, state, and local planning agencies promote compact land-use arrangements in the belief that these will contribute to less auto use and cleaner air. Yet the theory behind this multi-billion dollar effort remains weak.

5. *Inner city poverty is not a consequence of low-density suburbs.*[59] Poverty is a human capital problem exacerbated by poor inner city schools. Moreover, equity loses out when controls limit housing availability and push up prices. It is no accident that the planners' showcase—Portland, Oregon—is now among the least affordable of U.S. cities in housing, with the fastest-growing house prices in the 1990s.[60] A related issue is how the costs and benefits of alternative settlement patterns are distributed. The brute fact is that there are, in most cases, gainers and losers from any market or institutional change. The point is that market forces minimize costs to losers. Yes, CIDs may be more expensive, and the poor may not have access, but the suburban exit has created significant housing opportunities for central-city households.

6. *There are no clear infrastructure savings from high residential densities.* The few available studies reveal a "U-shaped" cost function that bottoms at relatively low residential densities, below 1,250 people

[56]David T. Hartgen and Daniel O. Curley, "Beltways: Boon, Bane or Blip?" *Factors Influencing Changes in Urbanized Area Traffic, 1990-1997* (Charlotte, NC: University of North Carolina Center for Interdisciplinary Transportation Studies: WP 190, 1999).

[57]C. Kenneth Orski, "In Search of Livability," *Innovation Briefs* 10 (Sep/Oct 1999): 1.

[58]Crane, "Cars and Drivers in the New Suburbs: Linking Access to Travel in Neotraditional Planning," pp. 51-65.

[59]Anthony Downs, "Some Realities about Sprawl and Urban Decline," *Housing Policy Debate* 10 (1999): 955-974.

[60]Staley and Mildner, "The Price of Managing Growth," 18-22

per square mile.[61]   Scale economies in areas such as power
generation are probably a thing of the past. In any event, cost
minimization is not the full story. People compare and trade off
marginal costs with marginal benefits whenever they can.

7. *The social interactions of suburbanites are no different from central-city
   residents.*[62] A standard argument is that more compact living
   encourages civil society. Yet, few people agree on what
   "community" means. We do know, however, that the residents of
   U.S. central cities and suburbs take precisely the same proportion
   of trips for "social" reasons. Robert Nelson found substantial
   community involvement in private neighborhoods, and argued
   that this is a much more plausible outcome than promoting
   community via top-down planning. [63]

8. *Providing expensive rail-transit systems does nothing for traffic
   congestion.* After more than $360 billion of public subsidies, most
   of it to rail transit, over the last 35 years, per capita transit use in
   the United States is at a historic low.[64] Yet, new rail-transit systems
   are routinely proposed and built. This waste is explained by
   political pork-barrel. The overwhelming majority of Americans
   prefer personal transportation, a fact that planners and
   politicians continue to ignore.

9. *The downtown revival stories may be much exaggerated.* There have
   been many media reports about the revival of the central city in
   general and downtown in particular. Also, the 2000 census results
   have revealed remarkable resilience in several central cities. So,
   are the central cities coming back? Our belief is that in the
   large-city cases, the explanation was the tight labor market of
   the late 1990s. Some of the small cities have done well by
   promoting their downtowns as tourist centers.[65] In the long run,
   the central cities require all the stars to come into constellation.
   The large majority of non-traditional households have to swear
   off children forever (no rational analysis can expect the vast
   majority of central-city schools to improve soon); central cities
   have to create their mini-Manhattans of good restaurants and
   recreational and cultural amenities; they have to address the
   other central-city social problems, apart from education; and

[61]Helen Ladd, "Population Growth, Density, and the Costs of Providing Public Services,"
Urban Studies 29 (April 1992): 273-295.

[62]Peter Gordon and Harry W. Richardson, "Critiquing Sprawl's Critics," *CATO Policy Analysis* 365 (2000).

[63]Robert H. Nelson, *The Privatization of Local Government: From Zoning to RCAs in Residential Community
Associations: Private Governments in the Intergovernmental System?* (Washington DC: U.S. Advisory Commission
on Intergovernmental Relations, 1989).

[64]*www.publicpurpose.com*

[65]Peter Gordon and Harry W. Richardson, "The Destiny of Downtowns: Doom or Dazzle?" *Lusk Review*
3 (1997): 63-76

significant job growth has to occur in downtowns (a little easier
in the information technology age than in the industrial age).
There are serious doubts that this constellation can come into line.

The arguments for more land-use controls are, of course, much more extensive (some are even silly, such as the assertion that Atlantans are the most obese because of that city's suburban sprawl, a hypothesis that has inspired research projects at the Centers for Disease Control).[66] The current favorite is "global warming" with proposals that seek to implement drastic lifestyle changes to counter it ("get people out of their cars"). Yet the evidence for climate change remains very controversial,[67] and the cost-benefit ratios of the policy proposals from the Kyoto Conference have been seriously questioned. Another issue is the relative importance of increasing land-use consumption per household relative to population growth as the major contributors to sprawl. This is a recurrent internal debate among anti-sprawl analysts that is, for example, tearing the Sierra Club apart. Some argue that land use is four times as important as population growth.[68] Others argue that population growth accounts for more than one-half of the problem.[69] Still others find significant variations among individual metropolitan areas.[70] Some of the confusion relates to a temporary glitch in the 1997 land-use database from the U.S. Department of Agriculture's Natural Resources Inventory. Because this is an internal discussion among those who take a different position on land-use controls, we remain neutral, except when they take the leap from population growth is the problem to immigration is the problem. In our view, the cliché that the United States is a "nation of immigrants" does not do full justice to the net benefits conferred on society as a whole and to individuals from recent immigration.

CONCLUSION

The agenda of the regulators cannot be justified on either equity or efficiency grounds. It is not clear what social benefits can reasonably be expected from their programs. Events in Eastern Europe and other places at the end of the twentieth century showed that markets will eventually prevail because the alternatives are not tenable. There is no reason to believe that land

[66]June Manning Thomas, "The Forces of Urban Heterogeneity Can Triumph," *American Quarterly* 46 (March 1994): 49-54, sees "racial and income segregation, oppression of women and ecological rape" as a consequence of suburbanization. James Kunstler mentions sprawl as an explanation of the Littleton, Colorado, shootings (quoted in Neal R. Peirce, "Littleton's Legacy: Our Suburban Dream Shattered," *The Washington Post*, 6 June 1999); Ann Carns and James R. Hagerty, "On a Rainy Night In Georgia, What Can You Do But Eat? – There Are More Obese People All Over, but Peach State Really Takes the Cake," *The Wall Street Journal*, 29 October 1999, p. A1.

[67]*www.co2science.org*

[68]David Rusk, *Inside Game, Outside Game: Winning Strategies for Saving Urban America* (Washington, DC: Brookings Institution Press, 1999).

[69]Roy Beck and Leon Kolankiewicz, *Weighing Sprawl Factors in Large U.S. Cities* (Arlington, VA: NumbersUSA, 2001).

[70]Rolf Pendall, William Fulton, and Alicia Harrison, "Losing Ground to Sprawl? Density Trends in Metropolitan America," (Paper presented at the Fannie Mae sessions at the Association of Collegiate Schools of Planning Conference, Atlanta, October 2000).

markets are exempt from this generalization. Innovations and improvements in most of humanity's material conditions, including their housing and living arrangements, spring from the profit-seeking impulses of entrepreneurs when allowed to operate in an environment of economic freedom. This is why minimalist local planning is preferred.

What then is the local government equivalent of Robert Nozick's Nightwatchman State? It is clear that planners should do few things and do them well. Several writers[71] have proposed that land markets (developed and undeveloped land) be freed while city planners focus on improving infrastructure planning. In this way, they would set and publicize the preconditions (the "rules of the game") for land markets. Planners would need to concern themselves only with trunkline infrastructure planning because anything below that level could be privately supplied by developers. Developers have already demonstrated their ability to create large-scale "planned communities" (that made up almost two-thirds of the CID housing stock in 1998).

It is a truism that everyone plans and that planning is essential. The important question is: what is the optimal division of labor between private and public planners? Our proposal (i.e., focus on infrastructure, set the rules of the game, and liberalize land markets) suggests one answer. The optimal division of responsibilities deserves further thought. The problem is that the city planning profession is unprepared. The public and planners are pulling in opposite directions. It is ironic that many writers suggest Canadian and Western European cities as models for U.S. planners. Short visits to tourist-oriented town centers are misleading. European and Canadian cities are also spreading out via the suburbanization of people and jobs. Automobile use is increasing, and transit use is declining.[72] This occurs in spite of much tougher policies than in the United States designed to promote the opposite trends. Rather than pursuing the hopeless goal of getting people to give up strongly preferred freedoms and lifestyles, U.S. planners may want to ponder how they can increase their effectiveness by doing less.

Finally, how does all this affect federalism and related issues? First, the federal government is a bystander in all this unless it can create a wedge issue (e.g., air quality, water quality, endangered species, or central-city disinvestment) to justify intervention on other grounds. Second, with respect to intergovernmental relations, the arena is a debate between states and

---

[71]Robert H. Nelson, *Zoning and Property Rights: An Analysis of the American System of Land-Use Regulation* (Cambridge: The MIT Press, 1980); Randall G. Holcombe, "Growth Management in Action: The Case of Florida," *Market Strategies for Land Use Planning for the 21st Century*, eds. Randall Holcombe and Sam Staley (Westport, CT: Greenwood Press, 2001).

[72]Christian Gerondeau, *Transport in Europe* (Norwood, MA: Artech House, 1997).

local jurisdictions, with the federal government almost irrelevant. Third, in our view, the constitutional issues that emphasize individual rights are the most critical. The sprawl debate, at its most fundamental level, hinges on whether one believes that people have the right to choose where they want to live, what they want to drive, where they want to shop, and soon—if they are willing to pay the full costs involved.

THE CHARTER OF THE NEW URBANISM

New Urbanism is a relatively recent entry into the long-standing debate about sprawl. Beginning in 1993, this movement has grown to include urban designers, architects, planners, environmentalists, economists, landscape designers, traffic engineers, elected officials, sociologists, developers, and community activists, to start an incomplete list. It represents the interests of a broad coalition of environmentalists concerned with farmland preservation, habitat enhancement, and air quality as well as inner-city advocates concerned with urban reconstruction and social equity. It weds these groups and interests with a design ethic that spans from region to building.

Put simply, the New Urbanism sees physical design—regional design, urban design, architecture, landscape design, and environmental design—as critical to the future of our communities. While recognizing that economic, social, and political issues are critical, the movement advocates attention to design. The belief is that design can play a critical role in resolving problems that governmental programs and money alone cannot.

The "new" in New Urbanism has several aspects. It is the attempt to apply the age-old principles of urbanism—diversity, street life, and human scale—to the suburb in the twenty-first century. It is also an attempt to resolve the apparent conflict between the fine grain of traditional urban environments and the large-scale realities of contemporary institutions and technologies. It is an attempt to update traditional urbanism to fit our modern lifestyles and increasingly complex economies.

The Charter of the New Urbanism specifically structures its principles at three telescoping scales: the region, the neighborhood, and the building. But perhaps most important is its assertion that the three scales are interconnected and interdependent. The Charter is simply twenty-seven principles organized by these three scales. The three elements of this book—the emerging region, the maturing suburb, and the revitalized urban neighborhood—each benefit from the principles articulated in the Charter.

The regional section of the Charter posits principles similar to those described in this book as the foundation of the Regional City. Its neighborhood-scale principles go to an urban-design philosophy that reasserts mixed-use, walkable environments. Its principles of design at the scale of the street and building seek to recreate places in which continuity and public space are reestablished for the pedestrian.

Urbanism advances the fundamental policies and goals of regionalism: that the region should be bounded, that growth should occur in more compact forms, that existing towns and cities should be revitalized, that affordable housing should be fairly distributed throughout the region, that transit should be more widespread, and that local taxes should be equitably shared. Each of these strategies is elaborated in this book as fundamental to the Regional City. Each of these strategies has become central to the larger agenda of New Urbanism.

This larger agenda gives clarity to the precarious balance at the regional scale between inner-city investments, suburban redevelopment, and the appropriate siting of greenfield development. This balance is one of the least understood aspects of New Urbanism and one of its most important. It addresses the question of where development is appropriate at the regional scale.

New Urbanism is best known (and often stereotyped) for its work at the neighborhood and town scale. At this scale the Charter's principles describe a new way of thinking about and structuring our cities and towns. Rather than the simplistic single-use zoning of most contemporary city plans, the Charter proposes a structure of three fundamental elements—neighborhoods, districts, and corridors. The Charter does not sidestep the scale of modern business and retailing. It simply calls for their placement within special districts when they are not appropriate to the scale and character of a neighborhood. In this taxonomy, the special-use district and the corridor (natural, auto, or transit) provide complements to and connections for the basic urban tissue—complete and walkable neighborhoods.

It is at the scale of the city block, its streets, and individual buildings that the test of integrating the auto and the need for more pedestrian-friendly environments is resolved. The Charter does not call for the simplistic elimination of the car, but instead challenges us to create environments that can simultaneously support walking, biking, transit, and the car. It outlines urban design strategies that reinforce human scale at the same time that they incorporate contemporary realities. Jobs no longer need to be isolated in office parks, but their integration into mixed-use neighborhoods calls for sensitive urban design. Differing types of housing no longer need buffers to separate and isolate them, but they do need an architecture that articulates a fundamental continuity within the neighborhood. Retail and civic uses do not need special zones, but they do need block, street, and building patterns that connect them to their community.

The Charter calls for an architecture that respects human scale, respects regional history and ecology, and respects the need for modesty and continuity within a physical community. Traditional architecture has much to teach us about these imperatives without prescribing nostalgic forms. And these imperatives can lead to the use of historical precedents, especially in infilling and redeveloping areas that have a strong and preestablished character. On the other hand, climate-responsive design that honors the history and culture of a place, when combined with new technologies, can lead to innovative rather than imitative design. The "seamless" integration of new and old, and a respect for existing urban patterns and scale are the imperatives of the Charter.

Too often, New Urbanism is misinterpreted simply as a conservative movement to recapture the past while ignoring the issues of our time. It is not understood as a complex system of policies and design principles that operate at multiple scales. To some, New Urbanism simply means tree-lined streets, porch-front houses, and Main Street retail—the reworking of a Norman Rockwell fantasy of small-town America, primarily for the rich.

But nostalgia is not what New Urbanism is actually proposing. Its goals and breadth are much grander, more complete and challenging. Many of the misconceptions are caused by focusing only on the neighborhood-scale prescriptions of the Charter without seeing how they are embedded in regional structures or understanding that those neighborhoods are supported by design principles at the street and building scale that attend more to environmental imperatives and urban continuities than to historical precedent.

The Charter shares its central thesis with that of this book—sprawl and social inequity must be addressed comprehensively. A fundamental tenet of the Charter speaks to the critical issue of affordability and social integration through the principles of economic diversity and inclusive neighborhoods. Economic diversity calls for a broad range of housing opportunities as well as uses within each neighborhood—affordable and expensive, small and large, rental and ownership, single and family housing. This is a very radical proposition. It implies more low-income and affordable housing in the rich suburbs at the same time that it advocates more middle-class opportunities in urban neighborhoods. It advocates mixing income groups and ethnic groups in a way that is very frightening to many communities. It is a principle that is rarely realized in practice and, given the current political climate, is almost always compromised. But it is a central tenet of the Charter and *The Regional City*—and it sets a direction quite different from most new development in the suburbs and many urban renewal programs.

New Urbanism outlines a set of design and policy principles that provide the means to reintegrate the segregated geography of our cities and suburbs. In so doing, it raises a complex set of issues. When does "economic diversity" in a distressed inner-city neighborhood become gentrification? What is the appropriate mix of inclusionary housing in a suburban town? These are tough questions that only have local answers. Gentrification may be mitigated by more affordable housing at the regional level, but what of the coherence and identity of the old neighborhood and its unique culture? There are no simple solutions. Perhaps the appropriate amount of economic diversity for a low-income neighborhood is reached when success doesn't mean moving out. Perhaps the definition for a rich neighborhood is when the schoolteacher and the fireman no longer have to drive in.

The Charter sees the physical design of a region—like the physical design of a neighborhood—as either fostering opportunities, sustainability, and diversity or inhibiting them. Such design cannot mandate a civil and vibrant culture, but it is a necessary framework. Much like healthy soil, the coherent design of a region and its neighborhoods can nurture a more equitable and robust society—or it can stunt them. This is not environmental determinism. It is simply an attempt to find a better fit between our current realities and their physical armature.

THE CHARTER

The Congress for the New Urbanism views disinvestment in central cities, the spread of placeless sprawl, increasing separation by race and income, environmental deterioration, loss of agricultural lands and wilderness, and the erosion of society's built heritage as one interrelated community building challenge.

We stand for the restoration of existing urban centers and towns within coherent metropolitan regions, the reconfiguration of sprawling suburbs into communities of real neighborhoods and diverse districts, the conservation of natural environments, and the preservation of our built legacy.

We recognize that physical solutions by themselves will not solve social and economic problems, but neither can economic vitality, community stability, and environmental health be sustained without a coherent and supportive physical framework.

We advocate the restructuring of public policy and development practices to support the following principles: neighborhoods should be diverse in use and population; communities should be designed for the pedestrian and transit as well as the car; cities and towns should be shaped by physically defined and universally accessible public spaces and community institutions; urban places should be framed by architecture and landscape design that celebrate local history, climate, ecology, and building practice.

We represent a broad-based citizenry, composed of public and private sector leaders, community activists, and multidisciplinary professionals. We are committed to reestablishing the relationship between the art of building and the making of community, through citizen-based participatory planning and design.

We dedicate ourselves to reclaiming our homes, blocks, streets, parks, neighborhoods, districts, towns, cities, regions, and environment.

We assert the following principles to guide public policy, development practice, urban planning, and design:

The Region: Metropolis, City, and Town

1. Metropolitan regions are finite places with geographic boundaries derived from topography, watersheds, coastlines, farmlands, regional parks, and river basins. The metropolis is made of multiple centers that are cities, towns, and villages,

each with its own identifiable center and edges.

2. The metropolitan region is a fundamental economic unit of the contemporary world. Governmental cooperation, public policy, physical planning, and economic strategies must reflect this new reality.

3. The metropolis has a necessary and fragile relationship to its agrarian hinterland and natural landscapes. The relationship is environmental, economic, and cultural. Farmland and nature are as important to the metropolis as the garden is to the house.

4. Development patterns should not blur or eradicate the edges of the metropolis. Infill development within existing urban areas conserves environmental resources, economic investment, and social fabric, while reclaiming marginal and abandoned areas. Metropolitan regions should develop strategies to encourage such infill development over peripheral expansion.

5. Where appropriate, new development contiguous to urban boundaries should be organized as neighborhoods and districts, and be integrated with the existing urban pattern. Noncontiguous development should be organized as towns and villages with their own urban edges, and planned for a jobs/housing balance, not as bedroom suburbs.

6. The development and redevelopment of towns and cities should respect historical patterns, precedents, and boundaries.

7. Cities and towns should bring into proximity a broad spectrum of public and private uses to support a regional economy that benefits people of all incomes. Affordable housing should be distributed throughout the region to match job opportunities and to avoid concentrations of poverty.

8. The physical organization of the region should be supported by a framework of transportation alternatives. Transit, pedestrian, and bicycle systems should maximize access and mobility throughout the region while reducing dependence upon the automobile.

9. Revenues and resources can be shared more cooperatively among the municipalities and centers within regions to avoid destructive competition for tax base and to promote rational coordination of transportation, recreation, public services,

housing, and community institutions.

The Neighborhood, the District, and the Corridor

1. The neighborhood, the district, and the corridor are the essential elements of development and redevelopment in the metropolis. They form identifiable areas that encourage citizens to take responsibility for their maintenance and evolution.

2. Neighborhoods should be compact, pedestrian friendly, and mixed use. Districts generally emphasize a special single use, and should follow the principles of neighborhood design when possible. Corridors are regional connectors of neighborhoods and districts; they range from boulevards and rail lines to rivers and parkways.

3. Many activities of daily living should occur within walking distance, allowing independence to those who do not drive, especially the elderly and the young. Interconnected networks of streets should be designed to encourage walking, reduce the number and length of automobile trips, and conserve energy.

4. Within neighborhoods, a broad range of housing types and price levels can bring people of diverse ages, races, and incomes into daily interaction, strengthening the personal and civic bonds essential to an authentic community.

5. Transit corridors, when properly planned and coordinated, can help organize metropolitan structure and revitalize urban centers. In contrast, highway corridors should not displace investment from existing centers.

6. Appropriate building densities and land uses should be within walking distance of transit stops, permitting public transit to become a viable alternative to the automobile.

7. Concentrations of civic, institutional, and commercial activity should be embedded in neighborhoods and districts, not isolated in remote, single-use complexes. Schools should be sized and located to enable children to walk or bicycle to them.

8. The economic health and harmonious evolution of neighborhoods, districts, and corridors can be improved through graphic urban design codes that serve as pre-

dictable guides for change.

9. A range of parks, from tot-lots and village greens to ballfields and community gardens, should be distributed within neighborhoods. Conservation areas and open lands should be used to define and connect different neighborhoods and districts.

The Block, the Street, and the Building

1. A primary task of all urban architecture and landscape design is the physical definition of streets and public spaces as places of shared use.

2. Individual architectural projects should be seamlessly linked to their surroundings. This issue transcends style.

3. The revitalization of urban places depends on safety and security. The design of streets and buildings should reinforce safe environments, but not at the expense of accessibility and openness.

4. In the contemporary metropolis, development must adequately accommodate automobiles. It should do so in ways that respect the pedestrian and the form of public space.

5. Streets and squares should be safe, comfortable, and interesting to the pedestrian. Properly configured, they encourage walking and enable neighbors to know each other and protect their communities.

6. Architecture and landscape design should grow from local climate, topography, history, and building practice.

7. Civic buildings and public gathering places require important sites to reinforce community identity and the culture of democracy. They deserve distinctive form, because their role is different from that of other buildings and places that constitute the fabric of the city.

8. All buildings should provide their inhabitants with a clear sense of location, weather, and time. Natural methods of heating and cooling can be more resource-efficient than mechanical systems.

9. Preservation and renewal of historic buildings, districts, and landscapes affirm the continuity and evolution of urban society.

American Political Science Review

Vol. 101, No. 3   August 2007

DOI: 10.1017/S0003055407070323

Vote Choice in Suburban Elections

J. ERIC OLIVER   *University of Chicago*
SHANG E. HA   *University of Chicago and Public Policy Institute of California*

*D*espite the importance of local elections in the United States, political scientists have little knowledge of what shapes vote choice in most municipalities and special districts, particularly in the suburbs where a majority of Americans live. This article develops and tests models of local voting behavior using unique survey data of over 1,400 voters in 30 different suburban communities. Suburban electoral politics are dominated by a nonrepresentative group of "stakeholders," who are highly informed and interested in local affairs. Because of this, vote choice in suburban elections ends up sharing many characteristics with larger contests (i.e., issue salience, partisanship, and candidate likeability), although their impact varies with the size and diversity of the particular community (e.g., in smaller suburbs, voters are more engaged in local politics, more likely to know candidates personally, and more likely to vote against incumbents). These findings suggest the importance of developing new theories about voting behavior in micro-electoral contexts.

merica is a suburban nation.[1] Over the past 50 years, the suburban portion of the population has nearly doubled, and today, over one in two Americans calls a suburb home. This transformation has fundamentally altered the American landscape. Rather than either being crowded in diverse, large cities or isolated in rural towns, most Americans now live in small municipalities that are highly singular in their social composition and land use. Despite the enormity of this change, political scientists know little about how democracy operates in these locales or how their unique social composition affects their political life. Most commentary on suburban politics consists largely of journalistic speculation, architectural criticism, or popular impressions. In these critiques, suburbs are typically lambasted as conformist, overly privatized, alienating landscapes, with residents who are parochial in their political concerns and disinterested in public life (Ehrenhalt 1995; Langdon 1994). With a few exceptions (e.g., Gainsborough 2001; Oliver 2001), social scientists have not systematically analyzed how democratic politics in suburbia differs from other locales.

Nowhere is this information gap greater than with respect to local elections. Every year, thousands of suburban municipalities, townships, and special districts in the United States hold elections for local councils, mayoral offices, board members, and other posts. Although these elections arguably represent the most immediate democratic experience for a majority of Americans, political scientists have little understanding of what determines vote choice in these settings. Among the voluminous literature on electoral choice since the beginning

of American National Election Studies (ANES), the vast majority of articles and books have concentrated on national and, particularly, presidential elections.[2] Of the relatively smaller body of research on local elections, most studies have focused on a handful of very large cities (e.g., Kaufman 2004; Sonenshein 1993) with virtually no analysis of vote choice in rural or suburban localities.

Nor have local elections figured prominently in the field of urban politics. Outside of research on political machines and ethnic coalitions in large cities (e.g., Erie 1988; Jones-Correa 2001), previous studies of urban politics have relegated the topic of vote choice to a place of minor consideration. The most prominent studies of local politics have focused primarily on the role of elites (Dahl 1961; Stone 1989), the impact of municipal competition (Peterson 1981), or the potential of minority empowerment (Browning, Marshall, and Tabb 1997; Welch and Bledsoe 1988), with research drawn largely from bigger cities. Indeed, some theories, such as Tiebout's (1956) seminal public choice model, discount the local electoral process entirely, assuming that citizens in fragmented metropolitan areas express their preferences by voting "with their feet" rather than at the ballot box. Among the few studies of suburban politics (e.g., Dreier, Mollenkopf, and Swanstrom 2001; Lewis 1996), none have examined local electoral behavior, focusing instead on institutions and their relationships with the larger metropolis.

This paucity of research actually reflects a much larger gulf in the political science literature on democracy in a variety of smaller contexts. In voluntary civic associations, in many workplaces, corporate boards, churches, and schools, and in countless smaller social units within American society, people are called on to participate and vote in democratic elections. Such micro-elections may be the "schoolrooms of

---

J. Eric Oliver is Professor of Political Science, University of Chicago, 5801 Ellis Avenue, Chicago, IL 60637 (eoliver@uchicago.edu).

Shang E. Ha is a doctoral candidate, University of Chicago, 5801 Ellis Avenue, Chicago, IL 60637; (sha1@uchicago.edu).

We gratefully acknowledge the Financial support of a National Science Foundation career award (SES-0332139) and comments from the American Politics Workshop at the University of Chicago.

[1] By suburb, we mean generally any incorporated municipality or township that is within or very close to a metropolitan area but not in a central city.

[2] Berry and Howell (2006) estimate that 99% of articles in the leading political science journals that investigated the dynamics of elections (i.e., campaigns, electoral behavior, and electoral system) focused on presidential, congressional, or gubernatorial elections.

democracy," the places where citizens learn the basics of collective decision making (Putnam 2000), but as with suburban municipal elections, political scientists know very little about how people make their vote choice, especially when partisanship or economic evaluations are not germane.

Looking to explain how democracy works in such smaller contexts, this article develops and tests new theories about voter behavior in American suburban elections. After reviewing the literature on both vote choice and suburbanization, we question whether prevalent vote choice models will be germane in most local elections and theorize on how a community's political institutions and social composition will affect its electoral politics. Contrary to popular stereotypes, we find that suburban voters represent a highly engaged, yet unrepresentative portion of the citizenry. Like voters in other contests, suburban voters base their choices on issue positions, subjective candidate evaluations, partisanship, and general evaluations of administrative performance. These patterns of citizen engagement and voter behavior differ, however, with the social and institutional composition of the place. From these findings, we update perspectives on suburban politics in particular and on electoral behavior in micro-contexts in general.

WHAT DIFFERENTIATES SUBURBAN ELECTIONS FROM OTHER ELECTIONS

Most of our knowledge about the way ordinary people vote comes from the vast body of literature on presidential elections. Ever since the development of the "Michigan model," scholars have explained national voting, to a greater or lesser extent, relative to four factors: partisan affiliation, evaluations of national economic conditions, the candidates' stances on salient issues, and candidate likeability (Campbell et al. 1960; Miller and Shanks 1996). There are many reasons, however, to question whether this robust model of presidential voting is applicable for most local elections in the United States. First, over three-quarters of its municipalities have nonpartisan elections (Wood 2002). Although nonpartisan elections do not necessarily preclude the formation of local political organizations, such groups tend to be local coalitions of various neighborhood groups or slates of candidates that have little relationship to the national parties (Lee 1960). In the absence of a party moniker, one of the most salient cues for voters on the ballot, and a fundamental predictor of vote choice, is gone.

Second, suburban electoral decisions may reflect voter evaluations of incumbent performance, but the criteria they will utilize to make their judgments are hard to know. In national elections, such retrospective judgments hinge primarily on the economy and foreign military involvement (Aldrich, Sullivan, and Borgida 1989; Nadeau and Lewis-Beck 2001), yet it is unlikely that concerns of "peace and prosperity" will have the same impact on local contests. Some evidence suggests that local economic circumstances, such as a deflated

real estate market, may be harmful to local incumbents (Mondak, Mutz, and Huckfeldt 1996), but it is doubtful that suburbanites will hold their local council officials accountable for the deteriorating economy or unsuccessful wars. Although some locally elected officials have specific responsibilities, such as with mosquito zones or school boards, most mayors and council members are responsible for a wide range of tasks, thus making it difficult to specify any one barometer of incumbent performance, barring a particular scandal or malfeasance, that would hold across all municipalities at all times.

Third, the influence of specific issues or subjective candidate appraisals in suburban elections is also questionable given the low visibility of politics in most localities. The American citizenry is already notoriously underinformed about national issues, candidates and their policy positions, or politics in general (Delli Carpini and Keeter 1996); thus it is hard to imagine that they would be any more attentive to or informed about local issues. And even if voters can overcome information shortfalls (Sniderman, Brody, and Tetlock 1991), it is unclear how well citizens can recognize candidate positions on pedestrian issues as zoning ordinances, bond issues, road maintenance, and so forth (Lowery and Lyons 1989; Teske et al. 1993). This information deficit may be exacerbated in suburban places without indigenous news sources or local political organizations.

In short, for electoral contests where partisan cues are usually absent, candidates have few resources for self-promotion, and issues are of questionable salience, the "classic" determinants of vote choice may simply be irrelevant. If this is the case, then what factors might be shaping voter behavior? Studies of city and congressional elections have identified other factors relating to vote shares, including incumbency advantages (e.g., Jacobson 2001; Krebs 1998), campaign spending (e.g., Arrington and Ingalls 1984), and support of local party organizations and newspapers (e.g., Ansolabehere, Lessem, and Synder 2006; Lieske 1989). In addition, racial and gender cues also exert considerable influence over local voting decisions, with black, white, or female voters typically choosing black, white, or female candidates, respectively (Svara 1991; Welch 1990). Although it is likely that incumbency and some of these other factors are also important for suburban elections, it is not self-evident that they will operate across all suburban locales in the same manner as in large cities or congressional races. Most suburban communities do not have their own papers or news sources; many are racially homogeneous (thus removing racial cues), and campaign spending would be less important where television advertising is not a prerequisite for electoral success.

The existing literature on local elections provides few other clues about what might drive vote choice in suburban contests. Partly, this is because the distinct patterns of *individual* voting behavior in local elections are largely unknown: most studies of local elections utilize aggregate vote shares in precincts or council districts (e.g., Lieske 1989) and any individual inferences drawn from such data are subject to ecological fallacy (Achen and Shively 1993). Meanwhile, the few studies that have data on individual voters are nearly all of one or two cities (e.g., Kaufmann 2004; Sonenshein 1993), thus making it impossible to gauge the impact of different electoral or social environments. Scholars of big-city elections rightly presume a plurality of interests, significant divisions along racial or economic lines, a relatively large electorate, and high political coverage by local news sources; yet, such assumptions may not be met in many suburban locales, which are highly varied in their population sizes, racial and economic composition, land usages, age, and institutional arrangements (Oliver 2001).

Given these considerations, it is essential to identify factors specific to electoral politics in suburban locales or other micro contexts that would, in turn, affect the suitability of existing models or demand the formation of new hypotheses. The first of these is the social and institutional composition of the suburb itself. Suburbanization has had seemingly contradictory effects on the local political life of metropolitan America. On the one hand, it has fragmented America's sprawling urban areas into a patchwork of small and independent polities. This fragmentation tends to draw people into local politics: residents of smaller places tend to participate more and be more engaged in community affairs (Oliver 2001). On the other hand, political fragmentation has created a number of communities that are quite homogeneous in their racial and economic composition. When suburban municipalities use zoning codes, deed restrictions, and other mechanisms to exclude large portions of the metropolitan population, they effectively preempt much of the political conflict that occurs within larger cities. As a result, residents of more homogeneous communities are typically less interested in local politics and less active in civic affairs (Oliver).

These internal dynamics are also affected by the institutional arrangements of the suburban governments. Many suburban municipalities have adopted "reform-style" practices of governance: replacing mayors with councils and professional managers, eliminating council districts for at-large jurisdictions, and holding nonpartisan elections. Forged in response to the perceived corruption of urban machines, these reform practices also serve to pacify local politics, making it difficult for local interests to organize political campaigns, mobilize key constituents, and practice patronage politics (Bridges 1997). Not surprisingly, voter turnout in places with reform-style institutions is usually lower than turnout in places with pre-reform governments (Hajnal and Lewis 2003). Because the social and institutional composition of a suburb has such profound effect on its political life, these factors should also influence both the dynamics of local campaigns and elections and the residents' electoral decisions.

Therefore, our first hypothesis is that the impact of traditional determinants of vote choice (i.e., incumbency evaluations, partisanship, candidate issue positions, and likeability) will vary in relation to two contextual dimensions of the particular suburb: its population size and the amount of internal political conflict it encompasses. In larger places, voters will be less interested or informed about local elections and thus more likely to support incumbents, in the absence of any other information (Zaller 2004). In smaller places, voters should be more interested and informed, thus more likely to know and support challengers to office. In places with more articulated conflict (i.e., more socially diverse suburbs with mayoral and partisan elections), we expect political campaigns to be more active, candidates and political groups to be more visible, and voters to be more interested in the elections and mobilized by partisan groups. As a result, they will be less likely to reflexively support incumbents and more likely to have particular issue positions that inform their vote choices. Conversely, in places with less articulated conflict (i.e., more homogeneous suburbs with reform-style institutions), voters are probably less likely to be interested or aware of local political controversies, more likely to support incumbents, and be less informed by issues positions.

Suburban electoral behavior also should be differentiated by the particular character of the suburban electorate. Electoral turnout is significantly lower in local elections, particularly when they are nonconcurrent with presidential or congressional election cycles (Hajnal and Lewis 2003; Wood 2002). Voters in off-cycle elections are less representative of the general population and are more likely to be those "stakeholders" within their communities, that is, parents of school-age children and older, home-owning, long-term residents (Fischel 2001). These nonrepresentative distortions may be exacerbated in many suburbs that have reform-style political arrangements, which serve to depress turnout even further. Thus our second hypothesis is that the distinctive composition of the electorate will have a major impact on the determinants of vote choice. "Stakeholders" are likely to be more informed and interested in local politics, and they are more likely to have their vote choices shaped by particular issues or knowledge about the different candidates. In other words, the greater the level of selective differences in participation, the more likely that information shortfalls and lower levels of political mobilization will be offset. This higher level of information will tend to benefit challengers who otherwise suffer from poor name recognition or other disadvantages relative to incumbents.

DATA

To test these hypotheses, we utilize data from the Study of the Suburban Voter (SSV), a survey of voters we administered in 30 different suburban municipalities from five different states (California, Georgia, Illinois, New Jersey, and North Carolina) in the period immediately following their elections in 2004 and 2005. The SSV selected municipalities that had competitive elections and that provided a wide range of social and institutional forms.[3] As illustrated in Appendix A, 9 of the 30 suburbs had partisan elections,[4] and 15 had mayoral elections (with the other 15 only electing council members).[5] The population size of the communities ranged from 1,191 in Colma, California, to 97,687 in Edison, New Jersey.[6] The median household income of the communities varied from a low of $35,322 in Union City, Georgia, to $146,537 in Oak Brook, Illinois. The racial composition of the municipalities also varied widely, with 7 predominantly white (i.e., 80% or more) places, 14 additional places with a white plurality, 4 places that were majority African American, and 1 place with a majority of Asian Americans. Four of the places were at least 30% Latino, and 6 were at least 20% Asian American. Ten places in California had elections concurrent with the presidential election in the fall of 2004, whereas the others had their elections in 2005.

Once the cities were selected, a phone survey was conducted by the Roper polling firm among randomly selected lists of registered voters. All interviews were conducted by telephone (CATI) at interviewing facilities on November 3–24; 2004, April 6–22; 2005; and November 11–29, 2005. Each interview took approximately 10 minutes, on average, to administer. In the fall 2004 and fall 2005 waves, the sample was drawn on an "nth" name basis from lists of registered voters maintained by and purchased directly from the counties surveyed. In the April 2005 wave, lists were used in most selected cities, but random digit dial (RDD) was used in three communities (Deerfield, Oak Park, and Sauk Village) because such lists were not available for their respective counties. In 27 of the 30 suburbs, interviews were conducted until 50 respondents were gathered. In three places, however, the small size of the community precluded that ability to gather all 50 interviewees.[7] Cooperation rates were

22% for fall 2004, 14% for spring 2005, and 20% for fall 2005. These low rates were largely attributable to the small portion of voters in the respective communities.

Because the SSV survey only sampled among registered voters and only interviewed those who had reported voting in the previous *local* election, the demographic composition of the study is distinct from that of the general population. Comparing the survey sample with 2000 Census data on each of the suburbs, as illustrated in Appendix B, we find that the differences between the survey respondents and the general population of the suburb tend to replicate the differences between voters and nonvoters in most general elections (Wolfinger and Rosenstone 1980). The respondents in the SSV survey are better educated, more likely to be homeowners, are older, and are disproportionately white: on average, 25% of the residents have a college degree, compared to 45% of the SSV sample; 68% of the residents are homeowners, compared to 85% of the SSV sample; the median age of the population in the communities is 36, whereas the median age of the SSV sample is 54; and 60% of the residents are white, compared to 82% of the SSV sample, whereas as a corollary, non-white residents are generally underrepresented in the data.[8]

Despite these differences, the sample appears to be representative of the voters in each of these jurisdictions, because the distribution of reported vote choice among the SSV sample generally reflects the actual distribution of votes in each election. For example, 161 out of 165 council candidates in the SSV had reported vote percentages that within 10 percentage points of the actual vote percentages they had received; 146 out of 165 candidates had reported vote percentages within 6 percentage points. Thus, although the SSV sample may not be representative of the general population of the communities that were surveyed, it appears to be representative, at least by the barometer of vote choice, of the voters in each community.

SUBURBAN ELECTORAL CULTURE

To understand how suburban voters make their decisions, it is important first to identify any systematic differences in the nature of electoral politics across suburbs or differences among the voters themselves. Therefore, we start our analysis with some descriptive

---

[3] Social characteristics of each city are extracted from the 2000 U.S. Census (SF1 and SF3). For simplicity's sake, we excluded the municipalities with district elections for city council. Also, an election was classified as concurrent only if it included a national race.

[4] Political parties in the suburbs of Illinois are local parties, whereas those in the suburban locales of New Jersey are identical to two major national parties (i.e., Democratic and Republican parties).

[5] Although the forms of city government can be roughly categorized into either mayor-council or council-manager type, they vary depending on several structural characteristics, for example, whether the mayor has veto power, whether the mayor is a regular member of city council, whether the mayor is full time, or whether the chief administration officer is mayor, a council member, or city manager (Frederickson and Johnson 2001; Wood 2002). In this paper, we distinguish the suburbs that had mayoral elections from those that had only city council elections. This is a reasonable distinction because when mayoral elections did not occur, the patterns of city council elections in the cities with mayor-council form of government may not significantly differ from those in the cities with council-manager type of government.

[6] Edison had two separate city council elections in 2005: one for four-year term and the other for 2-year term. We did not count the latter to simplify our analyses.

[7] These were Colma, California (23 respondents), Sauk Village, Illinois (43 respondents), and Norwood, New Jersey (47 respondents). In the following five cities, we gathered 51 respondents: Yorba Linda, California, Union City, Georgia, Mount Holly, North Carolina, Bound Brook, New Jersey, and Chatham, New Jersey.

[8] A simple comparison of the median age between the Census and the SSV data does not make sense because the SSV sample is limited to people whose age is at least 18. Unfortunately, it is not possible to calculate the median age among the residents who are older than 18 in the 2000 Census because the number of people is available not per age but per several sets of age brackets. However, we can say that relatively older people were sampled because the additive value (the median age from the Census plus 18, which indicates the most extreme case) is smaller than the median age from the SSV sample in most cities.

Vol. 101, No. 3

TABLE 1.   Differences in Political Interest, Mobilization, and Information by Place and Individual Level Traits

	Are Very or Somewhat Interested in Local Politics	Know a Lot or a Fair Amount about City Council Candidates	Know a Council Candidate Personally	Were by Contacted by Local Organizations	Agree that Local Issues Influenced Vote Choice
Racial diversity (IQV)					
Very homogeneous	74.4	47.5	34.7	54.9	87.3
Somewhat mixed	75.0	48.4	38.3	52.1	92.4
Very diverse	76.9	43.1	28.6	45.5	87.4
Population size					
Less than 15,000	79.4	51.5	43.8	52.2	89.2
15,000–30,000	76.4	42.5	28.4	54.9	88.1
More than 30,000	70.2	41.0	23.9	46.3	90.5
Mayoral election					
No	71.3	48.1	34.5	45.1	85.3
Yes	79.7	44.7	33.8	55.4	93.5
Partisan ballot					
No	74.6	48.0	34.7	46.8	89.4
Yes	77.7	42.5	32.9	58.3	89.6
Concurrent election					
No	78.4	47.3	38.0	53.5	92.2
Yes	69.6	44.3	26.3	43.7	82.5
Homeownership					
No	64.4	28.0	21.6	38.1	74.1
Yes	77.7	49.6	36.1	52.8	91.4
Live +10 years					
No	72.0	35.2	27.1	48.5	89.1
Yes	77.6	52.1	37.5	51.9	89.6
Total	75.6	46.3	34.2	50.4	89.5

Source: The 2004–2005 Study of Suburban Voter (SSV).
Note: Cell entries are percentages; the total number of cases is 1,468.

statistics of the respondents' reported knowledge of local candidates, interest in local affairs, and patterns of political mobilization. In each of the 30 suburbs, respondents were asked a series of questions about their familiarity with each of the council candidates and, where applicable, mayoral candidates and some questions about their interest and feelings about local politics.[9] As illustrated in the totals of Table 1 (listed in the bottom row), respondents in the SSV survey report a high level of interest in and familiarity with local politics. About 46% of the respondents say they knew "a lot" or "a fair amount" about one or more council candidates. Although not listed, over half of the SSV respondents who lived in towns with mayoral elections knew this much about one of the mayoral candidates. Roughly a third (34%) of the respondents personally knew a city council candidate, a rate that was roughly the same in mayoral elections. Not surprisingly, over three-quarters of the respondents rated themselves as either somewhat or very interested in the local campaign. Suburban voters were also highly mobilized: about 50% said they had been contacted by a party, candidate, or some other organization urging them to vote in a particular way. Almost 90% said that the biggest problem or problems that were facing their community were also important in influencing their vote choice.

Given the nature of the sample and the responses to these items, it would appear that the typical suburban voter (at least as represented in the SSV sample) is

[9] The interviewer said, "I'm going to read the names of some candidates who ran in the last election. After I say the name, I'll ask you a few questions about him or her. First is [Candidate Name]. How much would you say you know about that candidate? Would you know a lot, a fair amount, only a little, only know the name, or never heard of [Candidate]?." If the respondent had never heard of the candidate, the questioner would move to the next candidate. If the respondent had heard of the candidate, they were asked (1) if they liked him or her as a person, (2) if they agreed with him or her on the issues, (3) if they knew him or her personally, (4) if they were in the same political party as the candidate, and (5) if they voted for the candidate. The respondents were also asked questions of how interested they were in the political campaign (very interested, somewhat interested, not very interested, or completely uninterested) and whether anyone from an organization or a candidate contacted them about supporting a particular local candidate during the campaign. Finally, respondents were asked a series of open-ended questions about the most important problems facing their community (they could list up to two). They were then asked follow-up questions as

to whether that problem was an important issue in influencing their voting.

397

someone who is politically active, fairly knowledge-able about local politics, and concerned about some particular issues. Of course, there is an inherent problem with such generalizations: it is nearly impossible to call any one person a typical suburbanite. Partly, this is because of the diversity of people who live in suburbs, and partly this is because of the diversity of places that fall under the heading of suburb—the sample communities in the SSV are all technically suburbs, yet vary considerably in their size and social composition. Consequently, the rest of Table 1 lists the percentage of responses to the questions above across five community- and institution-level characteristics, that is, racial diversity (see Appendix C), population size, type of government, type of ballot, and timing of election (whether it was concurrent with a national election in the fall of 2004 or not), and two individual-level traits, that is, homeownership and length of residence.

At the community level, the largest differences occur by population size. Residents of smaller suburbs are generally more interested in politics, more likely to recognize local candidates, and more likely to know a candidate personally. For example, comparing residents in suburbs under 15,000 in population to those over 30,000 in size, we find a 9-percentage-point increase in political interest, a 10-point increase in candidate name recognition, and a 20-point increase in personal acquaintance with a city council candidate. Residents of smaller places are also more likely to be mobilized by a political organization or candidate. There are no consistent patterns in the cross-tabulations along the racial diversity scale, but there are some important differences by virtue of the institutional arrangements in the community. People who live in places that had mayoral elections are more likely to be interested in politics and be contacted by local organizations. Also, people who live in places with partisan ballots are far more likely to be mobilized during the campaign. Similarly, people whose elections were concurrent with the national elections of 2004 are less interested in local politics, less likely to know a candidate personally or be mobilized, and less likely to say that an important problem influenced their vote choice. At the individual level, the differences in these items generally conform to conventional wisdom: homeowners and, to a lesser extent, long-term residents are more likely to be interested in local politics, know about candidates, be mobilized, and report that issues influenced their vote choice (Verba, Schlozman, and Brady 1995; Wolfinger and Rosenstone 1980).

Although these results suggest that suburban voters' political experiences differ across environmental and individual traits, it is impossible to determine, from these cross-tabulations, which of these traits is more important or how they compare with other factors. To examine the relative effects of both the contextual and the individual-level variables, we employ a set of hierarchical linear models (HLM) with some additional controls, that is, individuals' education, race, age, and gender, in conjunction with the log of the median household income (MHI) of the community. The specifications of the models are reported in Appendix C, and the results are listed in Table 2.

Even when the individual-level characteristics and other demographic characteristics of the suburbs are taken into account, the patterns illustrated in the cross-tabulations remain: the social characteristics of the suburb and the individual characteristics of the suburban voter relate to interest, information, and mobilization levels. As in the cross-tabulations, community size remains one of the most important determinants of local electoral politics. People in larger suburbs are, on average, less interested in politics, less knowledgeable of city council candidates, and are less likely to be mobilized during the campaign. The multivariate analyses suggest that people in more racially heterogeneous suburbs are more interested in local politics. Furthermore, the institutional structure of the suburb makes a difference: voters in places with mayoral elections are more interested in local politics, more likely to know a city council candidate personally, and more likely to be mobilized; voters in places with partisan elections (also, those in relatively affluent cities) are more likely to be mobilized, and voters in places with off-cycle elections have particular issues that shaped their vote choice.

At the individual level, the biggest factors relating to voters' local political engagement were homeownership, length of residence, education, and race. As in the cross-tabulations, homeowners exhibited greater interest in politics, more knowledge of local candidates, higher mobilization rates, and more animation from local issues. Given that the models controlled for length of residence in the community (which is also positively related to political interest and knowledge of candidates), the effects of homeownership seem even more impressive. Education is also correlated with political knowledge, mobilization, and attention to local issues, which is unsurprisingly consistent with the existing literature (Verba, Schlozman, and Brady 1995; Wolfinger and Rosenstone 1980). Interestingly, racial minorities reported less knowledge of candidates, Asian Americans were less interested in local campaigns, and African Americans were less mobilized during local elections (although Latinos in the sample were more mobilized).

In sum, these findings suggest that suburban electoral politics vary in relation to the community's social composition and municipal institutions, even after controlling for several individual-level determinants. Even though larger places presumably have more community issues before them, their bigger populations seem to be a deterrent to their residents' interest in local politics. This can be offset, to some extent, by their institutional design. Local governments that provide more structure to local elections, either through partisan ballots or mayoral elections, enjoy greater voter interest and more active candidates and local organizations. In other words, where the institutional structures allow for more political organization, political activity increases and voters become better informed.

TABLE 2. Multilevel Model Results of Suburban Electoral Culture

		Interest in Local Campaigns 1 = Completely Uninterested; 4 = Very Interested	Mean Knowledge of City Council Candidates 1 = Never Heard of; 5 = Know A Lot	Personal Acquaintance of A Local Council Candidate	Contact by Local Organizations	Vote choice Influenced by Local Issues
Intercept (β_{0j})	Intercept (γ_{00})	2.64**	1.87**	−1.43**	−.74*	.14
		(.12)	(.10)	(.38)	(.27)	(.25)
	IQV (γ_{01})	.37^	.30	.77	.13	−.40
		(.19)	(.25)	(.57)	(.63)	(.55)
	Population (γ_{02})	−.14**	−.25**	−.76**	−.25	.12
		(.04)	(.05)	(.12)	(.15)	(.18)
	MHI (γ_{03})	.09	.22	.46	.59*	−.14
		(.15)	(.13)	(.40)	(.25)	(.28)
	Partisan election (γ_{04})	.01	−.11	−.17	.52^	−.11
		(.10)	(.12)	(.26)	(.25)	(.29)
	Mayoral election (γ_{05})	.33**	.02	.67*	.92**	−.12
		(.09)	(.12)	(.24)	(.25)	(.35)
	Off-cycle election (γ_{06})	−.04	−.16	−.06	−.27	.78^
		(.12)	(.12)	(.28)	(.31)	(.41)
Education (β_{1j})	Intercept (γ_{10})	.01	.07**	.01	.16**	.09^
		(.02)	(.02)	(.05)	(.06)	(.05)
Own home (β_{2j})	Intercept (γ_{20})	.23**	.40**	.57^	.48**	.88**
		(.08)	(.06)	(.31)	(.16)	(.21)
Live +10 Yrs (β_{3j})	Intercept (γ_{30})	.13*	.25**	.49**	.16	.05
		(.05)	(.04)	(.16)	(.13)	(.16)
Female (β_{4j})	Intercept (γ_{40})	.07	−.01	−.01	.21^	−.29*
		(.06)	(.05)	(.13)	(.12)	(.12)
Age (β_{5j})	Intercept (γ_{50})	.01	−.01	−.01	−.01	−.01**
		(.01)	(.01)	(.01)	(.01)	(.004)
Black+ (β_{6j})	Intercept (γ_{60})	−.07	−.31**	−.79**	−.51*	.10
		(.12)	(.08)	(.28)	(.21)	(.26)
Latino+ (β_{7j})	Intercept (γ_{70})	−.17	−.29*	−.50^	.47*	−.03
		(.13)	(.11)	(.29)	(.22)	(.32)
Asian+ (β_{8j})	Intercept (γ_{80})	−.35**	−.43**	−2.35*	−.51	−.73^
		(.11)	(.11)	(.95)	(.34)	(.38)
Other race+ (β_{9j})	Intercept (γ_{90})	.08	−.13	.14	−.07	.17
		(.10)	(.10)	(.32)	(.22)	(.21)
N (level 1)		1,371	1,374	1,241	1,359	1,378

Source: The 2004–2005 Study of Suburban Voter (SSV).
Note: All variables at the level 1 are centered around their group means, except for dummy variables. All variables at level 2 are grand-centered. The results from the unit-specific models are reported in the case of Bernoulli model. Robust standard errors are in parentheses.
** p < .01; * p < .05; ^ p < .1 (two-tailed). + "White" used as a baseline category.

Suburban electoral politics also vary in relation to a person's individual status in the community. Stakeholders in the community, that is, older, educated, homeowners; and long-term residents, are more engaged by local affairs, familiar with candidates, and mobilized in local politics. Thus these people not only are more likely to vote, but also are at the center of democratic life. This bias in the suburban electorate presumably shapes the local political agenda, putting concerns of homeowners and long-term residents to the forefront of any electoral contest. The SSV data also reveal a racial bias to suburban electoral politics—minorities are generally less informed about local candidates and are less likely to be recruited. Even in racially mixed places, as the ones we sampled from, electoral politics in suburbia is circumscribed by race.

DETERMINANTS OF INCUMBENCY SUPPORT

So, how does the electoral culture of these suburban communities translate into particular voting behavior? In suburbs, as in many local and congressional elections, incumbency is perhaps the most important factor shaping people's ballot decisions. Incumbent candidates have numerous benefits of office, including opportunities to enhance their name recognition, to perform various acts of retail politics, and to link with various constituencies, and, by one estimate, are overwhelmingly favored by local newspapers (Ansolabehere, Lessem, and Synder 2006). Not surprisingly, they also do a good job at getting reelected. In the municipalities of the SSV sample, 47 of 56 incumbents running for reelection in city council elections were returned to office as were 10 of the 11 mayoral incumbents. Depending on the amount of conflict within the suburb and the information and interest levels of the particular voter, it is reasonable to assume that local elections are, first and foremost, referendums on incumbent performance (Zaller 2004).

If evaluating of the status quo, and hence incumbents, is the default voting position of people in low information contexts, then the central question for explaining electoral behavior is what drives suburbanites to deviate from this trend and vote for challengers. Is it because of some general dissatisfaction with the way the suburb is being governed? Does it reflect a particular concern with local economic conditions? Or, do other determinants of vote choice, such as partisanship, community issues, or candidate likeability come into play?

To answer these questions, we examine city council races in the SSV sample where at least one incumbent was running and where all the elections were for at-large seats.[10] As a dependent variable, we constructed a scale of incumbency support: because voters had opportunities to vote for numerous candidates in the city council elections, we constructed a three-point vote scale of (1) supporting only incumbents, (2) supporting some incumbents and some challengers, and (3) supporting only challengers.[11] As predictors of incumbency support, we use several variables assessing the differences in voters' perceptions of the candidates, including their likeability, issue agreement, personal acquaintance, and shared partisanship. Given that voters in city council races had a choice of numerous incumbents and that most voters had numerous choices among challengers, we constructed four three-point ordinal variables relative to incumbent support. Taking candidate likeability, for example, -1 denotes that the number of incumbents a respondent liked was greater than that of challengers, 0 denotes that the number of incumbents he or she liked was equal to that of challengers, and 1 indicates that the number of incumbents he or she liked was smaller than that of challengers. We also use two items measuring the subjective impression that voters had of local economic conditions and government performance.[12]

Table 3 lists cross-tabulations showing the differences in incumbent support for city council elections by various evaluations of candidate traits as well as community conditions. As expected, candidate likeability, issue agreement, and shared partisanship correspond with voting patterns—the more a voter liked or agreed with challengers or incumbents, the more likely he or she voted for challengers or incumbents, respectively. For example, among respondents who only voted for incumbents, 51% liked incumbent candidates more, 66% agreed more with incumbents on issues, 26% knew incumbents personally, and 35% shared party affiliations with incumbents. Among those who voted only for challengers, 47% personally liked more challengers, 66% agreed more with challengers on issues, 21% knew more challengers personally, and 33% were closer to challengers in terms of partisanship. From these simple cross-tabulations, it appears that many of the same factors shaping voting behavior in national elections (partisanship, candidate likeability, issue positions) are also present in suburban elections. Their relative effects, however, are different. Whereas presidential elections hinge largely on partisan affiliations and subjective appraisals of candidate likeability (Miller and Shanks 1996), in suburban elections, the candidates' issue positions seem to be the most important determinant of voter support: a significantly higher percentage of voters were likely to share issue positions with the candidates they supported than to know candidates personally, like candidates or share a party affiliation with them.

Suburban voting behavior is also similar to national voting behavior in another key respect: evaluations of local economic conditions or government performance correspond with incumbent support. The overall impact of retrospective evaluations are comparatively small because, unlike in national politics, most suburban voters seem pretty happy with their communities. In the SSV sample, 76% of the respondents thought their city economy had done the same or better in the past year and about 80% thought that local government performance was good. Although such contentment may be a function of the higher social status of voters compared to nonvoters, it nevertheless shows that suburban *voters* are a generally satisfied lot. And, among the large majority who are more satisfied with the economy or government performance, incumbent support is higher; conversely, among the small percentage who are dissatisfied with local government performance, support for challengers is greater.

To compare these various influences, we return to multivariate analysis using a hierarchical generalized linear model predicting support for challengers. Once again, the dependent variable is a three-point scale of challenger support (1 = incumbents only; 3 = challengers only). For explanatory variables, the baseline model (Model 1) includes the three-point measures of likeability, issue agreement, and

---

[10] By doing so, we lose three cities, that is, Oak Brook, Oak Park, and Pittsburg, where no incumbent ran for reelection.

[11] When constructing vote choice variables, we exclude all invalid votes, which means that a respondent reported to cast more than the number of votes allowed in the city council election: for instance, if a respondent reported to vote for three city council candidates when only two seats were open, then his or her vote is considered invalid. Also, the votes of the respondents whose number of vote in city council election is zero are considered invalid. The percentage of valid vote in city council elections ranges from 42 (Hazel Crest) to 86 (Milpitas and Solana Beach).

[12] SSV respondents were asked about their impression of local economic conditions over the past year whether it had gotten better, stayed the same or gotten worse. Respondents were also asked how well they thought, "local government in [their community] is work-

ing: very well, somewhat well, somewhat badly, or very badly." For the later measure, the variable was recoded into two categories.

TABLE 3. Key Determinants of City Council Vote Choice (Column Percentage = 100)

	Vote for Incumbents Only (n = 317)	Vote for Both Challengers and Incumbents (n = 323)	Vote for Challengers Only (n = 217)
Likeability (n = 857)			
Prefer incumbents	50.5	17.0	1.8
Like both	16.1	53.3	18.0
Prefer challengers	1.3	8.7	46.5
No response	32.2	21.1	33.6
Issue agreement (n = 857)			
Agree w/incumbents	66.3	9.6	0.0
Agree w/both	13.3	76.2	14.8
Agree w/challengers	1.0	6.2	65.9
No response	19.6	8.1	19.4
Personal acquaintance (n = 857)			
Know incumbents	25.6	15.8	2.8
Know both	4.4	23.8	9.7
Know challengers	0.3	11.2	20.7
No response	69.7	49.2	66.8
Shared partisanship (n = 857)			
Share w/incumbents	34.7	7.1	2.8
Share w/both	6.3	24.8	6.5
Share w/challengers	1.6	7.4	33.2
No response	57.4	60.7	57.6
Mean familiarity score with challengers (n = 855)			
1 = Never heard of; 5 = Know a lot	3.05	2.64	3.70
Perceptions on city economy* (n = 813)			
Worse	30.9	38.8	30.3
Same/better	39.1	38.7	22.2
Perceptions on local government Performance* (n = 832)			
Good	38.8	39.3	21.9
Bad	25.4	33.3	41.3

Source: The 2004–2005 Study of Suburban Voter (SSV).
* Row percentage = 100.

shared partisanship in conjunction with a five-point scale variable of candidate familiarity, and several other individual-level measures including perceptions of the city economy, local government performance, homeownership, length of residency, interest in local campaigns, mobilization, education, age, and gender. We also added institution-related measures (off-cycle, mayoral, and partisan elections), and measures of the suburbs' social composition (racial diversity and the natural log of its population size and median household income). The model specifications are in Appendix C, and the results are presented in Table 4.

As in the cross-tabulations, results from the hierarchical linear models show that voters' perceptions of the candidates were related to their vote choices. Voters who were more familiar with challengers or who thought that challengers were either more likeable or shared their party affiliations or issue stances were more likely to vote for challengers. Among these four variables, shared issue positions exhibit the strongest

relationship to support for challengers: compared to voters who preferred incumbents, voters who personally liked challengers were, according to our estimates, 15% more likely to vote for only challengers; those who shared partisanship with challengers were 19% more likely to vote for only challengers; meanwhile, those who agreed with challengers on issues were 45% more likely to vote for only challengers.[13] Interestingly, personal familiarity with challengers had the smallest correlation with vote choice. Thus although suburban elections may be distinct because of the high levels of personal familiarity with candidates, this does not seem to have as large an impact on vote choice as other factors such as issue

[13] These predicted probabilities are calculated from ordered probit models estimated in Stata, using CLARIFY software (King, Tomz, Wittenberg 2000; Tomz, Wittenberg, and King 2003). The probit models used the same set of variables as the HLM models, although the coefficients do not taken into account the biases arising from a limited set of contexts. Nevertheless, they provide a convenient way of generating some predicted probabilities.

TABLE 4. Vote Choice for Challengers in City Council Elections

		Model 1	Model 2	Model 3	Model 4
Intercept (β_{0j})	Intercept (γ_{00})	−2.13**	−2.33**	−2.18**	−1.95**
		(.49)	(.48)	(.49)	(.39)
	IQV (γ_{01})	2.05^	1.98^	3.04*	2.15^
		(1.08)	(1.09)	(1.11)	(1.08)
	Population (γ_{02})	−.60**	−.61**	−.76**	−.60**
		(.20)	(.20)	(.24)	(.20)
	MHI (γ_{03})	−.08	−.12	−.08	−.08
		(.77)	(.78)	(.80)	(.77)
	Partisan election (γ_{04})	.37	.38	.33	.39
		(.50)	(.51)	(.51)	(.52)
	Mayoral election (γ_{05})	.94^	.95^	.83^	.92^
		(.47)	(.47)	(.46)	(.48)
	Off-cycle election (γ_{06})	−.01	−.01	.13	.01
		(.66)	(.67)	(.67)	(.67)
Likeability (β_{1j})	Intercept (γ_{10})	.54**	.53**	.55**	.55**
		(.11)	(.12)	(.12)	(.11)
Issue agreement (β_{2j})	Intercept (γ_{20})	1.66**	1.73**	1.70**	1.66**
		(.16)	(.17)	(.16)	(.16)
	Population (γ_{21})		.39*		
			(.16)		
	IQV (γ_{22})		.59		
			(.60)		
Shared partisanship (β_{3j})	Intercept (γ_{30})	.88**	.89**	.86**	.84**
		(.18)	(.19)	(.18)	(.16)
	Partisan election (γ_{31})				.84*
					(.37)
Familiarity (β_{4j})	Intercept (γ_{40})	.30*	.31**	.29*	.30*
		(.12)	(.12)	(.12)	(.12)
Perception on city economy; Positive (β_{5j})	Intercept (γ_{50})	.07	.02	.06	.06
		(.10)	(.10)	(.10)	(.09)
Local gov't performance; Positive (β_{6j})	Intercept (γ_{60})	−.52**	−.45*	−.54**	−.52**
		(.18)	(.19)	(.17)	(.40)
Education (β_{7j})	Intercept (γ_{70})	.12^	.13^	.11	.11
		(.07)	(.07)	(.07)	(.07)
Own home (β_{8j})	Intercept (γ_{80})	.24	.32	.29	.24
		(.26)	(.24)	(.26)	(.26)
Live +10 years (β_{9j})	Intercept (γ_{90})	−.20	−.20	−.21	−.24
		(.18)	(.18)	(.18)	(.17)
Interest (β_{10j})	Intercept (γ_{100})	.40**	.39**	.37**	.41**
		(.14)	(.14)	(.14)	(.14)
Mobilization (β_{11j})	Intercept (γ_{110})	.33^	.39*	.33*	.31
		(.20)	(.20)	(.15)	(.20)
	Population (γ_{111})			.44**	
				(.16)	
	IQV (γ_{112})			−1.95**	
				(.66)	
Female (β_{12j})	Intercept (γ_{120})	.17	.17	.17	.17
		(.17)	(.18)	(.16)	(.17)
Age (β_{13j})	Intercept (γ_{130})	−.01	−.01	−.01	−.01
		(.01)	(.01)	(.01)	(.01)

Source: The 2004–2005 Study of Suburban Voter (SSV).
Note: All variables at the level 1 are centered around their group means, except for dummy variables. All variables at the level 2 are grand-centered. Robust standard errors are in parentheses. The number of cases is 738.
** $p < .01$; * $p < .05$; ^ $p < .1$ (two-tailed).

positions or partisanship. Most significantly, these results demonstrate the preeminent importance of issues in suburban elections. Although suburban politics are routinely characterized as issueless, we find that issue positions are the strongest predictor of vote choice.

Other individual-level factors also had a relationship to voting for challengers. For example, voters were more likely to support challengers if they were more interested in local campaigns: voters who reported being very interested in the local campaigns were 10% more likely to vote for only challengers than those who were completely uninterested in the campaigns. The multilevel analyses confirm a finding from the cross-tabulations that voters who have negative perceptions on local government performance were more likely to vote for challengers, although evaluations of economic conditions had no impact.

Support for challengers was also related to the social composition and institutional structure of the suburb. Voters were more likely to vote against incumbents if they lived in a suburb that was racially diverse or was smaller in population size: compared to people in the least racially diverse cities, residents of the most diverse cities were 11% more likely to support only challengers; compared to those in largest places, residents of the smallest places were 19% more likely to support only challengers according to predicted probabilities calculated separately. The multilevel analyses also show that, compared to voters in council-manager governments, and voters living under mayor-council governments were more likely to support challengers, although these differences were small.

The biggest surprise in the multivariate models is the absence of differences among the individual-level demographic traits. Although homeowners, the educated, and long-term residents were more interested in local affairs and more knowledgeable about candidates, thus presumably more likely to be supportive of challengers, there were no significant differences in the challenger support scale along any of these dimensions (except for education). Nor were there any significant differences in incumbency support between voters in off-cycle versus concurrent elections, which is probably the result of the sampling screens (respondents were taken only if they said they voted in local elections) and voter roll-off (only those interested in local elections continued voting past the national ticket; see Wattenberg, McAllister, and Salvanto 2000).[14] Either way, whatever differences that occur between homeowners and renters, short- and long-term residents, or voters in national and strictly local elections seem to be subsumed by other individual-level factors such as candidate issue positions or subjective evaluations of candidates. These differences reinforce the importance of the distinct character of the suburban voter: when only the most informed and interested portion of the electorate casts a ballot, the determinants of vote choice tend to be more like those in high visibility elections.

In addition to these individual-level effects, we also hypothesized that the differences in challenger support would be related to the local political climate, which, as we saw earlier, is affected by the social and institutional composition of the community. Because people in smaller places are more involved in local politics, more informed about local issues, and more familiar with candidates, they should be more likely to support challengers. Similarly, in places with more political conflict, voters are more likely to know candidates, be animated by particular issues, or mobilized to vote in particular ways. As a result, we would also expect them to be more likely to support challengers than to reflexively support incumbents. To test these ideas more directly, we ran additional multilevel models with interaction terms between three key individual variables (shared issue positions, shared partisanship, and mobilization) and three contextual variables (population size, partisan elections, and racial heterogeneity). The results from these equations are listed in the remainder of Table 4.

The first equation (listed as Model 2) measures the effect of shared issue positions relative to the suburb's population size and racial diversity. In this equation, the relationship of voters' issue perceptions to vote choice do not change with the racial composition of their community (voters were no more or less likely to support challengers if they agreed with them on issues as the racial diversity of their community increased), but they do work to counteract the impact of population size. The strong correlation between incumbency support and population size attenuates among voters who express more issue agreement with challengers. The second set of interaction terms (Model 3) measure the relative impact of voter mobilization (i.e., was the voter asked to vote a particular way by a group or candidate). Voters who were mobilized tended to support challengers more often, although this effect varies with the size and racial diversity of the community. In larger cities, mobilization offsets the positive impact of population size on incumbency support. Mobilization also attenuates the impact of racial diversity on challenger support—voters in diverse cities typically are more likely to support challengers except when they have been mobilized. The third interaction term (Model 4) examines the relative impact of partisanship across partisan and nonpartisan elections. In general, partisanship seems most important for challengers—voters who share party affiliations with candidates are much more likely to support challengers than those who do not. This effect, not surprisingly, is higher in places with partisan elections.

These tests demonstrate the importance of campaign dynamics for suburban elections. As in all elections, challengers in suburban contests face greater hurdles than incumbents for getting elected. Their ability to clear these hurdles depends on whether they can link themselves to salient issues or shared partisan affiliations (even in nonpartisan elections) or to mobilize their supporters. The impact of these campaign dynamics varies, however, with a community's social composition. In larger places, challengers seem to have a harder time, possibly because voters are less interested or more difficult to reach, thus making credible campaigns more difficult and expensive to run. Such handicaps require challengers in larger places to expend even

---

[14] In the SSV sample, the proportion of the respondents who participated in the November 2004 presidential election, but did not cast valid votes in the local council election was 27%. Among those who did not vote in local elections, 48% were reported that they were "somewhat" or "very" interested in local campaigns, which is significantly smaller than the 77.7% who cast votes in both presidential and local election.

more resources mobilizing voters and finding issues to connect with.

Conversely, in racially diverse places, it is the incumbents who may face greater electoral difficulties. Challengers in racially diverse places consistently do better, possibly because there are more readily available social divisions to exploit, although these divisions do not seem to be based around any particular issues. As in many larger contests, electoral politics in racially diverse suburbs may hinge more on "symbolic" issues of race and ethnicity. Unfortunately, testing these ideas with data on the racial characteristics and specific issue positions of candidates is beyond the scope of this paper and awaits further research. Nevertheless, the findings suggest that, as in many large cities, racial and ethnic politics may be operative in suburban elections and that such patterns may offset some of the typical advantages of incumbency.

CONCLUSION

Taken together, these findings provide an interesting picture of both suburban politics in particular and voting behavior in micro-elections more generally. Vote choice in suburban elections has some important similarities and differences to vote choice in presidential, congressional, and big-city contests. Like these larger races, suburban electoral decisions are based partly on a combination of subjective appraisals of candidates, candidates' stances on issues, and cues regarding salient groups, although suburban voters are more likely to base their decisions on the candidates' stances on specific issues rather than party affiliation or personal traits. Much of this is due to the particular character of the suburban voter. As turnout in local elections is often under 25% of the population, suburban voters overrepresent populations with more resources and greater stakes in their communities, that is, educated, older, homeowners and long-term residents. Because the selected differences in local participation are so great, suburban voters end up sharing many behavioral patterns of voters in more visible contests—they have greater knowledge of candidates, associate their votes with particular issues, and, perhaps most remarkably, a very high percentage tend to know candidates personally.[15] Suburban electoral behavior is also differentiated by the composition of the particular suburb. In suburbs that are larger or less diverse, voters are less informed about or interested in local politics and tend to support incumbents more often. However, as a suburb diminishes in size, its voters become more animated by issues, involved in local politics, and are more likely to support challengers for office.

Such findings dispel some common misperceptions about suburban politics. In many popular commentaries, suburbanites are often criticized for being disinterested and apolitical while suburbs writ large are accused of destroying the vibrancy of local democracy in the United States (e.g., Langdon 1994). These views are informed largely by personal feelings, anecdotes, or aesthetic biases. When looking at actual evidence, however, political life in suburbia is more complicated than the common stereotypes suggest. On the one hand, suburban *voters* exhibit very high levels of interest and involvement in local affairs. Among this group of active participants, vote choice is driven more by specific issue concerns than either subjective impressions of candidates or knee-jerk adherence to party positions. In that such pro-democratic tendencies are heightened in smaller places, suburbanization, which is functionally the fragmentation of metropolitan areas into smaller political units, would seem to be a boon to democracy in America.

On the other hand, most suburbanites are not so active in politics; in fact, participation is limited typically to a small fraction of the voting age population. The social homogeneity and reform-style political practices that often accompany suburban political fragmentation are a further deterrent to both citizen involvement in local politics and to issue-driven voting. According to the SSV data, this disengagement is born most heavily among minorities, the uneducated, and renters, who are all less informed about community issues and less active in local politics. Thus suburbanization may empower one element of the population (i.e., stakeholders) but further disenfranchise the already most marginalized portions of the citizenry.

These findings also allow for some initial generalizations about voting patterns in micro-elections. In sofar as the suburbs in the SSV represent a sample of different smaller democracies, we might conclude that voting in micro-elections hinges primarily on the characteristics of the particular context. In settings that are smaller or more diverse, or that allow for the articulation of more conflict, voters are more likely to be interested, informed, and motivated by particular issues. In contests that are larger or less diverse, or where the rules inhibit the articulation or coalescence of different partisans, voters will be less engaged, challengers will have a harder time mounting credible campaigns, and, with less information or fewer viable choices, voters will be more likely to reflexively support incumbents. We might also conclude that micro-elections are shaped by selective differences in participation. Where turnout is low, elections will be driven more by the concerns of motivated stakeholders rather than by the general group membership. In other words, the lower the turnout, the less likely that an election will hinge on a "median voter" and the more likely that it will be determined by a highly motivated group. Although these conclusions await testing across a variety of different electoral contexts, if suburban voting is any indication, the politics of small democracies can be as issue specific, partisan, and candidate centered as many larger elections.

---

[15] Interestingly, nearly all the respondents who reported knowing a candidate personally also reported having a favorable opinion of the candidate. This would suggest that suburban politics are not as personally vindictive as some accounts would suggest.

APPENDIX A

TABLE A1. City Characteristics in the Study of the Suburban Voter (SSV)

City	Election Date	Election Type	Mayoral Election	Total Pop.	MHI ($)	White (%)	Black (%)	Asian (%)	Latino (%)
Colma, CA	Nov. 2004	NP	No	1,191	58,750	27.7	0.9	23.5	43.9
Danville, CA	Nov. 2004	NP	No	41,715	114,064	83.0	0.9	8.9	4.7
Fountain Vly., CA	Nov. 2004	NP	No	54,978	69,734	58.5	1.1	25.6	10.7
Imperial Beach, CA	Nov. 2004	NP	No	26,992	35,882	43.5	5.0	6.2	40.1
Milpitas, CA	Nov. 2004	NP	Yes	62,689	84,429	23.8	3.5	51.5	16.6
Pittsburg, CA	Nov. 2004	NP	No	56,769	50,557	31.2	18.4	12.4	32.2
Sausalito, CA	Nov. 2004	NP	No	7,330	87,469	89.4	0.6	4.1	3.3
Solana Beach, CA	Nov. 2004	NP	No	12,979	71,774	79.0	0.5	3.3	14.8
Westminster, CA	Nov. 2004	NP	Yes	88,207	49,450	36.2	0.9	38.0	21.7
Yorba Linda, CA	Nov. 2004	NP	No	58,918	89,593	74.8	1.1	11.0	10.3
Carol Stream, IL	Apr. 2005	NP	No	40,438	64,893	73.0	4.2	11.1	10.0
Deerfield, IL	Apr. 2005	Partisan	Yes	18,420	107,194	94.6	0.3	2.5	1.7
Flossmoor, IL	Apr. 2005	NP	Yes	9,301	94,222	65.0	26.8	4.2	2.4
Hazel Crest, IL	Apr. 2005	Partisan	Yes	14,816	50,576	18.3	75.8	0.9	3.3
Oak Brook, IL	Apr. 2005	NP	No	8,702	146,537	74.5	1.4	20.1	2.4
Oak Park, IL	Apr. 2005	Partisan	Yes	52,524	59,183	66.2	22.2	4.1	4.5
Riverdale, IL	Apr. 2005	Partisan	Yes	15,055	38,321	10.2	86.0	0.2	2.4
Sauk Village, IL	Apr. 2005	NP	Yes	10,411	46,718	53.2	32.1	0.7	11.8
Wheeling, IL	Apr. 2005	NP	Yes	34,496	55,491	66.4	2.3	9.2	20.7
Avondale Ests., GA	Nov. 2005	NP	No	2,609	70,625	87.6	8.4	1.0	1.5
Clarkston, GA	Nov. 2005	NP	Yes	7,231	37,436	17.3	55.1	12.4	4.6
Union City, GA	Nov. 2005	NP	Yes	11,621	35,322	25.4	69.3	1.3	5.2
Huntersville, NC	Nov. 2005	NP	Yes	24,960	71,932	86.1	7.3	1.5	3.9
Kannapolis, NC	Nov. 2005	NP	Yes	36,910	35,532	75.2	16.4	0.8	6.3
Mount Holly, NC	Nov. 2005	NP	Yes	9,618	39,459	84.8	9.2	2.5	2.1
Bound Brook, NC	Nov. 2005	Partisan	No	10,155	46,858	58.7	2.2	2.8	34.9
Chatham, NJ	Nov. 2005	Partisan	No	8,460	101,991	93.6	0.1	2.8	2.6
Edison, NJ	Nov. 2005	Partisan	Yes	97,687	69,746	55.8	6.6	29.2	6.4
Norwood, NJ	Nov. 2005	Partisan	No	5,751	92,447	75.7	0.8	19.0	3.0
Somerville, NJ	Nov. 2005	Partisan	No	12,423	51,237	60.6	12.5	7.3	17.0

APPENDIX B

TABLE B1. Demographic Composition of SSV Respondents and General Population (A Simple Comparison)

City	Percentage of College Degree Holders		Percentage of Homeowners		Median Age		Percentage of Whites		Percentage of Other Race (b=Black, a=Asian, l=Latino)	
	Census	SSV	Census	SSV	Census	SSV	Census	SSV	Census	SSV
Colma	8.65	30.43	50.29	69.57	36.9	55.0	27.7	47.8	43.9 (l)	17.4
Danville	40.53	78.00	91.15	95.92	39.9	53.5	83.0	88.0	8.9 (a)	2.0
Fountain Valley	23.47	53.06	75.63	88.00	38.1	53.0	58.5	92.0	25.6 (a)	4.0
Imperial Beach	6.61	28.00	28.22	51.02	28.6	47.0	43.5	70.0	40.1 (l)	14.0
Milpitas	23.94	52.00	67.22	70.83	33.4	45.5	23.8	50.0	51.5 (a)	24.0
Pittsburg	8.66	38.00	64.50	83.67	30.9	52.0	31.2	64.0	32.2 (l)	14.0
Sausalito	63.79	76.60	52.26	63.04	45.4	55.0	89.4	82.0	4.1 (a)	4.0
Solana Beach	43.80	80.00	61.38	81.63	41.6	61.0	79.0	86.0	14.8 (l)	2.0
Westminster	11.77	46.94	58.25	81.63	34.1	51.0	36.2	70.0	38.1 (a)	12.0
Yorba Linda	26.37	50.98	85.82	92.00	37.4	50.0	74.8	92.2	11.0 (a)	2.0
Carol Stream	19.19	20.00	75.66	83.33	31.3	50.5	73.0	90.0	11.1 (a)	0.0
Deerfield	45.44	38.00	91.20	100.00	39.6	53.5	94.6	90.0	2.5 (a)	0.0
Flossmoor	40.42	40.00	93.42	98.00	42.2	54.5	65.0	76.0	26.8 (b)	16.0
Hazel Crest	13.37	16.33	83.92	91.67	34.6	57.5	18.3	26.0	75.8 (b)	50.0
Oak Brook	43.50	38.00	93.53	86.00	50.0	67.0	74.5	92.0	20.1 (a)	0.0
Oak Park	43.10	52.00	66.40	88.00	36.0	50.5	66.2	92.0	22.2 (b)	0.0
Riverdale	6.32	18.37	59.31	82.00	27.5	52.0	10.2	32.0	86.0 (b)	60.0
Sauk Village	5.05	13.95	81.19	88.37	30.1	56.0	53.2	69.8	32.1 (b)	25.5
Wheeling	21.35	12.24	72.65	88.00	34.5	55.0	66.4	88.0	20.7 (l)	2.0
Avondale Estates	54.16	70.00	91.22	98.00	42.9	55.0	87.6	90.0	8.4 (b)	2.0
Clarkston	12.13	62.00	18.72	82.00	28.1	45.0	17.3	46.0	55.1 (b)	42.0
Union City	12.00	44.00	37.93	69.39	32.2	56.0	25.4	37.3	69.3 (b)	54.9
Huntersville	30.52	65.31	79.80	89.58	32.8	48.5	86.1	82.0	7.3 (b)	10.0
Kannapolis	7.89	28.57	65.22	80.43	34.3	57.5	75.2	86.0	16.4 (b)	6.0
Mount Holly	10.13	33.33	64.78	91.84	33.3	60.0	84.8	90.2	9.2 (b)	5.8
Bound Brook	16.46	38.78	50.88	91.84	34.2	53.0	58.7	80.4	34.9 (l)	7.8
Chatham	45.09	78.43	82.71	94.00	36.3	56.0	93.6	86.3	2.8 (a)	0.0
Edison	29.32	54.00	66.56	93.75	35.3	52.5	55.8	68.0	29.2 (a)	12.0
Norwood	28.99	55.32	83.72	97.87	40.3	57.0	75.7	85.1	19.0 (a)	2.1
Somerville	21.83	50.00	52.77	84.00	34.3	57.0	60.6	82.0	17.0 (l)	6.0
Mean	25.46	45.42	68.21	85.18	35.9	53.9	59.6	82.0	N/A	N/A

Political Behavior, Vol. 18, No. 4, 1996

COMPARING ABSENTEE AND PRECINCT VOTERS:
Voting on Direct Legislation

Jeffrey A. Dubin and Gretchen A. Kalsow

This paper addresses issues related to how absentee voters actually cast their ballots on propositions. If the liberalization of absentee laws changed either the composition or behavior of the electorate, then the outcome of the election may be affected. This paper tests whether the electoral behavior of absentee and precinct voters differs in regards to voting on propositions. The analysis is based on a sample of actual absentee and precinct voter ballots drawn from the approximately three million ballots cast in Los Angeles county for the 1992 general election. The analysis uses a nested model of voter participation and is estimated using the weighted exogenous sampling maximum likelihood method. We find that precinct and absentee voters do differ on both the propositions on which they cast votes and in their propensity to vote "Yes" for a proposition. For example, absentees appear to vote on fewer bonds and initiatives than do precinct voters. They also vote on fewer propositions dealing with state taxes, food taxes, and property taxes. In addition, given that a voter casts a valid vote, the propensity for absentee voters to vote "Yes" is higher on initiatives and propositions related to education, welfare, and health care than it is for precinct voters.

It has been asserted that absentee voters have been the decisive group in several recent statewide candidate elections. While campaign organizers in California have demonstrated their prowess at attracting the absentee vote for candidates, they have not actively sought absentee votes for propositions. Proposition outcomes are potentially affected in at least three different ways by the recent increase in absentee voting. First, an interest group supporting a proposition could have its own absentee voter drive, or coordinate such a drive with a major candidate. Although this has not happened yet, it is surely one of the next moves being considered by proposition supporters. Second, to the extent that candidate absentee drives are successful, they may alter the composition of the electorate.

A third influence may result from absentees modifying their voting behav-

Jeffrey Dubin and Gretchen A. Kalsow, California Institute of Technology.

0190-9320/96/1200-0393$09.50/0 © 1996 Plenum Publishing Corporation

ior, as compared to their behavior as precinct voters. Hamilton (1988, p. 860) lists several advantages of all-mail elections, including "an increase in the integrity of elections as a result of more time for voters to consider issues before casting their ballots." If Hamilton is correct, then the additional time spent by absentee voters considering how to cast their ballots may result in absentees voting on different measures and casting their votes differently than if they had voted at the precinct. Thus, the pattern of votes cast and the propensity to vote "Yes" may differ when voters switch from voting at the precinct to voting at home.

In this paper we examine the voting behavior of absentee voters, as compared to precinct voters, in voting on direct legislation. Specifically, we examine differences in proposition voting behavior by analyzing the effect of proposition form (bond, legislative proposal, or initiative) and proposition content.[1] In our model of proposition voting, voters first determine whether or not the issue is important, and if so, how to cast their vote on the specific proposition. This model is depicted in Figure 1. The first decision we analyze empirically is the decision to cast a vote on a proposition. We control for a voter's demographics and socioeconomic characteristics while examining the effect of proposition form and content on the probability of casting a vote. Next we analyze the propensity to vote "Yes" conditional on voting, again investigating the impact of form and content.

Because little is known about absentee voters from prior studies of voter behavior, the focus of this paper is on discovering the rudimentary differences in the ballots cast by absentee and precinct voters. Mueller's (1969) pioneering study of voter fatigue and drop-off off employed a sample of ballots that was primarily from absentee voters, and concluded that voters do indeed drop off between candidate races and propositions.

To date, we have reached three preliminary conclusions regarding absentee voting in California. First, in more recent California elections (1988 through 1992) absentee voters in Los Angeles county voted on approximately 5% fewer propositions than did their precinct voting counterparts. Second, Dubin

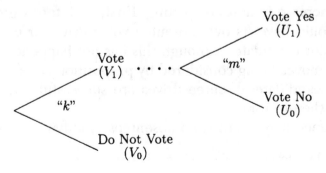

FIG. 1. Model of proposition voting.

and Kalsow (1995) find that absentee voting is a substitute activity for precinct voting in general elections, although they are not perfect substitutes. This implies that the composition of the electorate may have changed. In addition, Dubin and Kalsow find that the pool of absentee voters is not random. The propensity to vote absentee is positively related to being over 64 years old and to the presence of young children in the home. Absentee voting is also negatively related to education, being unemployed, and homeownership.

More generally, we know that voters respond differently to propositions of varying lengths, complexity, content, and form.[2] This paper addresses the question of whether the drop-off that Mueller found was an artifact of his use of absentee ballots, or if the pattern of votes on propositions is similar for absentee and precinct voters. We analyze the voting behavior of precinct and absentee voters in terms of their propensity to vote on particular propositions and their propensity to vote "Yes," given the form and content of the proposition.

The next section of this paper outlines the theory of proposition voting. The third section briefly describes the data sources and independent variables employed. The Estimation Techniques section discusses the econometric approach used to estimate our model of proposition voting and the next section highlights prior results regarding proposition voting behavior that are applicable to our model. The Hypotheses section describes the hypotheses that will be tested. The last two sections present the results, their implications on future policy, and directions for further research.

THEORY OF PROPOSITION VOTING

Relatively few studies of proposition voting have been reported. Price (1975) finds that Western states are more likely to provide for the use of initiatives, and their electorate votes on initiatives with greater frequency as compared with the behavior in Eastern states. Owens and Wade (1986) find that the probability that a proposition passes and the inflation-adjusted campaign-related expenditures have both been stable over time.[3] Zisk (1987) examines the decrease in participation on propositions compared to top candidate races by using aggregate election results and survey data from four states over five years. She finds that a voter's decision to cast a vote, vote negatively, or abstain is unrelated to proposition position. Zisk also finds support for increased levels of voting on citizen-initiated propositions over legislative proposals.

In addition to proposition voting, ballot roll-off and voter fatigue theories are relevant to our analysis. Burnham (1965) determines that roll-off and split-ticket voting have increased from 1907 to 1962. Mueller (1969) attributes roll-off to campaign spending and voting behavior on surrounding propositions. His analysis also concludes that the number of negative votes increases with ballot position.

Magleby's (1984) book, *Direct Legislation*, explores many aspects of proposition voting and reports the drop-off percentages for California propositions from 1970 to 1982. He finds evidence that longer ballots impact drop-off, but his results were not consistent across time. Magleby also reports that non-white voters vote on fewer issues, as do older voters, blue-collar voters, and low-income voters. In addition, he finds that education is positively correlated with ballot completion. These results are consistent with those of Clubb and Traugott (1972). They confirm that white, educated, higher-income, higher-social-class individuals who read the newspaper and are more interested in politics vote more often on referenda. Magleby also reports that proposition readability affects participation level, and that voters have an increased propensity to vote on initiatives over legislative proposals.

More recent work has been published by Vanderleeuw and Engstrom (1987), Darcy and Schneider (1989), and Bowler, Donovan, and Happ (1992). Vanderleeuw and Engstrom report that African-Americans roll off at faster rates than whites, even when controlling for age and education. Darcy and Schneider find that confusing and complex ballots lead to more roll-off. Bowler, Donovan, and Happ demonstrate that aggregate proposition voting is related to the total campaign spending, type of proposition, source of the proposition, length, and turnout.[4]

Using Los Angeles county data, Dubin and Kalsow (1994a) find evidence of both roll-off and ballot fatigue. *Ceteris paribus*, the probability of a voter abstaining increases further into the ballot, as does the propensity to cast a "No" vote. In addition, they find that both the form and the content of a proposition affect the propensity to vote and the propensity to vote "Yes" on a given proposition.

DATA SOURCES AND INDEPENDENT VARIABLES

The primary data source for this analysis is the ballot image files prepared by the California Secretary of State. These files contain one record for each ballot cast in the 1992 general election in Los Angeles county. A secondary data source is the decennial book on congressional districts published by Congressional Quarterly. It provides the demographic information for each congressional district. In addition, the California Secretary of State publishes the *Statement of Vote* (SOV), which provides registration and vote totals by precinct. These totals are used as a validation of the ballot image decoding process described below. The Secretary of State also provides an election ballot book that contains proposition-specific information, such as the official ballot description.

Ballot Images

Our primary data source comes from a sample of the 2,831,077 actual punch-card ballots cast in Los Angeles county in the 1992 general election. As voters turn a page in the ballot book, they also move one column to the right on the punch card, perforating the card in a specified box to indicate their vote. The evening of the election the cards are collected and transported to a central location where a machine reads the cards. As a by-product of tabulating the votes, a binary image of each ballot is written to a magnetic tape. This tape, after extensive manipulation, provides the data for this analysis.

There are several factors that complicate the decoding of ballots from the ballot image tape.[5] The first is that the ballot image tape is not used for official purposes, so its creation is often an *ad hoc* procedure. For example, if some ballots within a processing group are misfed into the reader, the entire group may be re-read. Our procedures were designed to identify and eliminate such duplications. Another complication comes from the use of ballot groups. Each unique combination of contests and rotation sequences constitutes a ballot group.[6] An additional complication is that up to four card readers can be processing ballots simultaneously, and the ballot images are written to the same tape, which means that the ballot images on the tape must be "unshuffled" into distinct precincts prior to processing.

The last step of the decoding process is to match a "correction" tape to the original precinct ballot images and compare vote counts to the SOV. The completeness and accuracy of this correction tape, and hence the match rate to the SOV, vary by election.[7]

Sampling from the Data

Since the actual 1992 general election had almost three million ballots, a sample was selected for econometric analysis. The sampling process selects ballots from each precinct whose ballot count matches that found in the SOV, and from each absentee ballot group whose ballot count matches that found in the SOV. The number of ballots selected from each precinct is proportionate to the total number of ballots cast from that precinct. A 0.21% sample of the valid precinct ballots is combined with a 1.29% oversample of the absentee ballots to create a data set of 5,028 precinct ballots and 5,009 absentee ballots. This sample of ballots is then pooled across the thirteen propositions appearing on the ballot, resulting in a total of 130,481 observations.[8]

Dependent Variables

The dependent variable for the vote decision is based on the coded response of the subject; voting either "Yes" or "No" on a specific proposition sets the "vote" indicator to "1", while abstaining or invalidating the vote sets the "vote" indicator to "0". The dependent variable for the outcome decision is set to "1" if the voter votes "Yes", and "0" otherwise, as long as the voter casts a valid vote for that proposition.

Explanatory Factors

The independent variables are one of two types: proposition-specific characteristics (Z_j for proposition j), or individual-specific variables, that is, demographics (W_i for individual i), as reported in Table 1. The proposition-specific factors include the proposition form, content, and characteristics of the official ballot description. Individual-specific variables are matched to each ballot image using an identifier for the voter's congressional district that is located on the ballot image. This is necessary since individual-level demographic information is, of course, not contained on the ballot image data.

The proposition-specific variables included in the analysis are the proposition form, content, reading ease score, and word count. The proposition form conveys information on the author or source of the proposition, as well as its relative ballot position. Bonds appear first on the ballot, then legislative proposals, and last are the initiatives.[9] Both the bonds and the legislative proposals are placed on the ballot by the state legislature, while initiatives qualify through a process involving a petition requiring an appropriate number of registered voter signatures.[10] We group the propositions into major content areas: humanitarian (education, welfare, health, and physician-assisted death), taxes (food taxes, property taxes, and state taxes), and "other" (term limits, toll roads, rail transit, and state government). The reading ease score is the Flesch score, as described in Magleby (1984). It serves as a proxy for the comprehension of the proposition's impact, while the number of English words appearing in the official ballot description is a proxy for the patience and time required to muddle through the proposition's description.

The individual-specific variables include race, socioeconomic, social connectedness, and party affiliation variables. The race variable in our model is the percentage of the population that report African-American on the census.[11] The socioeconomic factors considered are the median family income (in 0000's) and the percentage of adults over age 25 that did not complete high school. The social connectedness factors (Teixeira, 1992) include the percentage of households residing in owner-occupied housing units. We measure the conservativeness of the congressional district using the percentage of regis-

TABLE 1. Independent Variables

Variable	Definition
Absentee	Indicator for absentee voters.
Proposition Form	
Bond	Indicator for bonds.
Initiative	Indicator for initiatives.
Proposition Content	
Humanitarian	Indicator for propositions whose content deals with education, health, welfare, or physician-assisted death.
Taxes	Indicator for propositions whose content deals with state taxes, food taxes, or property taxes.
Proposition Characteristics	
Reading Ease	Flesch index score for the proposition's official ballot description (divided by 100).
English Words	Word count of the English version of the proposition's official ballot description (divided by 100).
Demographics	
African-American	% of population reporting African-American.
Median Income (0000's)	Median family income in 1989.
Low Education	% of population over age 25 not completing high school.
Homeownership	% of households residing in owner-occupied homes.
Party Affiliation	
Republican	% of registered voters that are Republican.

tered voters that are Republican. Finally, we employ an indicator for whether the voter cast an absentee ballot or not.

ESTIMATION TECHNIQUES

In this section we develop our model of proposition voting using a discrete choice econometric framework. Since, by design, our sample of the ballots cast in the 1992 general election has oversampled absentee voters, we employ a weighted exogenous maximum likelihood estimator.

Discrete-Choice Model of Proposition Voting

There are two decisions required of a voter in the voting booth—whether to cast a vote on a particular contest or not, and declaring their position on that contest. Refer to Figure 1. Let $i = 1, \ldots, I$, represent the individuals, $j = 1, \ldots, J$, the propositions. Further, let $k = 0, 1$ and $m = 0, 1$ represent the choices made by an individual voter. In the first decision $k = 1$ represents the decision to vote on a specific proposition, and $k = 0$ represents the decision to abstain. The act of voting "Yes" on a proposition is represented by $m = 1$, and "No" by $m = 0$. Recall that W_i represents the individual-specific factors and Z_j the proposition-related factors.

Let V_k represent the utility an individual voter receives from voting on a proposition. If the errors are independent, identically distributed, and from an extreme value distribution, then McFadden (1981) demonstrates that the probability of voting by the ith individual on the jth proposition is given by:

$$P_1^{ij} = \frac{e^{V_1(W_i, Z_j)}}{e^{V_1(W_i, Z_j)} + e^{V_0(W_i, Z_j)}}, \tag{1}$$

where P_1^{ij} TRIPLE LINE $P_{(k=1)}^{ij}$. We assume that $V_k(W_i, Z_j)$ is linear in its parameters, with $V_k(W_i, Z_j) = \alpha'_k W_i + \beta'_k Z_j$, where α_k and β_k are the weights given to factors W_i and Z_j, respectively. Then,

$$P_1^{ij} = \frac{e^{\alpha'_1 W_i + \beta'_1 Z_j}}{e^{\alpha'_1 W_i + \beta'_1 Z_j} + e^{\alpha'_0 W_i + \beta'_0 Z_j}}. \tag{2}$$

We impose the normalization, $\alpha_0 = \beta_0 = 0$, and let $\alpha = \alpha_1$ and $\beta = \beta_1$, so that equation (2) may be rewritten:

$$P_1^{ij} = \frac{1}{1 + e^{-[\alpha' W_i + \beta' Z_j]}}. \tag{3}$$

Similarly, if U_m denotes the utility of voting "Yes" on a proposition, then the conditional probability of voting "Yes" given that a vote is cast is given by:

$$P_{(m=1|k=1)}^{ij} = \frac{1}{1 + e^{-[\delta' W_i + \gamma' Z_j]}} \tag{4}$$

where we impose the normalizations $\delta_0 = \gamma_0 = 0$, $\delta = \delta_1$, $\gamma = \gamma_1$, and where $U_{(m|k=1)}(W_i, Z_j) = \delta'_m W_i + \gamma'_m Z_j$.

Weighting

Since our sample of absentee and precinct voters is not random, it is necessary to reweight the data in the log-likelihood function to compensate. For a random sample, the sample average log likelihood converges to

$$E[L(y; \theta)] = E[E(L(y; \theta)|x)]$$
$$= \int E[L(y; \theta)|x] r(x) dx \tag{5}$$

where $r(x)$ is the distribution of x in the population, and $L(y; \theta)$ is the sample average log-likelihood function.

When the observations come from a nonrandom sample with probability density $s(x)$, the sample average log likelihood converges to

$$\int \mathrm{E}[L(y;\theta)|x]s(x)dx. \tag{6}$$

Optimization of equation (6) with respect to θ will not in general lead to the true parameter θ_0, which is obtained when optimization is done with respect to equation (5).

When sampling weights are observed, it is possible to reweight the sample log likelihood using the weights $w(x) = r(x)/s(x)$. The weighted log likelihood $w(x)L(y; \theta)$ converges to

$$\int \mathrm{E}[L(y;\theta)w(x)|x]s(x)dx = \mathrm{E}[L(y; \theta)]. \tag{7}$$

The weighting $w(x)$ corrects for the nonrandom nature of the original sample. Let P_i^S be the probability of precinct voting in the sample for congressional district i and let $(1 - P_i^S)$ be the probability of absentee voting in the sample. Let Q_{ij}^S be the probability of voting "Yes" in the sample for congressional district i on initiative j, and let $(1 - Q_{ij}^S)$ be the corresponding probability of voting "No" in the sample. Let P_i^A and Q_{ij}^A denote the true probabilities of precinct-voting and yes-voting in the population. Then $R(x_i) = P_i^A Q_{ij}^A$ and $S(x_i) = P_i^S Q_{ij}^S$ are the unconditional sample and population probabilities for precinct and yes-voting respectively. The weighting to correct for nonrandom sampling sets

$$w(x_i) = \frac{P_i^A Q_{ij}^A}{P_i^S Q_{ij}^S} \tag{8}$$

for observations that the precinct votes "Yes." Similar weights are calculated and applied for other combinations of precinct/absentee voting and voting yes/no.[12] Estimation is performed within the *Statistical Software Tools* econometric package (Dubin and Rivers, 1988).

FACTORS AFFECTING VOTING BEHAVIOR

Prior studies of proposition voting suggest that there is a relationship between voting behavior and both proposition-specific and individual-specific variables, independent of the effects of voting absentee or voting at the precinct. The anticipated impact of the proposition-specific variables is described first. Although the individual-specific variables are not the focus of this paper, a brief discussion of their impact on voting and "Yes" is also given below.

The proposition-specific variables analyzed in previous studies include the proposition form, content, reading ease, and number of English words in the official ballot description. Voters tend to vote more often on bonds and initiatives than legislative proposals (Dubin and Kalsow, 1994a). Because many hundreds of thousands of registered voters must sign the petition for an initiative, there tends to be wider preelection visibility of initiatives as compared to legislative proposals.[13] Bonds also tend to reflect "pocketbook voting" theories since the issuance of bonds has an economic impact on each voter. In addition, as compared to legislative proposals, bonds and initiatives receive more "Yes" votes. Legislative proposals may receive higher numbers of "No" votes simply because of the reason the legislature placed those issues on the ballot. Although some legislative proposals are constitutional amendments that are required to be put before the people, many of the legislative proposals are extremely controversial issues. In fact, in some cases the legislature determines that it would cost them more political capital to cast a public vote in the legislature on the issue than it would to turn the issue over to their constituents. If this is the case, then we expect that there are more "Yes" votes on bonds and initiatives as compared to legislative proposals.

Proposition content also impacts the propensity of voters to cast votes and to vote "Yes" for a proposition. Dubin and Kalsow (1994a) find that voters tend to vote more often on issues that affect their daily lives, such as education, welfare, health, and taxes. They also find that people vote "Yes" more often on issues such as welfare and education. Although suggesting that voters will vote "Yes" less often on tax issues is consistent with "pocketbook voting," there are tax issues, such as those for cigarette and alcohol, that tend to be less related to a voter's checkbook than others such as property taxes. There are also tax issues such as proposition 163 in 1992 that repeal a tax on certain food products. As a result, it is difficult to predict the reaction of voters to tax issues in general.

The proposition characteristics also affect the propensity to vote and to vote "Yes." A proposition's reading ease and number of English words are positively and negatively related, respectively, to proposition voting (Dubin and Kalsow, 1994a). Based on our previous work we also anticipate that voting "Yes" will be positively related to reading ease and negatively related to the number of English words in the official ballot description (Dubin and Kalsow, 1994a).

The individual-specific variables that have been considered in prior studies include race, socioeconomic, and social connectedness factors. Their impact on voting and voting "Yes" on propositions varies. We anticipate a negative relationship with voting and the percentage of African-Americans (Vanderleeuw and Engstrom, 1987), a negative relationship with income (Dubin and Kalsow, 1994b), a negative relationship with education (Wolfinger and

Rosenstone, 1980), and a positive relationship with homeownership (Dubin and Kalsow, 1994b). In addition, we expect that African-Americans will vote "Yes" more often, as will those with higher incomes and lower levels of education. A negative relationship between voting "Yes" and homeownership would be consistent with our prior work.[14]

HYPOTHESES

The effect of the voting method (absentee or precinct), proposition form, content, and ballot characteristics on voting and voting "Yes" are the primary focus of this study. In this section we provide hypotheses for each of these variables as they relate to our analysis of proposition voting. In addition, we briefly discuss the impact of demographic factors and party affiliation that may be specific to absentee voters.

Since we know that absentee voters complete less of the ballot than their precinct voting counterparts, we anticipate a negative relationship between voting on propositions and absentee voting (Dubin and Kalsow, 1994a). Whether absentees actually voted "Yes" more or less often in the 1992 election depends on the specific propositions.[15] For example, if the election were to contain propositions that are conservative or pro-business, then one might expect a positive relationship between absentees and voting "Yes." This would follow if absentee voters are more conservative than precinct voters, as Cook (1991) and Willis (1994) suggest. However, the correlation at the election level depends on the composition of the entire slate of propositions.

At this point it is difficult to predict any relationship between either voting or voting "Yes" on a proposition with the proposition's form or content. Since the press attributes absentees with conservative tendencies, we might expect propositions that impose direct costs on taxpayers to receive fewer "Yes" votes by absentees. Of course, this expectation implies that absentees "suffer" from a more severe case of "pocketbook voting" than do their precinct voting counterparts. The tendency to vote "No" more often would be extended to bonds in general (proposition form) and any other propositions with potential costs, that is, those related to taxes (proposition content).

If voters select their method of voting based on an opportunity cost of time model, and if absentee voting is more convenient, then we anticipate a negative relationship between the number of English words and voting on propositions for absentees. It could also be argued that absentee voters can rely on their sample ballots and the election information sent to every registered voter in California. However, if absentee voters are truly rushed for time, the tendency to skip the propositions with the longest descriptions will outweigh any advantage of voting at home.

As far as the race, socioeconomic, and social connectedness factors are concerned, we do not hypothesize any difference in either voting or voting "Yes" between absentee and precinct voters. Prior theoretical and empirical work on absentees does not suggest any direction or significance for these relationships.

Although the popular press would project a positive relationship between absentees and Republican Party support, Dubin and Kalsow (1995) find a lack of evidence for this supposition. As the relationship between Republican registration and absentee voting is not completely described by income, education, or race, party affiliation may impact the propensity to vote and vote "Yes."[16] If we follow the pattern of higher Republican turnout in elections down to the ballot level, then Republican Party affiliation will be positively related to voting on propositions. However, as noted above with respect to the absentee variable, the statistical significance and direction of the relationship of voting "Yes" and party affiliation depends on the specific propositions on the ballot.

RESULTS

The estimated proposition voting model is given in Table 2. To analyze the effects of proposition form and content for absentee voters as compared to precinct voters we have constructed a series of hypotheses tests based on the estimated model reported in Table 2. The results of the hypothesis tests for proposition form are summarized in Table 3 and those for proposition content are in Table 4.[17] Inspecting Table 3 we find that absentee voters cast fewer votes on bonds and initiatives than do precinct voters. (Refer to the rows labeled BOND and INITIATIVE and the column labeled VOTE in Table 3.) Both cells contain negative signs, demonstrating a decreased propensity for absentee voters to cast votes for these proposition types as compared to precinct voters. Similarly, the entry found in the row labeled LEGISLATIVE PROPOSAL and the column labeled VOTE contains a zero, implying that there is no distinguishable difference in the voting behavior between absentee and precinct voters for legislative proposals. The results summarized in Table 4 indicate that absentee voters also vote more frequently on tax-related issues than do precinct voters, perhaps related to their higher incomes (Dubin and Kalsow, 1995). In addition, there does not appear to be any difference in the propensity to vote on HUMAN and OTHER propositions between absentee and precinct voters.

The results related to proposition characteristics, demographics, and party affiliation are also given in Table 2. As anticipated, the easier a proposition is to comprehend, the more often people cast votes. Our hypothesis that absentee voters may be rushed and therefore unwilling to wade through long

TABLE 2. Propensity to Vote

Variable	Estimated Coefficient	T-Statistic
Constant	1.763°°°	5.98
Absentee	−0.148	−1.25
Proposition Form		
Bond	0.187°°°	3.67
Bond ° Absentee	−0.112°	−1.65
Initiative	0.190°°°	4.13
Initiative ° Absentee	0.131°°	2.39
Proposition Content		
Humanitarian	0.453°°°	14.56
Taxes	0.237°°°	6.86
Taxes ° Absentee	0.092°°	1.99
Proposition Characteristics		
Reading Ease	0.605°°°	7.00
English Words	0.344°°	1.87
English Words ° Absentee	−0.643°°°	−2.73
Demographics		
African-American	−0.263	−1.51
Median Income	−0.124°°°	−3.08
Low Education	−0.865°°°	−2.67
Homeownership	0.505°°°	3.58
Party Affiliation		
Republican	0.755°°°	3.17
Log Likelihood—Initial		−90443
Log Likelihood—Convergence		−44543
Number of Observations		130481

°*p* = .10.
°°*p* = .05.
°°°*p* = .01.

TABLE 3. Effect of Proposition Form on Absentee Voters

Proposition Form	Vote	Vote Yes
Bond	−	−
Legislative Proposal	0	−
Initiative	−	+

Note: "+" represents an increased propensity for absentee voters to perform the specified task. A "−" implies a decreased propensity for absentee voters to perform the specified task. A "0" indicates no statistically significant effect. These measurements are made relative to the group of precinct voters.

TABLE 4. Effect of Proposition Content on Absentee Voters

Proposition Content	Vote	Vote Yes
Human: Educ., Welfare, Health	0	+
Taxes: State, Property, Food	+	−
Other	0	−

Note: "+" represents an increased propensity for absentee voters to perform the specified task. A "−" implies a decreased propensity to perform the specified task. A "0" indicates no statistically significant effect. These measurements are made relative to the group of precinct voters.

TABLE 5. Propensity to Vote Yes Conditional on Voting

Variable	Estimated Coefficient	T-Statistic
Constant	1.138°°°	5.06
Absentee	−0.118°°°	−4.54
Proposition Form		
Bond	0.102°°°	2.90
Bond ° Absentee	−0.226°°°	−5.50
Initiative	0.998°°°	31.38
Initiative ° Absentee	0.309°°°	9.90
Proposition Content		
Humanitarian	−0.560°°°	−23.30
Humanitarian ° Absentee	0.171°°°	5.38
Taxes	0.477°°°	20.35
Taxes ° Absentee	−0.096°°°	−2.98
Proposition Characteristics		
Reading Ease	0.402°°°	6.53
English Words	−3.579°°°	−30.33
Demographics		
African-American	0.507°°°	3.86
African-American°Absentee	−0.374°°°	3.77
Median Income (000's)	0.087°°°	2.86
Low Education	0.396	1.56
Homeownership	−0.457°°°	−4.35
Party Affiliation		
Republican	−0.354°°	−1.98
Log Likelihood—Initial		−79918
Log Likelihood—Convergence		−77885
Number of Observations		113359

°$p = .10.$
°°$p = .05.$
°°°$p = .01.$

propositions is supported by the negative relationship between number of English words and voting for absentees. The Republican registration variable is positively related to voting on propositions. However, Republicans who use the absentee format are no more or less likely to vote for a proposition than are the precinct-voting Republicans.

The estimates for the voting "Yes" model are given in Table 5. Tables 3 and 4 provide a summary of the results for proposition form and content on voting "Yes," under the column heading VOTE YES. The INITIATIVE row in Table 3 shows that absentee voters support initiatives more often than do precinct voters. However, the other two rows indicate that absentee voters are more inclined to oppose bonds and legislative proposals than are their precinct-voting counterparts. Absentee voters also seem to have benevolent tendencies when it comes to issues related to education, welfare, health care, and physician-assisted death. However, as the TAXES and OTHER rows indicate in Table 4, absentee voters consistently oppose taxes and other issues related to state government, toll roads, rail transit, and term limits.

The results regarding the reading ease and number of English words are consistent with our hypothesis. We find that the easier the proposition text is to read on the ballot, the more voters will support that proposition. In addition, the longer the description of the proposition, the more impatient the voter becomes, and the less support the proposition receives. One surprising result is that related to African-American absentees. Although we did not hypothesize any difference between African-American absentee voters and precinct voters, it appears that African-American absentee voters vote "No" more often than do their precinct counterparts.[18] The results of the remaining demographic variables are similar to those obtained in Dubin and Kalsow (1994a). Since the previous Dubin and Kalsow study was not an analysis specific to 1992, we find evidence that our current results are not specialized to this specific election.

DISCUSSION AND CONCLUSION

Clearly the form and content of propositions do matter when a precinct or an absentee voter is considering her option to cast a vote and whether to cast a "Yes" or "No" vote. If absentee and precinct voting are substitute activities in general elections (Dubin and Kalsow, 1995), albeit not perfect substitutes, then some individuals are simply changing their mode of voting while others are becoming voters. In addition to the changes in the composition of the electorate, however, there appear to be shifts in typical voters' behavior when they vote absentee as compared to voting at the precinct. Thus, the switch from precinct to absentee voting is not as innocuous as it first appears. The representativeness of an election is affected not only by the composition of the electorate, but also by their behavior. While the supporters of liberalizing absentee laws have claimed that it would increase the number of voters, it does not appear to have done so. Moreover, participation has in fact decreased if one counts the number of propositions on the ballot that receive notice by voters.

An important conclusion from our study is related to the conventional wisdom regarding voters and nonvoters. If voters and nonvoters have similar demographics and political attitudes, and if this pattern extends to absentee and precinct voters, then we would not expect any difference in direct legislation voting based on those factors. Our research supports this notion as we do not find any differences in absentee and precinct voters' propensity to vote or vote "Yes" based on education, income, race, homeownership, or party affiliation.

We could speculate what would have happened without the liberalization of absentee voting laws, but a more useful exercise is to investigate who will now benefit from the legislative change. If the number of absentee voters continues to increase, and if they maintain the apparent differences in voting behavior that we have found, then it may be incumbent upon interest groups and other proposition campaign groups to examine the voting behavior of absentees. If it is feasible to identify potential supporters for certain propositions, and if interest groups have the fiscal resources, then they have the opportunity to join the "get out the absentee vote" movement. Both proposition supporters and opposition groups could begin to encourage absentee voting either by independent efforts or in an alliance with a larger partisan candidate effort.

To date we have found that the representativeness of proposition outcomes may be affected by the extent of absentee voting. If absentee voters are more conservative and have higher incomes and educational levels, combined with the fact that they behave differently when voting on propositions, then election outcomes may be different than they would have been without the liberalization of absentee laws. Since ballot completion can also be considered as a stage in a political participation model, the ability to cast an absentee ballot may have actually decreased participation.

Further research is required to determine the impact of absentee voters on partisan and nonpartisan candidate races. Additionally, in recent years Californians have begun employing opposing or strategic propositions as a method for defeating other propositions. This situation leads to an opportunity for voters to vote either sincerely or strategically. Because absentee voters are voting in the comfort of their homes, their ability to sort through such competing propositions may be different than that of precinct voters. The patterns of voting on competing propositions should be examined in light of differences in voting behavior between absentee and precinct voters.

Acknowledgments. The helpful comments of Santa Traugott and seminar participants are gratefully acknowledged. An earlier version of this paper was presented at
the 1995 Annual Meeting the Midwest Political Science Association, Chicago, IL,
April 6–8, 1995.

NOTES

1. Differences in behavior related to proposition form and content may be related to the phenomenon known as roll-off and voter fatigue. See Dubin and Kalsow (1994a) for additional
   information on these topics.

2. Refer to Dubin and Kalsow (1994a) for additional information regarding an analysis of ballot
   roll-off and voter fatigue.

3. See also the studies of Wolfinger and Greenstein (1968) and Hamilton (1970) on the repeal
   of the Fair Housing Act in California.

4. Matsusaka (1992) considers the decision by elected officials to either resolve issues or place
   them before the people, and if they opt for a popular vote on an issue, why some voters then
   abstain is discussed.

5. See Dubin and Gerber (1992) for additional information on decoding these ballot images.

6. There were 235 ballot groups in the 1992 general election. The candidates are "rotated" to
   minimize any order effects. In this way any advantage to being first on the list of candidates
   is distributed among all the candidates. Each ballot group locates a particular contest in a
   different punch position, depending on both the number of previous contests and on the
   number of candidates in the previous contests.

7. For the 1992 general election we were able to match 99.5% of precincts exactly when comparing total vote counts as reported in the SOV to the number of ballot images determined
   from the ballot image tapes.

8. The mean sample and L.A. county voting percentages are 86.9% and 88.1%, respectively.
   The mean frequency of voting "Yes" on a proposition in the sample is 46.2%, and 45.8% in
   L.A. county. The completion rate across all propositions for absentee voters is 84.9%, and
   89.6% for precinct voters.

9. Since California law stipulates the order of propositions by form on the ballot, we are unable
   to identify both the form and proposition position in our model. Because bonds appear first,
   the indicator for bonds may also be viewed as an indicator for the "beginning" of the propositions. Similarly, the legislative proposal and initiative indicators could be construed as the
   "middle" and "end" of the propositions, respectively. This problem would exist in any analysis
   using a single election or series of elections where the legislature passed the bond bill before
   the required date. One notable exception to the ordering of propositions occurred in the
   1990 general election when the legislature failed to pass the bond bill in a timely fashion,
   which resulted in bonds being placed last on the ballot.

10. Refer to Fitzgerald (1980) for additional information on qualifying a proposition for the
    ballot in California.

11. Los Angeles county is racially and ethnically diverse, with large populations of Asian-Ameri-
    cans and Latino-Americans. Our models were tested with factors reflecting the percentage of
    Asian-Americans and Latino-Americans and neither factor was found to be statistically signif-
    icant.

12. Refer to Manski and Lerman (1977) for additional details regarding the weighted exogenous
    sampling maximum likelihood method.

13. California law requires signatures from registered voters to place an initiative on the ballot.

The number of signatures ranges from at least 5% of the number of ballots cast in the last gubernatorial election for statutes to 8% of the same number for constitutional amendments.

14. For a complete discussion of the effects of race and socioeconomic factors on proposition voting, see Dubin and Kalsow (1994a).

15. This analysis is conditional on the decision to vote absentee or at the precinct. Given that choice, the next decisions of whether or not to vote on a proposition and to vote "Yes" versus "No" are temporally separate. One could also examine the decision by individuals to cast absentee ballots using this data set. However, given the level of demographics that can be matched to absentee ballots, our previous county-level time-series series cross section model of absentee voting provided a better analysis of that decision. See Dubin and Kalsow (1995).

16. A regression of the log odds of Republican registration on the demographic variables accounts for approximately 46% of the variance.

17. Note that Tables 3 and 4 summarize the results in Table 2 for absentee voters relative to precinct voters. For example, the effect of voting on a bond by precinct voter is measured by the coefficient of "Bond" as reported in Table 2. However, for an absentee voter, the effect of voting on a bond is the summation of the coefficients on the "Absentee," "Bond," and "Bond • Absentee" variables reported in Table 2. Table 3 provides a summary of the net effect ("Absentee" plus "Bond • Absentee" coefficients) and the statistical significance of that net effect. For example, in the row labeled BOND and the column labeled VOTE, there is a negative sign, implying that absentee voters vote on bonds less often than do precinct voters, and this difference is statistically significant.

18. Since the effect of the other socioeconomic factors we examined did not differ between absentee and precinct voters, we tend to discount this result and regard it as plausibly spurious.

REFERENCES

Bowler, Shaun, Donovan, Todd, and Happ, Trudi (1992). Ballot propositions and information costs: Direct democracy and the fatigued voter. *Western Political Quarterly* 45: 559–568.

Burnham, Walter Dean (1965). The changing shape of the American political universe. *American Political Science Review* 59: 7–28.

California Secretary of State (1992). *Ballot Book.*

California Secretary of State (1992). *Ballot Image Rental File.*

California Secretary of State (1992). *Election Results Rental File.*

Clubb, Jerome M., and Traugott, Michael (1972). National patterns of referenda voting: The 1968 election. In *People and Politics in Urban Society* (pp. 137–169). Beverly Hills, CA: Sage Publications.

Congressional Quarterly (1993). *Congressional Districts in the 1990's.* Washington, DC: Congressional Quarterly.

Cook, Gale (1991). Mail-order voters tip the balance in close elections. *California Journal* 22: 101–103.

Darcy, R., and Schneider, Anne (1989). Confusing ballots, roll-off, and the black vote. *Western Political Quarterly* 42: 347–364.

Dubin, Jeffrey A., and Gerber, Elisabeth (1992). Patterns of voting on ballot propositions: A mixture model of voter types. Social Science Working Paper 795, California Institute of Technology.

Dubin, Jeffrey A., and Kalsow, Gretchen A. (1994a). Participation in direct legislation: Evidence from the voting booth. Mimeo, California Institute of Technology.

Dubin, Jeffrey A., and Kalsow, Gretchen A. (1994b). Racial and ethnic differences in political participation. Mimeo, California Institute of Technology.

Dubin, Jeffrey A., and Kalsow, Gretchen A. (1995). Comparing absentee and precinct voters: A view over time. Mimeo, California Institute of Technology.

Dubin, Jeffrey A., and Rivers, R. Douglas (1988). *Statistical Software Tools*. Pasadena, CA: Dubin/Rivers Research.

Fitzgerald, Maureen S. (1980). Computer democracy. *California Journal* 11: 1–15 (Special Report).

Hamilton, Howard D. (1970). Direct legislation: Some implications of open housing referenda. *American Political Science Review* 64: 124–137.

Hamilton, Randy (1988). American all-mail balloting: A decade's experience. *Public Administration Review* 48: 860–866.

Magleby, David B. (1984). *Direct Legislation*. Baltimore, MD: Johns Hopkins University Press.

Manski, C., and Lerman, S. (1977). The estimation of choice probabilities from choice-based samples. *Econometrica* 45: 1977–1988.

Matsusaka, John G. (1992). Economics of direct legislation. *Quarterly Journal of Economics* 107: 541–571.

McFadden, Daniel (1981). Econometric models of probabilistic choice. In Charles F. Manski and Daniel McFadden (eds.), *Structural Analysis of Discrete Data with Econometric Applications*. Cambridge, MA: MIT Press.

Mueller, John E. (1969). Voting on the propositions: Ballot patterns and historical trends in California. *American Political Science Review* 63: 1197–1212.

Owens, John R., and Wade, Larry, L. (1986). Campaign spending on California ballot propositions, 1924–1984: Trends and voting effects. *Western Political Quarterly* 39: 675–689.

Price, Charles M. (1975). The initiative: A comparative state analysis and reassessment of a Western phenomenon. *Western Political Quarterly* 28: 243–262.

Teixeira, Ruy (1992). *The Disappearing American Voter*. Washington, DC: Brookings Institution.

Vanderleeuw, James M., and Engstrom, Richard L. (1987). Race, referendums, and roll-off. *Journal of Politics* 49: 1081–1092.

Willis, Doug (1994). Absentee voting is increasing. *Pasadena Star-News*, October 17, Section B.

Wolfinger, Raymond E., and Greenstein, Fred I. (1968). The repeal of fair housing in California: An analysis of referendum voting. *American Political Science Review* 62: 753–769.

Wolfinger, Raymond E., and Rosenstone, Steven J. (1980). *Who Votes?* New Haven, CT: Yale University Press.

Zisk, Betty H. (1987). *Money, Media, and the Grass Roots*. Beverly Hills, CA: Sage Publications.

THREE

Twentieth-Century Voter Turnout in the United States

Most studies of twentieth-century voting in the United States are motivated by the statistic that only about half of the electorate routinely turns out to vote on Election Day. Although this may be true in the aggregate, once the data are disaggregated by region and then by state, we find much more variation than the national picture conveys. This point, often overlooked in national studies, is central to this book. By examining state participation over several decades, we can develop a finer-grained representation of national trends and better identify when and where the modern electorate began to take shape. Furthermore, disaggregating national turnout by region and state lets us begin to see how institutional configurations, created and enforced at the state level, create variability in participation rates. By offering a close examination of twentieth-century voter turnout in the American states, this chapter presents the first half of the story—variation in state voting rates.

Measuring State-Level Voter Turnout

This study examines trends in state-level voter turnout during presidential election years from 1920 to 2000 and nonpresidential election years from 1922 to 1998.[1] Voter turnout is measured as a percentage calculated by dividing the total number of votes for the highest office on the ballot by the state's voting age population.[2] For presidential election years, I used the total votes cast in the presidential race. For nonpresidential election years I used the total votes cast for a US senator. If no Senate race was held in the state, I used the total votes for governor. In a few instances a seat in the US House of Representatives was the highest office on the ballot.[3] National

Table 3.1 Regional Classification of the American States

	South
1	Alabama
2	Arkansas
3	Florida
4	Georgia
5	Louisiana
6	Mississippi
7	North Carolina
8	South Carolina
9	Tennessee
10	Texas
11	Virginia

	Midwest		West		Northeast
1	Illinois	1	Alaska	1	Connecticut
2	Indiana	2	Arizona	2	Delaware
3	Iowa	3	California	3	Maine
4	Kansas	4	Colorado	4	Maryland
5	Kentucky	5	Hawaii	5	Massachusetts
6	Michigan	6	Idaho	6	New Hampshire
7	Minnesota	7	Montana	7	New Jersey
8	Missouri	8	Nevada	8	New York
9	Nebraska	9	New Mexico	9	Pennsylvania
10	North Dakota	10	Oregon	10	Rhode Island
11	Ohio	11	Utah	11	Vermont
12	Oklahoma	12	Washington	12	West Virginia
13	South Dakota	13	Wyoming		
14	Wisconsin				

Note: This table presents the regional classification of the American states used throughout this book. It is also the regional schema employed in the American National Election Survey (ANES). As in Key (1949), in this book the South is defined as the eleven secession states.

figures were constructed by aggregating voting rates across the fifty states. Table 3.1 provides the regional classification I used.

Voter turnout is calculated as a percentage of the state's total voting age population to control for the varying sizes of states' voting age populations. The term voting age population (VAP) refers to the number of individuals who satisfy the national voting age requirement in a state.[4] Although the voting age population statistics could be inflated by including persons who satisfy the age requirement but are ineligible to vote, such as resident aliens and institutionalized citizens (Burnham 1986; McDonald 2002; McDonald and Popkin 2001), they are the most reliable measures for this project, given its eighty-year time span.

First, reliable statistics on the voting eligible population (VEP) do not exist throughout the period I studied, and they were not used in any of the historical work I cite (e.g., Black and Black 1987, 1992; Burnham 1970; Key 1949; Kleppner 1982; Lawson 1976, 1985). Employing them now would make meaningful comparisons with previous historical work difficult, and historical analysis is essential for seeing the jurisdictional variation in turnout. Additionally, the VAP and VEP statistics are highly correlated. During the years for which the VEP statistics are available, the national turnout trends (using VAP or VEP) correlate at .89, and the state-by-state trends correlate at .99. Furthermore, when the statistical models I present in this book were estimated using VEP as the dependent variable instead of VAP (for the years it is available), the findings were robust with those generated from the VAP model. This is consistent with evidence that turnout trends do not vary dramatically based on the denominator used (Patterson 2002; Wattenberg 2002). Because accurate systematic figures on eligible voters are lacking throughout the twentieth century, scholars regularly employ voting age population statistics in contemporary and historical assessments of voter registration and voter turnout (e.g., Althaus and Trautman 2008; Ansolabehere and Konisky 2006; Crocker 1996; Fitzgerald 2005; Gomez, Hansford, and Krause 2007; Knack and Kropf 2003; Teixeira 1992; Whitby 2007), and I follow suit.

Disaggregating National Turnout Trends, 1920–2000

As I noted in chapter 2, most studies of American voting point to national voting figures to demonstrate the "turnout problem" in the United States. In the aggregate, as was shown in figure 2.1, twentieth-century turnout rates appear low compared with statistics from the nineteenth century and also with rates in other industrialized democracies. By focusing solely on these aggregate figures, many conclude that Americans are characteristically nonparticipatory. This is a misleading generalization. In fact, once the national trends are disaggregated by region, as shown in figures 3.1 and 3.2, it is clear that voter turnout varied a lot throughout the century.

In fact, many regions have consistently had voter turnout well above the national average during most of the twentieth century. For example, voting rates in the Midwest were consistently, and impressively, above the national average during *all* election years from 1920 to 2000. Similarly, states in the West and Northeast had reasonably high turnout—above the national average during most of the period and converging with the national average during elections in the late 1970s through 2000. These high turnout regions, especially the Midwest, are particularly noteworthy considering

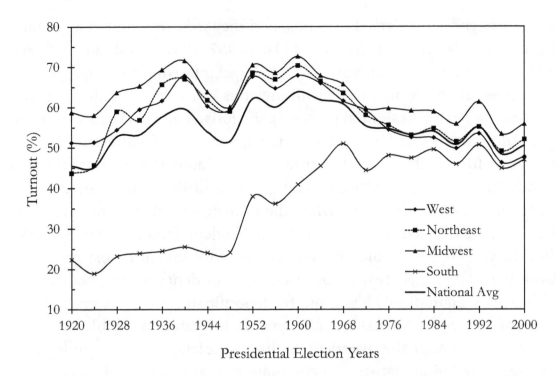

3.1. Presidential election year voter turnout trends by region, 1920–2000. (This graph and all others in this chapter are available in a larger color format at www.press.uchicago.edu/sites/springer/.)

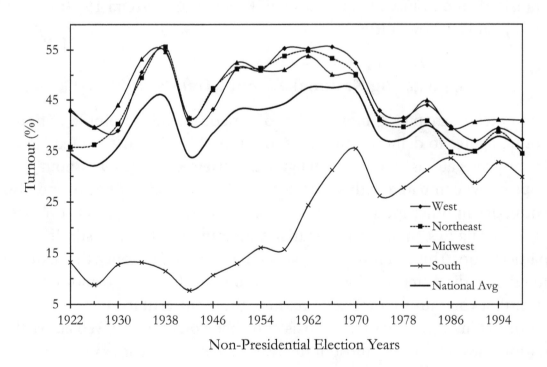

3.2. Nonpresidential election year voter turnout trends by region, 1922–98

the effect high turnout has on political outcomes. Since recent national elections have been decided by increasingly close margins, a region like the Midwest in 2000, with a turnout rate 10 percentage points above the national average, could have a real impact in determining political victories and losses. This distinction is important, yet it is routinely masked by the national figures.

Figures 3.1 and 3.2 also demonstrate that voting levels in the South were below the national average for the *entire* century. Although the regional trends begin to converge over time, narrowing the difference between southern and nonsouthern rates, especially since the late 1960s, after the enactment of the 1964 Civil Rights Act and 1965 Voting Rights Act, there is still a substantial difference between turnout in the southern and nonsouthern states (Burnham 1970; Kousser 1999; McDonald and Popkin 2001; Rusk and Stucker 1978). These figures suggest that southern voting rates have consistently depressed the national trends throughout the period. Of course voting in the South was institutionalized differently than voting in many of the other regions—a connection I will be evaluating throughout this book.

Additionally, since the regions are simply groupings of states, it is not surprising that even more variation appears when the regional trends are further disaggregated. Figures 3.3 through 3.10 illustrate that the voting rates of individual states, even within the same region, vary widely.[5] These

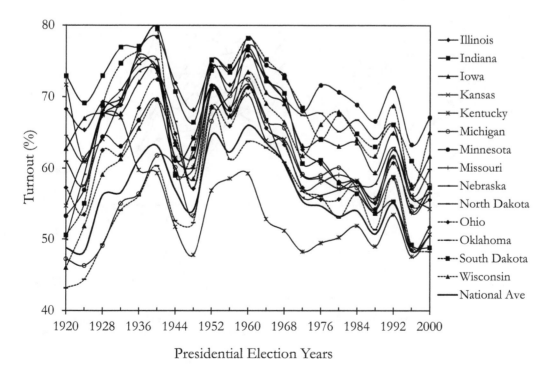

3.3. Midwestern presidential election year voter turnout trends by state, 1920–2000

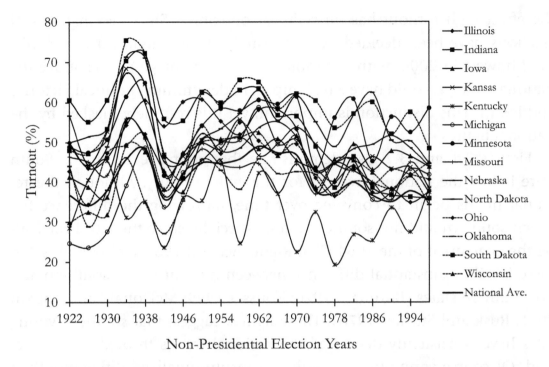

3.4. Midwestern nonpresidential election year voter turnout trends by state, 1922–98

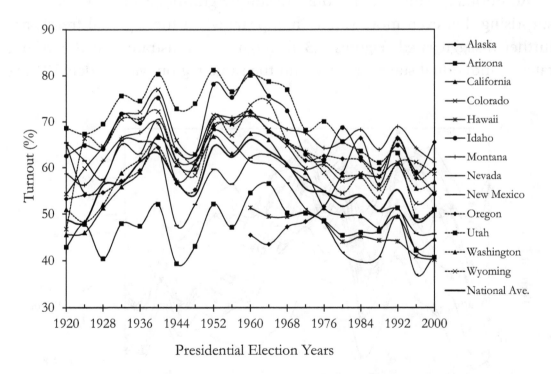

3.5. Western presidential election year voter turnout trends by state, 1920–2000

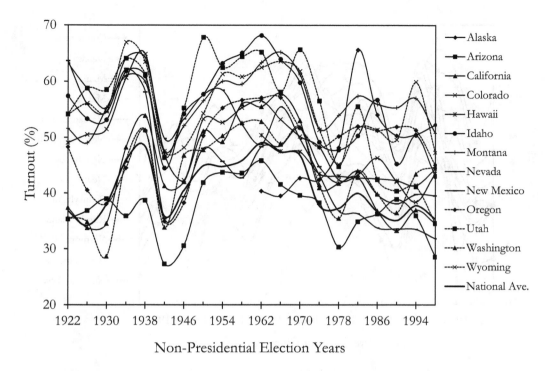

3.6. Western nonpresidential election year voter turnout trends by state, 1922–98

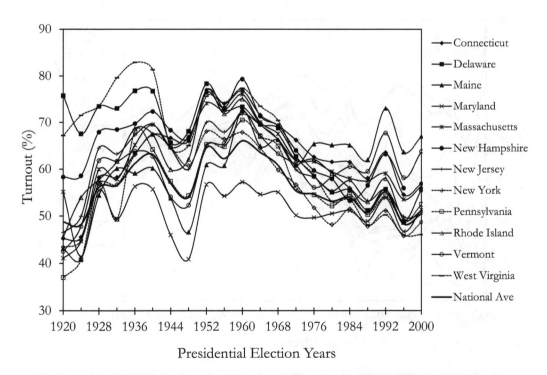

3.7. Northeastern presidential election year voter turnout trends by state, 1920–2000

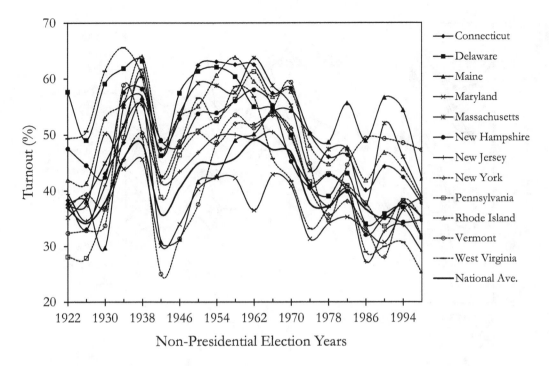

3.8. Northeastern nonpresidential election year voter turnout trends by state, 1922–98

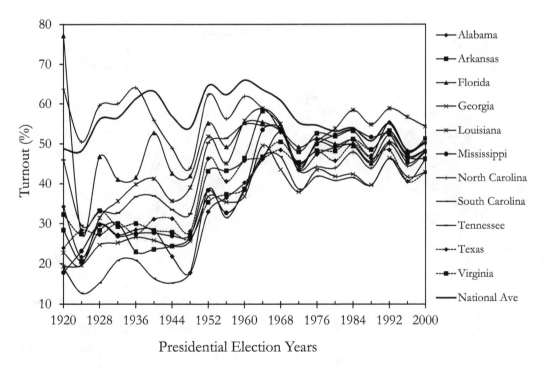

3.9. Southern presidential election year voter turnout trends by state, 1920–2000

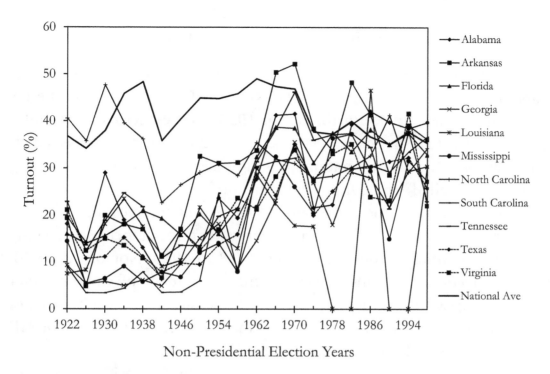

3.10. Southern nonpresidential election year voter turnout trends by state, 1922–98

disaggregated state-level trends provide an underappreciated lens for examining the nature of voting throughout the twentieth century, offering much more detail for our understanding of national turnout rates. These more nuanced trends help us identify similarities and differences between the states in political participation and also aid preliminary theorizing about why state turnout trends look the way they do.

How Do the States Fit into the National Story?

Twentieth-century voting trends have been described a number of ways, but such descriptions typically do not include the histories of individual states. This is unfortunate, since we can learn a great deal from the electoral tendencies of regions and states over time. Considering the nature of political change throughout history among, and within, the American states allows us to further examine the elements fueling political participation. Accordingly, this section situates the voting patterns of individual states within the national story, exposing the chronological boundaries of critical periods during presidential and nonpresidential election years at the state level. By evaluating the national trends from a state perspective, we gain a richer understanding of the norms of twentieth-century participation in the United States.

Presidential Election Years, 1920–2000

The American electoral landscape changed dramatically in 1920 when, after years of organization and protest, the Nineteenth Amendment to the US Constitution was ratified. In the fall of 1920, women across the country were able to vote in national elections. At first this had the unexpected effect of artificially lowering national voting rates as the size of the voting population swelled (the denominator in the turnout equation increased disproportionately to the numerator). The size of the electorate quickly normalized, however, and for the most part voter turnout increased steadily during presidential election years from 1928 to 1940. Notably, in 1928, just two elections after the universal enfranchisement of women, voter turnout increased in all the midwestern, northeastern, and southern states except Texas. In the West, voter turnout increased in all states except Arizona, Idaho, New Mexico, and Wyoming.

Then, in 1944 turnout declined at a striking rate, decreasing in all states except Arkansas, Mississippi, Texas, and Virginia. Many social and political factors may have contributed to this decline: for example, the nation's preoccupation with World War II and its aftermath, widespread internal migration throughout the United States, and perhaps most important, the fact that incumbent Franklin Delano Roosevelt was running for his fourth consecutive term as president. This decrease in voter turnout eventually bottomed out nationally in 1948 at 52%.

In 1952, during the presidential race between Dwight Eisenhower and Adlai Stevenson, voter turnout increased in all fifty states, and Eisenhower won by a landslide in every region but the South. This notable increase of nearly 10 percentage points in turnout in 1952 was likely due to Ike's unprecedented popularity and concerns regarding the Korean War. There is also some chance that turnout increased in 1952 because of the famous election miscall in 1948. Owing to a polling mishap, the headline of an early edition of the *Chicago Daily Tribune* famously read "Dewey Defeats Truman," much to Truman's glee after he won the election by 4.4%.[6] It is possible that the polling fiasco reminded people that actual votes matter more than polls, so more voters were motivated to turn out on Election Day in 1952. It is also worth noting that although at first glance the 1952 national turnout rates look unusually high, this is largely by juxtaposition with the lower than average rates in 1944 and 1948. Those low rates (54% and 52% respectively) are the outliers, not the rates for 1952. When we compare rates in 1940 (60%) with rates in 1952 (62% percent), the high in 1952 looks less striking.

Over the years that followed, participation rates experienced an ebb and flow, generally hovering around 61%, and during the close election between Kennedy and Nixon in 1960, they reached the high for the century with nearly 64% of the voting-age population turning out. In 1960 voter turnout increased in every state except Nevada. Even though many scholars use the 1960 election as a benchmark for gauging the subsequent decline in national turnout, that is somewhat misleading. In reality, the 1960 presidential election garnered the highest turnout in the United States since 1900, so one should expect rates to fall after this unprecedented peak. The 1960 election capped a nearly thirty-six-year rise in turnout and represents an impressive increase over the low points in 1920 and 1924. With the exception of 1944 and 1948, when the nation was preoccupied with World War II and its aftermath, the years between 1928 and 1960 reflect a fairly steady increase in voter turnout.

After the peak in 1960, there was a fairly steady decline in state voting rates. In 1964, the year of Lyndon Johnson's decisive victory over Barry Goldwater, voter turnout decreased in all the midwestern and northeastern states, and in 1968 turnout rates decreased again throughout these regions except in Kansas, Maine, and Maryland. During this period, however, the Civil Rights Act of 1964, the Voting Rights Act of 1965, and the subsequent ratification of the Twenty-Fourth Amendment had a pivotal and relatively swift positive effect on voting rates in the South. Indeed, in 1964, shortly after the federal legislation was implemented, turnout rates increased in ten of the eleven southern states (Alabama, Arkansas, Georgia, Louisiana, Mississippi, South Carolina, Florida, Tennessee, Texas, and Virginia), declining only in North Carolina. Turnout continued to climb in all the southern states during the 1968 election, but it fell throughout the rest of the nation—a trend that continued, more or less, for the rest of the century.

During the 1972 election, in the midst of the Vietnam War and a landslide Republican victory, turnout declined once again, in all states. This was the first election held after the Federal Voting Rights Act of 1970, which outlawed literacy tests, employed as a prerequisite for voting in many states, and also after the ratification in 1971 of the Twenty-Sixth Amendment, lowering the national voting age.[7] In fact, only 55.4% of the voting age population participated in the 1972 election, 54.7% went to the polls in 1976, and only 53.2% turned out in 1980. This marks a decrease of nearly 9 percentage points in national voter turnout since 1964—over the course of just five presidential elections. Notably, however, although turnout declined in most states in 1976, voting rates increased throughout the South, but the following years witnessed a fairly consistent decline. In 1980, 1988, and 1996, turnout was down in most states despite surprising gains in the southern states in 1984. In fact, apart from the anomalous 4% boost in national voter turnout during the 1992 election, when turnout rose in every state but Hawaii, presumably owing to Ross Perot's unprecedented third-party candidacy, and a small national increase in 2000, when states in the Northeast and South had fairly consistent increases, turnout in many states has declined or held steady during the latter part of the century.

Nonpresidential Election Years, 1922–98

Voter turnout typically is lower during nonpresidential election years than during presidential election years—averaging about 40% since 1920. Regional and state patterns are also somewhat harder to detect, given the more local aspect of these races. Although state experiences during nonpresidential election years tend to be more variable, there were a few notable trends throughout the twentieth century. For example, in 1934, amid excitement about the New Deal, voter turnout increased in all the states in the Midwest, Northeast, and West except Kentucky, Maryland, and Arizona. In 1942, during World War II, voter turnout declined in all states except Mississippi—and, conversely, in 1946 turnout rates increased in all states in the Northeast, West, and South except New Hampshire, Colorado, Mississippi, and Florida. Incidentally, in 1946 the Democrats lost a large number of seats in both the House and the Senate. In 1950 turnout rates further increased in all the northeastern, midwestern, and western states apart from Kentucky. In 1962, even before the enactment of federal civil rights and voting antidiscrimination legislation, turnout rates increased throughout the states in the South except Virginia, and in 1966, after the passage of the Civil Rights Act and Voting Rights Act, once again most southern states showed gains in participation. In 1966 voter turnout increased in Alabama, Arkansas, Georgia, Mississippi, South Carolina, Florida, Tennessee, and Virginia and declined in Louisiana, North Carolina, and Texas. In 1970, although voting rates continued to increase in Alabama, Arkansas, Georgia, Florida, South Carolina, Tennessee, Texas, and Virginia, they declined in a handful of other southern states: Louisiana, Mississippi, and North Carolina. Then in 1974, shortly after the national voting age was lowered, voter turnout declined in all states except Kentucky.

From 1978 through 1998, nonpresidential turnout rates varied considerably by state. There were not many consistent regional patterns during this time. For example, in 1982 one-third of the states in each region had increases in turnout, but in 1986 rates varied more substantially, although most of the states in the Northeast and West had declines. Similarly, in 1990 state rates in the Midwest and Northeast varied while turnout was down in all the western states but Arizona and Oregon and all the southern states except North Carolina and Texas. In 1994, turnout rates fluctuated widely outside the South, but they were up in all the southern states except Alabama and North Carolina. Finally, in 1998 regional turnout patterns varied substantially, although turnout in the Northeast was down in all states except Maryland and New Hampshire.

What States Had "High Turnout" or "Low Turnout" throughout the Century?

In this section I present state rankings to determine which states have exhibited consistently "high" or "low" turnout patterns throughout the century. To construct these rankings, I sorted the states according to their presidential and nonpresidential election year turnout, then constructed year-by-year state turnout rankings. The ten states with the highest and lowest turnout rates were identified for each election year from 1920 to 2000. Then these states were sorted based on the number of times, during the twenty-one presidential election years and twenty nonpresidential election years, they appeared in the "highest ten" or "lowest ten." Tables 3.2 and 3.3 present these rankings.

Table 3.2 shows that all the states with the most years in the highest ten category during the twentieth century were located outside the South. Remarkably, 40% of the states with consistently high turnout for 15% or more of the presidential election years from 1920 to 2000 were in the Midwest, and an additional 30% were in the Northeast and West. Further, five out of the eight states with turnout in the "highest ten" for over 50% of the presidential election years were in the Midwest.

The rankings, although similar, vary a bit more during nonpresidential election years. During these less salient elections, the western states dominated the high turnout category, with 40% of the states in the region ranking consistently high during 15% or more of the years. Additionally, 30% of these routinely high-ranking states were in the Northeast and in the West. Notably, almost all the same states were ranked in the highest ten during both presidential and nonpresidential election years. Of these twenty-six overlapping states, 38% were in the West and 31% were in the Midwest and Northeast.

On the other hand, table 3.3 reveals that all eleven southern states consistently dominated the lowest turnout category throughout the century.

Table 3.2 Ranking of States with Consistently High Turnout

State	Region	% of Years with Turnout in Highest Ten
Presidential election years:		
Utah	West	86
South Dakota	Midwest	71
Iowa	Midwest	71
North Dakota	Midwest	67
Indiana	Midwest	62
Idaho	West	57
Minnesota	Midwest	57
West Virginia	Northeast	57
Delaware	Northeast	48
Illinois	Midwest	48
Connecticut	Northeast	43
New Hampshire	Northeast	43
Montana	West	38
Maine	Northeast	33
Wisconsin	Midwest	29
Oregon	West	24
Wyoming	West	24
Alaska	West	19
Nebraska	Midwest	19
Vermont	Northeast	19
Colorado	West	14
Kansas	Midwest	14
Massachusetts	Northeast	10
Missouri	Midwest	10
New Mexico	West	10
Kentucky	Midwest	5
Nevada	West	5
New York	Northeast	5
Ohio	Midwest	5
Rhode Island	Northeast	5
Washington	West	5
Nonpresidential election years:		
Wyoming	West	85
Montana	West	80
South Dakota	Midwest	80
Idaho	West	70
North Dakota	Midwest	65
Utah	West	65
Indiana	Midwest	60
Connecticut	Northeast	50
Delaware	Northeast	40
Minnesota	Midwest	40
Nevada	West	40
Massachusetts	Northeast	35
Alaska	West	30
Maine	Northeast	30
Nebraska	Midwest	30

Oregon	West	30
Rhode Island	Northeast	30
West Virginia	Northeast	25
Illinois	Midwest	20
New Mexico	West	20
Vermont	Northeast	20
Colorado	West	15
Kansas	Midwest	15
California	West	5
New Hampshire	Northeast	5
Pennsylvania	Northeast	5
Washington	West	5
Wisconsin	West	5

Note: States in boldface were ranked in the "highest ten" during both presidential and nonpresidential election years from 1920 to 2000.

Table 3.3 Ranking of States with Consistently Low Turnout

State	Region	% of Pres Years with Turnout in Lowest Ten
Presidential election years:		
Georgia	South	100
South Carolina	South	100
Texas	South	100
Virginia	South	76
Alabama	South	71
Mississippi	South	71
Arkansas	South	67
Tennessee	South	67
Florida	South	62
Louisiana	South	62
Hawaii	West	82
Arizona	West	33
Nevada	West	33
North Carolina	South	33
California	West	24
Alaska	West	27
Kentucky	Midwest	10
New Mexico	West	10
New York	Northeast	10
West Virginia	Northeast	10
Pennsylvania	Northeast	5
Nonpresidential election years:		
Georgia	South	100
Louisiana	South	95
South Carolina	South	95
Texas	South	95
Virginia	South	95

(continued)

Table 3.3 (*continued*)

State	Region	% of Pres Years with Turnout in Lowest Ten
Mississippi	South	90
Florida	South	70
Tennessee	South	70
Alabama	South	65
Arkansas	South	50
North Carolina	South	50
Kentucky	Midwest	30
Arizona	West	20
West Virginia	Northeast	20
Maryland	Northeast	15
New Jersey	Northeast	15
Delaware	Northeast	5
Missouri	Midwest	5
Nevada	West	5
New Hampshire	Northeast	5
New York	Northeast	5

Note: States in boldface were ranked in the "lowest ten" during both presidential and nonpresidential election years from 1920 to 2000.

In fact, Georgia was ranked among the lowest ten during all the presidential *and* nonpresidential election years from 1920 to 2000. Similarly, South Carolina and Texas were among the lowest ten during all the presidential election years during this period. Also, a handful of nonsouthern states ranked among the lowest turnout states during several presidential election years. For example, Arizona and Nevada were both in the lowest ten during presidential and nonpresidential election years throughout the period, and so were New York and West Virginia.

State Turnout Trends Compared with the National Average

This section highlights both the consistency of the high and low turnout rankings throughout the century (How often is turnout in the state above or below the national average?) and the magnitude of the classifications (How high and low are state turnout rates comparatively?). Appendix A (available online only: www.press.uchicago.edu/sites/springer/) provides individual state-by-state graphs of state voter turnout compared with the national average from 1920 to 2000. Table 3.4 provides the national average statistics for each election year so that the turnout percentages (compared

Table 3.4 Average National Voter Turnout (%)

Year	Voter Turnout (%)
Presidential election years:	
1920	45.49
1924	45.19
1928	52.77
1932	53.25
1936	57.68
1940	59.65
1944	53.98
1948	51.63
1952	62.13
1956	60.08
1960	63.85
1964	61.86
1968	60.82
1972	55.38
1976	54.67
1980	53.20
1984	53.99
1988	50.73
1992	55.10
1996	48.33
2000	50.51
Nonpresidential election years:	
1922	34.42
1926	32.07
1934	43.17
1938	45.58
1942	33.90
1946	38.50
1950	43.04
1954	43.09
1958	44.28
1962	47.38
1966	47.37
1970	46.83
1974	37.73
1978	37.25
1982	39.96
1986	36.68
1990	35.08
1994	37.76
1998	35.35

with the national average) discussed can be translated into actual turnout statistics.

High Turnout during Presidential Election Years, 1920–2000

As shown in appendix A and summarized in table 3.5, several of the states in the Midwest and West had voter turnout above the national average during *all* the presidential election years from 1920 to 2000. Nine of the fourteen midwestern states had trends above the national average during all presidential election years. Of the thirteen western states, six are in this category. States in the Northeast and South do not fare as well in the high turnout category. In fact, only two northeastern states had high turnout during all presidential election years, and the South had no such states. There are six additional states with turnout trends above the national average in *all but one* of the presidential election years.

It is also important to assess the magnitude of these trends. Aside from having routinely high turnout, most of the midwestern states had particularly high turnout compared with the national average. This is especially true in the nine states listed in table 3.5. For example, appendix A shows that during *all* presidential election years Iowa's turnout ranged from 8% to 22% above the national average, Minnesota's rates were 7% to 17% above, North Dakota's were 5% to 18% above, and South Dakota's rates were 5% to 22% above. The magnitude of these trends demonstrates that not only were voting rates consistently high in the Midwest, they have been substantially higher than the national average during most of the presidential election years throughout the century.

As shown in appendix A, twelve of the thirteen western states had voter turnout above the national average during some subset of presidential election years from 1920 to 2000. Similar to the states in the Midwest, many of the western high turnout states, noted in table 3.5, routinely demonstrated turnout well above the national average. For example, during *all* presidential election years, Colorado's voting rates were 4% to 18% above the national average, and Idaho's rates were 4% to 20% above. Further, Montana's turnout ranged from 8% to 16% above the national average during all presidential years except 1944, and Wyoming's ranged from 4% to 21% above in all years except 1920 and 1980.

As also noted in table 3.5, five northeastern states were in the high turnout category, experiencing rates above the national average during all, or all but one, of the presidential election years from 1920 to 2000. Although the turnout trends in the Northeast vary a bit more in magnitude than those

Table 3.5 High Turnout States Compared with the National Average

Region/State	Presidential Election Years		Nonpresidential Election Years	
	Above National Average All Years	Above National Average All But 1 Year	Above National Average All Years	Above National Average All But 1 Year
Midwest:				
Illinois	X	...	...	X
Indiana	...	X	...	X
Iowa	X	...	...	...
Kansas	X	...	...	X
Kentucky	...	...	...	...
Michigan	...	...	...	...
Minnesota	X	...	X	...
Missouri	X	...	...	...
Nebraska	...	X	X	...
North Dakota	X	...	X	...
Ohio	X	...	...	...
Oklahoma	...	...	...	...
South Dakota	X	...	X	...
Wisconsin	X	...	...	...
West:				
Alaska	...	...	...	...
Arizona	...	...	...	...
California	...	...	...	...
Colorado	X	...	X	...
Hawaii	...	...	X	...
Idaho	X	...	X	...
Montana	X	...	X	...
Nevada	...	...	...	...
New Mexico	...	...	...	X
Oregon	X	...	...	X
Utah	X	...	...	X
Washington	...	X	...	...
Wyoming	X	...	X	...
Northeast:				
Connecticut	...	X	X	...
Delaware	X	...	...	...
Maine	...	...	...	...
Maryland	...	...	...	...
Massachusetts	...	...	X	...
New Hampshire	...	X	...	...
New Jersey	...	X	...	...
New York	...	...	...	...
Pennsylvania	...	...	...	...
Rhode Island	X	...	X	...
Vermont	...	...	...	...
West Virginia	...	...	...	...

Note: States in boldface had "above average" turnout during both presidential and nonpresidential election years from 1920 to 2000. None of the southern states had voter turnout trends warranting inclusion in this table.

in the Midwest or West, the northeastern voting rates tend to be substantially above average throughout the century and are particularly impressive during several presidential election years. For example, Delaware and Rhode Island are the only states in the Northeast with turnout well above the national average during all presidential election years. Notably, turnout in Delaware ranged a striking 7% to 30% above the national average from 1920 to 1972, and Rhode Island's rates ranged from 5% to 15% above from 1924 to 1980.

High Turnout during Nonpresidential Election Years, 1922–98

As shown in table 3.5, many states in the Midwest, West, and Northeast also demonstrated voter turnout well above the national average during *all* the nonpresidential election years from 1922 through 1998. When the classification is expanded to include states with turnout trends above the national average in *all but one* year, the list grows in the Midwest and West. There are no states in the South that can be classified as high turnout during nonpresidential election years from 1922 to 1998. One should also note that many of the high turnout states during nonpresidential election years were also high turnout states during presidential election years. These consistently high turnout states during both types of elections are noted in boldface in table 3.5. The South has no such states.

It is clear that most of the states in the high turnout classification during nonpresidential years are in the Midwest and West: 50% of the midwestern states had voting rates above the national average during nonpresidential election years, and the magnitude of these trends is impressive. For example, during all nonpresidential election years from 1922 to 1998, Minnesota's rates were well above the national average, ranging from 6% to 23% above, and Nebraska's turnout ranged from about 4% to 24% above. North Dakota's and South Dakota's rates also remained above the national average during all nonpresidential years from 1922 to 1998. North Dakota's turnout ranged between 6% and 28% above the national average, and South Dakota's rates were 3% to 32% above.

In addition to the midwestern states, eight of the fourteen western states also displayed voter turnout above the national average during nonpresidential election years from 1922 to 1998. For example, Hawaii's voting rates ranged about 1% to 9% above the national average from 1962, during its first nonpresidential election after gaining statehood, through 1998. And perhaps most striking, during *all* nonpresidential election years, Colorado's rates ranged from 1% to 19% above the national average, Idaho's voter turnout ranged from 8% to 23% above, Montana's rates ranged from 14% to 20% above, and Wyoming's rates ranged from 8% to 24% above.

Last, three of the twelve northeastern states displayed voting rates above the national average during *all* nonpresidential election years. Specifically, Connecticut's turnout ranged from 1% to 20% above the national average, rates in Massachusetts ranged from 1% to 17% above, and Rhode Island's turnout was 3% to 20% above the national average. So it appears that many states in the Northeast, like their western and midwestern counterparts, have been in the high turnout category during nonpresidential election years throughout the century and have had turnout rates substantially above the national average. Furthermore, many of these states displayed rates considerably above the national average during *both* presidential and nonpresidential election years.

Low Turnout during Presidential Election Years, 1920–2000

There is much more variation in states with "low voter turnout" during presidential election years. As shown in table 3.6, only a few states had turnout consistently below the national average during *all* presidential years from 1920 through 2000. In the West, Hawaii consistently experienced below average turnout since gaining statehood in 1959. In the South, seven states are in the low turnout category during *all* presidential election years from 1920 to 2000. Once the definition is expanded to include states with trends below the national average in *all but one* presidential year, four states—three southern and one western—are added to the list. None of the states in the Midwest or Northeast displayed voting rates consistently below the national average during all, or all but one, of the presidential election years.

As shown in table 3.6, only two of the thirteen western states consistently fall into the low turnout category throughout the period. In the West, Arizona's voting rates fell 3% to 15% below the national average during all years except 1924, and Hawaii's rates were 5% to 13% below during the first presidential election after it gained statehood in 1960 and remained low until 2000. The infrequency of low turnout trends in the nonsouthern states underscores the tendency of midwestern, northeastern, and western states to have high, or above average, voter turnout throughout the twentieth century.

The southern states, however, fell disproportionately into the low turnout category, and in most cases their turnout was substantially below the national average. For example, during *all* presidential election years,

Table 3.6 Low Turnout States Compared with the National Average

Region/State	Presidential Election Years		Nonpresidential Election Years	
	Below National Average All Years	Below National Average All But One Year	Below National Average All Years	Below National Average All But One Year
South:				
Alabama	. . .	X	. . .	. . .
Arkansas	X	. . .	. . .	. . .
Florida	X	. . .	. . .	. . .
Georgia	X	. . .	X	. . .
Louisiana	. . .	. . .	. . .	X
Mississippi	. . .	X	X	. . .
North Carolina	X	. . .	. . .	X
South Carolina	X	. . .	. . .	X
Tennessee	X	. . .	. . .	X
Texas	X	. . .	X	. . .
Virginia	. . .	X	. . .	X
West:				
Alaska	. . .	. . .	. . .	. . .
Arizona	. . .	X	. . .	. . .
California	. . .	. . .	. . .	. . .
Colorado	. . .	. . .	. . .	. . .
Hawaii	X	. . .	. . .	. . .
Idaho	. . .	. . .	. . .	. . .
Montana	. . .	. . .	. . .	. . .
Nevada	. . .	. . .	. . .	. . .
New Mexico	. . .	. . .	. . .	. . .
Oregon	. . .	. . .	. . .	. . .
Utah	. . .	. . .	. . .	. . .
Washington	. . .	. . .	. . .	. . .
Wyoming	. . .	. . .	. . .	. . .

Note: States in boldface had "below average" turnout during both presidential and nonpresidential election years from 1920 to 2000. None of the midwestern or northeastern states had voter turnout trends warranting inclusion in this table.

Georgia's turnout ranged from 7% to 42% below the national average, South Carolina's turnout fell 5% to 50% below, and Texas's rates were 4% to 34%. Several other southern states had turnout dramatically below the national average for a subset of years. For example, Arkansas's voting rates fell 10% to 41% below the national average from 1920 to 1964 and 1% to 8% below from 1968 to 2000, and Virginia's turnout fell 2% to 38% below from 1920 to 1992. These trends illustrate that not only was voter turnout in the South remarkably low, especially compared with the rates in most of the midwestern and western states, but the turnout trends are substantially below average throughout the entire presidential series.

Low Turnout during Nonpresidential Election Years, 1922–98

Voter turnout varies more during nonpresidential election years. As shown in table 3.6, only three states—all southern—had voter turnout below the national average during *all* the nonpresidential election years during the twentieth century. During these years, Georgia's turnout ranged from 5% to 42% below the national average, rates in Mississippi were 1% to 43% below, and Texas's rates ranged from 4% to 36% below. When states with trends below the national average in *all but one year* are included, five more states are added. As shown in appendix A, South Carolina's turnout rates ranged from 4% to 41% below the national average and exceeded the national average only once, in 1998. Similarly, Virginia's rates were 4% to 37% below the national average in all years but 1994, and Tennessee's rates ranged from about 1% to 31% below during all nonpresidential election years except 1994. It is worth noting that none of these states surpassed the national average during these election years by 5% or more. Like the presidential election year trends, the nonpresidential patterns illustrate that turnout rates not only are below average in most of the southern states, they are dramatically below average.

Taken together, the state trends described here and presented in appendix A reveal that most of the states have distinct patterns of change relative to the nation. Some start with higher turnout and then merge with the national level. For example, West Virginia begins with turnout higher than the nation and ends the century with below-average turnout, whereas some states like Utah and South Dakota are consistently higher than the nation. It also illustrates that the South's negative deviation from the national average throughout the twentieth century was far greater than the positive deviations in the Midwest and West. Many expect voter turnout in the South to be low, but appendix A demonstrates how severe the difference was. The following chapters aim to determine the extent to which changes in electoral rules versus population characteristics versus electoral competitiveness can account for the divergent patterns of state turnout relative to national turnout.

Conclusion

This chapter has shown the importance of studying variation in voter turnout across the American states, rather than only national trends, and of using a historical perspective to understand twentieth-century voting patterns. Most of the previous scholarship on voter turnout in the United States has focused on the national level, offering little information on how the states are distinctive within the national trends. This is a vital omission. As this chapter has demonstrated, a great deal of variation exists within regional and state-level turnout patterns; this variation has been masked by studies conducted at the aggregate level. When we disaggregate these trends it becomes clear that two radically opposed trends persisted throughout the century: the consistently high turnout rates in the nonsouthern states—especially in the Midwest—and the remarkably low turnout rates in the southern states during both presidential and nonpresidential election years. The components fueling this variation demand further analysis. The variation in turnout rates between the southern and nonsouthern regions, and the seeming consistency of high and low turnout tendencies within many individual states could be associated with several aspects of state and electoral politics. High or low turnout could be attributed to electoral institutions, political competition, mobilization, or—most realistically—some combination of these elements. This study focuses on the effects of political institutions and evaluates how they might have influenced participation in the states over time and contributed to the state-level variation this chapter illuminates.

Of course, we can make a preliminary assessment of the relationship between state turnout trends and electoral institutions. As this chapter has shown, most states with voter turnout consistently, and usually substantially, above the national average are in the midwestern and western United States. This tendency warrants further investigation. If the high turnout states in the Midwest and West tend to have disproportionately expansive voting laws, then perhaps there is a link between electoral institutions and participation rates.[8] Further, this chapter has demonstrated that the only states with consistently low turnout during all presidential and nonpresidential elections are in the South. This does not seem accidental. The southern tendency to discriminate against and disenfranchise blacks, and in many cases poor whites, was broad and relentless. Jim Crow laws in the South, particularly those relating to voting rights, surely affected political participation in the region. Accordingly, we might expect voter turnout to be disproportionately lower in the southern states because of racist disenfranchising rules that made voting exorbitantly costly for some citizens; and one might contend that turnout rates are higher in the western and midwestern states because voting laws there have been historically expansive, so that the costs of voting are comparatively low and a commitment to voting is high. Although these connections are speculative at this point, even a sweeping institutional characterization of voting laws and norms in these regions seems to connect with the observed voting patterns presented throughout this chapter. At a minimum, they warrant further investigation.

Chapter 4 examines the origin and historical evolution of a variety of restrictive and expansive electoral institutions that have structured voting and elections within individual states. This in-depth discussion character-izes state electoral institutions independent of participation trends, chroni-cles how dramatically state registration and voting processes have changed throughout the century, and frames the empirical analyses of the effects of state electoral institutions on state turnout presented in later chapters.

Getting Out the Vote in Local Elections: Results from Six Door-to-Door Canvassing Experiments

Donald P. Green
Alan S. Gerber
David W. Nickerson
Yale University

Prior to the November 6, 2001 elections, randomized voter mobilization experiments were conducted in Bridgeport, Columbus, Detroit, Minneapolis, Raleigh, and St. Paul. Names appearing on official lists of registered voters were randomly assigned to treatment and control groups. A few days before Election Day, the treatment group received a face-to-face contact from a coalition of nonpartisan student and community organizations, encouraging them to vote. After the election, voter turnout records were used to compare turnout rates among people assigned to treatment and control groups. Consistent with the recent experimental results reported by Gerber and Green (2000b), the findings here indicate that face-to-face voter mobilization was effective in stimulating voter turnout across a wide spectrum of local elections.

Among the many distinctive attributes of American federalism is the frequency with which elections are held. Due to a profusion of state, municipal, and primary elections, the American voter has more opportunities to cast ballots than citizens of any other country. However, few Americans avail themselves of these abundant opportunities. Voter turnout slumps from presidential election years to even-numbered midterm elections. And in off-years, during which many local and some state elections are held, turnout levels fall even lower (Morlan 1984). Despite the immediate relevance of local issues to voters' lives, the typical U.S. municipal election draws between one-fifth and one-half of the *registered* electorate.

As Harold Gosnell (1927) noted in his path-breaking study of voter mobilization in Chicago during the 1924 and 1925 elections, the quiescence of local elections makes them ideal laboratories for studying methods for increasing voter turnout. Amid limited campaigning and few newsworthy political events, the effects of interventions designed to increase turnout are more readily detected. In addition, low voter turnout rates reduce statistical uncertainty, which is maximal when half of the sample casts ballots. Despite these advantages, local elections tend to attract little attention from students of politics, except insofar

THE JOURNAL OF POLITICS, Vol. 65, No. 4, November 2003, Pp. 1083–1096
© 2003 Southern Political Science Association

as they involve heated racial politics or other circumstances that make them atypical.

In recent years, the study of electoral turnout has increasingly focused on the subject of voter mobilization. Building on the early works of Gosnell (1927) and Eldersveld (1956), the recent scholarship of Rosenstone and Hansen (1993), Verba, Schlozman, and Brady (1995), and Putnam (2000) has emphasized the responsiveness of voters to their social and political environments. A citizen's level of electoral participation and civic engagement more generally is said to respond to blandishments from family members, political parties, and social networks. By implication, a dearth of mobilization activities may account for the low voter turnout rates typical of local elections.

The present study is patterned after the recent field experimental work of Gerber and Green (2000b). Examining the effects of nonpartisan get-out-the-vote (GOTV) drives on voter turnout in the 1998 midterm elections in New Haven, Gerber and Green found that face-to-face canvassing raised turnout rates from approximately 44% in the control group to 53% among those canvassed. This randomized experiment, which involved tens of thousands of registered voters, provides the clearest indication to date of the effectiveness of face-to-face mobilization, although the authors point out that one must be cautious about drawing generalizations based on a single study.

This essay provides six replications of the Gerber and Green (2000b) experiments, spanning a range of competitive and uncompetitive local elections. During the months leading up to the November 6, 2001 election, we collaborated with a variety of nonpartisan organizations to examine the effectiveness of door-to-door canvassing. Names appearing on lists of registered voters were randomly assigned to treatment and control groups. Treatment groups were visited during the days leading up to the election. Control groups were not contacted. After the election, we obtained voter turnout records from each county and calculated the turnout rates in each control and treatment group. It should be stressed that in contrast to most survey-based analyses of voter mobilization, our study does not rely on voters' self-reported turnout or self-reported contact with GOTV campaigns.

This essay begins with a brief overview of our statistical model and estimation procedure. Next, we describe the experiments conducted at each of the face-to-face canvassing sites. We then analyze the effectiveness of the get-out-the-vote campaign in each site and for the sample as a whole. The results indicate that canvassing significantly increases voter turnout across a range of political and social environments. These mobilization effects are significant, both substantively and statistically, and similar in magnitude to other recent experiments (Gerber and Green 2000b; Michelson 2003).

Research Design and Statistical Model

Unlike observational studies of voter mobilization, which examine the correlation between voting and contact with campaigns, experimental studies randomly manipulate whether voters are approached by campaigns. Experimental control eliminates two problems associated with observational data. First, if campaigns target voters who are especially likely to go to the polls, the observed correlation between contact and voter turnout may be spurious. We might observe a strong correlation even if GOTV campaigns were ineffective. Second, if respondents' recollections of whether they were contacted is vague or distorted, the correlation between self-reported contact and turnout will misrepresent the true causal influence of contact.

The principal complication that arises in experimental studies of voter mobilization is that some citizens assigned to the treatment group cannot be reached. We must therefore distinguish between the intent-to-treat effect and the effects of actual contact. The intent-to-treat effect is simply the observed difference in voter turnout between those assigned to the treatment and control groups. If everyone in the treatment group is actually contacted, the intent-to-treat effect is identical to the actual treatment effect. In practice, however, contact rates are lower than 100% because target voters are often unavailable when canvassers visit their residences.

Consider the linear probability model,

$$Y = a + bX + u, \tag{1}$$

where Y is a dichotomous $\{0,1\}$ variable indicating whether a citizen cast a vote, and $X \in \{0,1\}$ represents whether he or she was actually contacted by a canvassing campaign. The coefficient b is the treatment effect, the boost in turnout caused by contact with the mobilization campaign. Contact is itself a function of whether a person was assigned to the treatment or control condition of the experiment. Let the variable Z, also a dichotomous $\{0,1\}$ variable, represent the random assignment to one of these experimental groups, such that

$$X = cZ + e. \tag{2}$$

To estimate the actual treatment effect (b) given a contact rate (c), we must adjust the intent-to-treat effect (t) as follows:

$$t/c \Rightarrow b. \tag{3}$$

In other words, to estimate the actual treatment effect, we take the intent-to-treat estimate and divide it by the observed contact rate. This estimator is equivalent to performing a two-stage least-squares regression of vote (Y) on actual contact (X) using randomization (Z) as an instrumental variable (Angrist, Imbens, and Rubin 1996; Gerber and Green 2000b). So long as we have information about the rate at which subjects assigned to the treatment group are actually contacted by the canvassers, we can accurately estimate the effects of contact.

A similar approach may be used for nonlinear probability models. One complication in studying local elections is that voter turnout tends to be very low, particularly among certain subgroups such as registered voters who did not vote in a previous national election. OLS may produce inadmissible predictions that voting will occur with less than zero probability. Rivers and Vuong (1988) propose a two-stage conditional probit estimator that parallels the instrumental variables estimator described above.[1] The probit transformation ensures that predicted vote probabilities are confined to the range between 0 and 1.

Door-to-Door Canvassing Sites

Using official lists of voters gathered immediately after the close of registration, we compiled a database of registered voters' names and addresses. Names of individuals residing at the same address were grouped into households, which were in turn grouped geographically into walk lists. We restricted our attention to households with fewer than five registered voters, and in two sites, Raleigh and St. Paul, the population was restricted to households with at least two voters. One registered voter from each household was selected for study, and these voters were randomly assigned to treatment and control groups. The walk lists given to canvassers contained the names and addresses of people in the treatment group, and they were instructed to approach only these residences.

Although the canvassing sites cannot be construed as a random sample of municipal elections occurring nationwide, our study is strengthened by the fact that the get-out-the-vote campaigns took place in very different political and demographic settings. Some elections were tightly contested; others were devoid of meaningful competition. Some sites have large populations of racial and ethnic minorities; others are predominantly white. Our aims in drawing from such a diverse collection of sites are twofold: to better gauge the average treatment effect of canvassing and to examine whether the treatment effects vary systematically with electoral competitiveness or other characteristics of the sites.

Site 1: Bridgeport, Connecticut. Bridgeport is a racially diverse, low-income urban area that votes overwhelmingly Democratic. The November 6 election featured a local school board election and local city council races. Due to the city's lopsided Democratic majority, all but one of these races were uncompetitive, and the remaining election occurred in a district that was outside the area we canvassed. Turnout, as expected, was low.

ACORN, a community organization championing the interests of low- and moderate-income families, conducted a door-to-door campaign in hopes of generating sufficient support among voters for a "living wage" ordinance (raising the minimum wage to $11.08 per hour) that had been introduced in the city council earlier in the year. Beginning on October 20th and each weekend thereafter, ACORN volunteers followed walk lists urging every treatment household to vote in the upcoming election.

ACORN did not field many volunteers, but those who participated were experienced and well trained. These volunteers, a diverse group of African Americans

---

[1] Estimates produced by the Rivers and Vuong method turn out to be almost identical to those obtained using maximum likelihood.

and Latinos, were largely female high-school graduates in their 30s and 40s. Some but not all of the canvassers spoke Spanish.

Site 2: Columbus, Ohio. The neighborhoods canvassed in Columbus were near The Ohio State University campus and tended to be heavily populated by students. Since the Franklin County Clerk only recently began collecting data on birth dates, the age of the voters contacted cannot be determined from voter registration records. Based on the observations of those who conducted the canvassing, it appears that the majority of those canvassed were 25 years old or younger. The only election on the slate was for City Council. Despite the at-large format of the city council election, the races were not competitive, and turnout was expected to be low.

Canvassing occurred during the weekend prior to the election. The canvassers were recruited from the local Public Interest Research Group (PIRG) chapter and volunteers from around campus. Unlike the canvassers in Bridgeport, the Columbus canvassers had little political experience. Only one of the volunteers had ever gone door-to-door for any purpose.

Site 3: Detroit, Michigan. With a closely contested mayoral race, the Detroit elections were among the most interesting in 2001. As in Bridgeport, canvassing was conducted under the auspices of ACORN. However, the crew of canvassers, who were predominantly young, African American, and female, had no previous political experience. After receiving a half-hour training session, the canvassers took to the streets during the weekend prior to Election Day, canvassing all day Saturday, Sunday, and Monday.

Site 4: Minneapolis, Minnesota. Minneapolis elected a wide array of officials in 2001: mayor, city council, school board, and the boards governing city parks, library, and taxation. Turnout was expected to be moderate by local election standards. The neighborhood canvassed was racially mixed and working class. Canvassing was conducted on the Saturday before Election Day by the Twin Cities PIRG chapter. Most canvassers were white college students with no previous experience with door-to-door activity.

Site 5: St. Paul, Minnesota. This election focused solely on the mayor's office, and the race was expected to be very close. As it happened, only 400 votes eventually separated the winner and the loser—a mere 0.6%. Two neighborhoods were canvassed, a poor racially mixed neighborhood and a predominantly white working-class neighborhood.

The local PIRG chapter again organized the canvassing effort with a slightly broader range of volunteers drawn from both colleges and community organizations. The canvassers were inexperienced but received a brief training session before venturing into the field during the Sunday before Election Day.

Site 6: Raleigh, North Carolina. In Raleigh, our canvassing experiment focused on a municipal run-off election. Rather than holding conventional municipal primary elections, Raleigh conducts an all-comers election the first Tuesday of October. In the event that no candidate receives an outright majority, the two top candidates advance to an Election Day run-off. Both the mayoral and the city council elections featured closely contested races.

Canvassing focused on two neighborhoods, one racially mixed and the other predominantly white. Raleigh was the only site where canvassers were paid an hourly wage ($10 an hour). Half of the canvassers assembled by the local PIRG group were students (mostly North Carolina State University), and half were members of the community. One-third of the canvassers were African American. Only 20% of the canvassers had any experience in canvassing, and the overwhelming majority responded to a precanvassing survey by indicating that their principal motive for canvassing was to earn money. On the Saturday before Election Day, the canvassers received twenty minutes of instruction before heading into the field.[2]

An overview of the six sites is presented in Table 1. Looking solely at the regions within each site that were targeted for canvassing, one sees that the variation across sites is considerable. Data from the 2000 Census indicate that the region canvassed in Detroit is 94% black, whereas Columbus is 82% white. Hispanics account for nearly half of the population in the canvassed regions of Bridgeport. St. Paul has a large Asian population. Home-ownership rates vary widely as well. The large student population in Columbus makes for a low median age and 9% rate of home ownership. St. Paul and Raleigh have higher median ages and home ownership rates of nearly 50%. While not a random sample of cities or elections, the sites in this study span a wide array of urban profiles.

Canvassing Scripts

Although the characteristics of the sites and canvassers varied, they tended to follow similar procedures when going door-to-door. Each canvasser was equipped a clipboard, a map, and a target list of names and addresses. The scripts used in Columbus were broadly representative of the kind of scripts used in other sites:

> Hi, how are you? I'm _____ with Ohio Youth Vote. We're reminding people that there's an election this Tuesday. Are you [Name]? [If yes:] Hi! I'd just like to give you this little reminder about voting this Tuesday. [Hand reminder sheet and check "reached" on disposition sheet.] [If no:] Oh, may I please speak with [Name]? And by the way, are you registered to vote? [When Name appears, repeat script with person listed on sheet. Check 'reached" if they are there, and record the number of voting age people you spoke with in "other."] Have a nice day!

---

[2] In contrast to the other sites, where canvassing occurred without incident, the canvassing effort in Raleigh encountered problems. Some white residents refused to open their doors to black canvassers. Two black canvassers were accosted by white residents and expelled from the neighborhood. A coincidental canvassing effort by white supremacists seeking to deport Arabs raised residents' general level of hostility to canvassers; indeed, the local police stopped and questioned some of the white canvassers in the PIRG campaign, thinking that they were white supremacists. Whether these events altered the effectiveness of the canvassing effort is a matter of speculation.

TABLE 1

Characteristics of Canvassing Sites, Focusing only on Regions of Each Site that Were Actually Canvassed

	Bridgeport	Columbus	Detroit	Minneapolis	Raleigh	St. Paul
Total City Population	139,529	771,470	951,270	382,618	276,093	287,151
Population in Canvassed Areas	19,115	8,222	17,412	12,177	43,030	17,904
White	37%	82%	4%	36%	70%	54%
Black	28%	5%	94%	26%	22%	20%
Asian	4%	9%	0%	6%	2%	17%
Hispanic	47%	3%	1%	23%	6%	7%
Median Age	26	24	35	26	37	29
Owners	20%	9%	28%	20%	49%	48%
Type of Election	School Board	City Council	Mayoral	Mayoral	Mayoral/City Council	Mayoral
Competitiveness	Low	Low	High	Medium	High	High
Voter Turnout Rate among Subjects in the Control Group	9.9%	8.2%	43.3%	25.0%	29.4%	37.6%
N of Subjects in the Control Group	911	1,322	2,482	1,418	2,975	1,104
N of Subjects in the Treatment Group	895	1,156	2,472	1,409	1,685	1,104

Source for Demographic Profile: 2000 Census.

Canvassers were thus responsible for conveying a brief reminder about the upcoming election, in some cases distributing a flyer, and recording the disposition of each visit.[3]

Data and Design Issues

The procedures by which subjects were assigned at random to treatment and control groups varied slightly across sites. Subjects in Detroit, Minneapolis, and St. Paul were stratified into walk lists before random assignment, while Bridgeport and Columbus were not, but in each of these sites subjects were assigned the same probability of receiving a treatment. In Raleigh, the proportion of subjects assigned to the treatment condition varied across walk lists.[4] This across-list variation means that the multivariate analyses that follow include dummy variables for each walk list. These walk-list dummy variables are useful for the other sites as well, since they absorb some intra-site variability in turnout rates.[5]

After the election, we obtained voting histories and registration lists from local registrars. These lists were merged with names in the treatment and control groups in order to calculate voter turnout rates. Since both the registration lists and the voter turnout lists came from the same sources, we experienced no difficulties merging the two lists into a unified database. We also obtained information about whether each citizen participated in the 2000 presidential election. This information enables us to check whether random assignment to treatment and control groups was indeed uncorrelated with past voting behavior. It also provides a useful covariate in a multivariate analysis, as past behavior helps reduce the disturbance variance in models predicting voting in 2001.

Results

Randomization Check

Randomization procedures are designed to create treatment and control groups with equivalent pretreatment vote propensities. In order to check that random

---

[3] The treatment thus comprises both a personal appeal and distribution of a leaflet. Other experimental evidence seems to show that leaflets alone have minimal effects on turnout (Gerber and Green 2000a). Not reported here are embedded experiments in which the content of the leaflet was varied randomly, sometimes urging subjects to vote and in other cases presenting them with a voter guide culled from a local newspaper. Varying the content of the flyer had small and statistically insignificant effects.

[4] This variation was introduced to enable us to study the interaction between the treatment given to any single individual and the quantity of treatment given to a particular block. In the end, this study proved too small to detect this interaction with any statistical power.

[5] Random assignment within walk lists give us the luxury of being able to discard walk lists (including both treatment and control subjects) when we suspected that canvassers had falsified their records of whom they contacted. In Raleigh, we discarded one walk list because a canvasser implausibly claimed to have contacted every other house in a rigid sequence. In Detroit, we discarded three lists from one canvasser whose records involved an implausible sequence of contacts and noncontacts. These lists were discarded before we gathered data on voter turnout in 2001.

assignment performed this function, we calculated voter turnout rates for treatment and control groups in the 2000 elections, a year before canvassing occurred. In five of the six sites, pretreatment differences are negligible. In three cases, the treatment group voted at slightly lower rates than the control group, and in two cases, slightly higher. In St. Paul, the treatment group voted at rates that were noticeably higher, with a two-tailed p value of .052. We checked the integrity of the randomization procedures used in St. Paul and found them to be sound. Nevertheless, it will be necessary to analyze the St. Paul results in two ways, one based on a simple comparison of treatment and control and the other using past voting behavior as a covariate.[6]

Intent-to-Treat Effects

The intent-to-treat effects of face-to-face canvassing can be calculated by examining the turnout rates among those assigned to the treatment and control groups, making no allowance for the fact that only some of those assigned to the treatment groups were actually contacted. Column two of Table 2 presents these turnout rates for treatment and control groups in each city. In every site, the treatment group turned out at a higher rate than the control group. For example, in Detroit, where over 40% of registered voters cast ballots, turnout in the treatment group was 2.4 percentage points higher than in the control group. In Bridgeport, where turnout in the control group was an abysmal 9.9%, turnout in the treatment group was 4.0 percentage points higher. The outlier in this set of experiments was Raleigh, where turnout was negligibly higher in the treatment group.

Taking all of the experiments into account, face-to-face canvassing has an intent-to-treat effect of 2.1 percentage points. This estimate is statistically significant at the .01 level using a one-tailed test. These intent-to-treat estimates give some indication of how much get-out-the-vote drives like the ones studied here tend to raise aggregate levels of turnout. As we note below, more intensive GOTV campaigns, which contact much higher proportions of the subjects in the treatment group (e.g., Michelson 2003), can be expected to have much larger intent-to-treat effects.

The Effects of Actual Contact

In order to estimate the mobilizing effect of canvassing among those who are contacted, one must make a statistical adjustment for the fact that many people in the treatment group were never contacted. As shown in Table 2, the limiting factor in these GOTV campaigns is the fact that they contact less than half of

---

[6] An additional test of randomization examined the joint significance of age, race, gender, party, and past voting history as predictors of assignment to treatment and control groups. Dummy variables were used to mark missing values in order to avoid deleting observations. Both the null and alternative models included dummy variables for walk lists. As expected, the test statistic is non-significant, $F(12,18729) = .66$, $p = .80$.

TABLE 2

Treatment Effects, by Site

	Pre-Treatment Difference in Voting Rates, 2000 Election	Post-Treatment Difference in Voting Rates, 2001 Election	Percentage of Treatment Group Actually Contacted	Effects of Actual Treatment on Voting in 2001
Bridgeport (n = 1,806)	−.3 (2.3)	4.0*** (1.5)	28.1	14.4*** (5.3)
Columbus (n = 2,478)	−.4 (2.0)	1.4 (1.1)	14.3	9.7 (7.9)
Detroit (n = 4,954)	.2 (1.4)	2.4** (1.4)	30.9	7.8** (4.5)
Minneapolis (n = 2,827)	−.4 (1.8)	1.9 (1.6)	18.5	10.1 (8.7)
Raleigh (n = 4,660)	.4 (1.4)	.1 (1.4)	44.6	.2 (3.2)
St. Paul (n = 2,208)	3.2* (1.6)	4.6*** (2.1)	32.1	14.4*** (6.4)
All Sites (n = 18,933)	.4 (.7)	2.1*** (.6)	29.6	7.1*** (2.2)

*p < .10, two-tailed test. **p < .05, one-tailed test. ***p < .01, one-tailed test. Standard errors in parentheses.

Notes: Differences between treatment and control groups were calculated from OLS regressions of voting in 2000 or 2001 on a dummy variable for experimental treatment, with dummy variables for each walk list as covariates. Contact rates (column 3) were calculated from an OLS regression of actual contact on a dummy variable for experimental treatment, with dummy variables for each walk list as covariates. Actual treatment effects (column 4) were estimated from a 2SLS regression of voting in 2001 on contact, with the experimental treatment as an excluded instrumental variable. Both stages of the 2SLS regression included covariates for each walk list.

their walk lists; indeed, in two of the sites, fewer than one citizen in five was actually contacted. It should be emphasized that for purposes of this calculation, contact is defined quite conservatively to include GOTV conversations with intended subjects or their housemates.[7] Excluded from the definition of contact are instances where canvassers found no one at home, could not locate the address, discovered that they had the wrong address, or were told to go away before making their GOTV appeal.

The rightmost column of Table 2 reports the actual contact effects. The influence of actual contact in Bridgeport, for example, is estimated to be a 14.4

[7] Of the 8,721 subjects assigned to the treatment group, 18% were contacted directly, and another 11% were contacted indirectly insofar as canvassers spoke with another voting-age member of the household. If one assumes that only direct conversations with canvassers influence turnout, the effects of actual treatment will be larger than what we report in Tables 2 and 3 because the estimated intent-to-treat effects are divided by .18 instead of .29.

percentage-point jump in the probability of voting. Four of the six estimates exceed the estimate of 8.7 percentage points reported by Gerber and Green (2000b), although the standard errors associated with the estimates for Columbus and Minneapolis are quite high. Combining all of the sites (but controlling for walk lists and therefore for inter- and intrasite variation), we find an average treatment effect of 7.1 percentage points. This estimate is statistically significant at the .01 level using a one-tailed test. This estimate also falls within one standard error of the Gerber and Green findings (2000b, 659).

In sum, the experimental results reaffirm the effectiveness of face-to-face canvassing as a means of mobilizing voters. Across a wide range of electoral settings, ranging from the sleepy local election in Bridgeport to the closely contested mayoral race in St. Paul, canvassing had a profound effect on voter participation. This effect turns up in places as different economically and demographically as Columbus and Detroit. Although Raleigh appears to be an outlier ex post, we cannot reject the null hypothesis of homogeneous treatment effects across the six sites [$F(5,18737) = 1.06$, $p = .38$]. Moreover, the findings square with the results of other experiments, such as Gerber and Green's (2000b) study of voter mobilization in New Haven's 1998 elections and Michelson's (2003) study of mobilization prior to a local election in a rural town with a large Latino population.

Multivariate and Nonlinear Models

These findings are underscored by a two-stage probit analysis, which is presented in Table 3. We report two versions of this analysis. The first model includes actual contact as a regressor and intended contact as an instrument. Dummy variables marking each walk list in each site are included as covariates at both stages

TABLE 3

Two-Stage Probit Coefficients, with and without Covariates

	Probit Estimates	Standard Errors
Model Without Covariates		
Canvassing	.211**	.069
Model Including Covariates		
Canvassing	.217**	.076
Voting in 2000	1.571**	.030
1 Registered Voter in the Household	.143*	.053
2 Registered Voters in the Household	.192*	.049
3 Registered Voters in the Household	.018	.053

Note: **$p < .01$, one-tailed test. *$p < .01$, two-tailed test. Both specifications include dummy variables (not shown) marking each walk list in each site. The dummy variables for the number of registered voters in each household treats four voter households as the base category. Estimation method is 2-stage conditional maximum likelihood, see Rivers and Vuong (1988).

of the regression. In the second model, we also control for a set of covariates that predict voter turnout in 2001: voting in 2000 and dummy variables marking whether a household contained one, two, three, or four registered voters.

The two models provide nearly identical estimates of the effectiveness of canvassing. The two probit coefficients are .211 and .217. These estimates imply that a person who would otherwise have a 50% chance of voting would vote with approximately a 58.5% probability after being canvassed face-to-face. Ordinarily, the inclusion of covariates reduces the standard errors associated with an experimental treatment by reducing the disturbance variance. Here, the standard error increases slightly, reflecting an unexpected correlation between voting in 2000 and the treatment for one of the sites (St. Paul). Nevertheless, the probit coefficients in both specifications suggest that contact with canvassers raises turnout by a statistically significant margin ($p < .01$, one-tailed test).

Conclusion

Building upon previous results, these experimental findings demonstrate that mobilization campaigns have the potential to increase turnout substantially in local elections. Each successful contact with a registered citizen raises that individual's probability of voting by approximately 7 percentage points, which is considerable given the fact that local elections often attract only 25% of the electorate to the polls. This figure, moreover, is a conservative estimate. When calculating the effects of actual treatment, we regarded any conversation with a member of the household as a "contact." Only about half of these conversations occurred directly with the subject in the treatment group; the remainder involved urging a housemate to vote and requesting that this message be passed along to the intended subject. Had we restricted the definition of contact to direct conversations with the subject, the apparent effects of canvassing would have been much greater.

The success with which these door-to-door campaigns mobilized voters is especially impressive given the meager budgets on which these campaigns operated. Our experimental results suggest that 12 successful face-to-face contacts translated into one additional vote. Consider what this finding implies for a large scale GOTV campaign. Suppose one were to hire campaign workers at a rate of $10 per hour. According to our records for Bridgeport and Columbus, where canvassers traveled in pairs but approached different doors, canvassers contacted eight voters per hour. In Raleigh and St. Paul, the rate was five contacts per hour, but this figure reflects the fact that in these sites canvassers not only traveled in pairs but also went in pairs up to every door. Had the teams of canvassers split up, the contacts per hour would presumably have doubled. If we imagine that the average canvasser makes eight contacts per hour, the cost per vote would be $15. This figure is quite similar to those reported in previous experimental studies using face-to-face canvassing and notably smaller than comparable cost-per-vote figures associated with commercial phone banks or direct mail (Gerber and Green 2000b, 2001).[8]

One of the paradoxes of local elections is that individual votes have a greater likelihood of affecting the outcome, yet fewer eligible voters participate. The same logic applies to arguments based on the indirect effects that voters can have on elections by mobilizing their friends and neighbors (Shachar and Nalebuff 1999). With such small numbers of voters casting ballots, mobilization campaigns would seem to be a promising strategy for influencing an election. And yet, the overall level of GOTV activity tends to be low in local elections. In lopsided contests, campaigns have little incentive to do this type of work; in competitive contests, campaigns seem content to focus their energies on persuading voters who regularly vote in local elections. This pattern tends to leave undisturbed the massive age and socioeconomic disparities between voters and nonvoters that have long been the focus of scholarship on local voter turnout (Hamilton 1971; Oliver 1999). The present study suggests that nonpartisan groups, as well as partisan groups that choose to use nonpartisan appeals, have the potential to alter this pattern through face-to-face contact with potential voters. Even in settings where the election outcome seems to be a foregone conclusion, this type of personal contact has a marked effect on voter participation.

Manuscript submitted 16 July 2002
Final manuscript received 9 October 2002

References

Angrist, Joshua D., Guido W. Imbens, and Donald B. Rubin. 1996. "Identification of Causal Effects Using Instrumental Variables." *Journal of the American Statistical Association* 91 (June): 444–55.

Eldersveld, Samuel J. 1956. "Experimental Propaganda Techniques and Voting Behavior." *American Political Science Review* 50(1): 154–65.

Gerber, Alan S., and Donald P. Green. 2000a. "The Effect of a Nonpartisan Get-Out-The-Vote Drive: An Experimental Study of Leafleting." *Journal of Politics* 62(3): 846–57.

Gerber, Alan S., and Donald P. Green. 2000b. "The Effects of Canvassing, Direct Mail, and Telephone Contact on Voter Turnout: A Field Experiment." *American Political Science Review* 94(3): 653–63.

Gerber, Alan S., and Donald P. Green. 2001. "Do Phone Calls Increase Turnout?" *Public Opinion Quarterly* 65 (Spring): 75–85.

Gosnell, Harold F. 1927. *Getting-Out-The-Vote: An Experiment in the Stimulation of Voting*. Chicago: University of Chicago Press.

Hamilton, Howard D. 1971. "The Municipal Voter: Voting and Nonvoting in City Elections." *American Political Science Review* 65(4): 1135–40.

---

[8] Naturally, a complete accounting of costs must take into account the fixed costs of sustaining organizations that can recruit and inspire canvassers. The canvassing campaigns studied here were put together with only a few weeks' preparation. Better organization and training could improve the hourly productivity of canvassers.

Michelson, Melissa R. 2003. "Getting Out the Latino Vote: How Door-to-Door Canvassing Influences Voter Turnout in Rural Central California." *Political Behavior* 25(3): 247–63.

Morlan, Robert L. 1984. "Municipal vs. National Election Voter Turnout: Europe and the United States." *Political Science Quarterly* 99(3): 457–70.

Oliver, J. Eric. 1999. "The Effects of Metropolitan Economic Segregation on Local Civic Participation." *American Journal of Political Science* 43(1): 186–212.

Putnam, Robert C. 2000. *Bowling Alone: The Collapse and Renewal of American Community*. New York: Simon and Schuster.

Rivers, Douglas, and Quang H. Vuong. 1988. "Limited Information Estimators and Exogeneity Tests for Simultaneous Probit Models." *Journal of Econometrics* 39(3): 347–66.

Rosenstone, Steven J., and John Mark Hansen. 1993. *Mobilization, Participation, and Democracy in America*. New York: Macmillan Publishing Company.

Shachar Roni, and Barry Nalebuff. 1999. "Follow the Leader: Theory and Evidence on Political Participation." *American Economic Review* 89(3): 525–47.

Verba, Sidney, Kay Lehman Schlozman, and Henry E. Brady. 1995. *Voice and Equality: Civic Voluntarism in American Politics*. Cambridge: Harvard University Press.

Donald P. Green is A. Whitney Griswold Professor of political science and Director, Institution for Social and Policy Studies, Yale University, New Haven, CT 06520-8209 (donald.green@yale.edu). Alan S. Gerber is professor of political science, Yale University, New Haven, CT 06520-8209 (alan.gerber@yale.edu). David W. Nickerson is a Ph.D. candidate in political science, Yale University, New Haven, CT 06520-8209 (david.nickerson@yale.edu).